THE TRAINING
AND DEVELOPMENT
STRATEGIC PLAN
WORKBOOK

RAYNOLD A. SVENSON
MONICA J. RINDERER

PRENTICE HALL
Englewood Cliffs, New Jersey 07632

Prentice-Hall International (UK) Limited, *London*
Prentice-Hall of Australia Pty. Limited, *Sydney*
Prentice-Hall Canada Inc., *Toronto*
Prentice-Hall Hispanoamericana, S.A., *Mexico*
Prentice-Hall of India Private Limited, *New Delhi*
Prentice-Hall of Japan, Inc., *Tokyo*
Simon & Schuster Asia Pte. Ltd., *Singapore*
Editora Prentice-Hall do Brasil, Ltda., *Rio de Janeiro*

10   9   8   7   6   5   4   3   2

Library of Congress Cataloging-in-Publication Data

Svenson, Raynold A.
    The training and development strategic plan workbook / Raynold A. Svenson and
Monica J. Rinderer.
        p.   cm.
    Includes bibliographical references (p.   ) and index.
    ISBN 0-13-853862-X
    1. Employees—Training of—Handbooks, manuals, etc.   2. Strategic
planning—Handbooks, manuals, etc.   I. Rinderer, Monica J.
II.   Title.
HF5549.5.T7S88   1991
658.3′12404—dc20   91-24575
                                                                              CIP

0-13-853862-X

PRENTICE HALL
Business Information & Publishing Division
Englewood Cliffs, NJ 07632
Simon & Schuster, A Paramount Communications Company

Printed in the United States of America

To all our colleagues at
Svenson and Wallace,
present and past.
Each and every one of you
has made a contribution
to us and to the making
of this book.

Our thanks to you.
Ray and Nikki

FOREWORD

Ten years ago, Motorola University was only a charter and a limited supply of resources. Today it is a full-fledged campus with an expanded charter; a comprehensive governance, development, delivery, evaluation, and maintenance system; and significant resources to back it all up. Reading this book has been like reliving the last ten years of my life.

Training is the hot-button of the 1990s. Today's training manager not only wants to build a world-class training system for his or her organization but also needs to do so to keep pace with the changing environment. Anyone trying to do what we have done at Motorola will find that there are few good models to follow and very little has been previously written to help. This book takes the reader, chapter by chapter, through all the stages an organization must go through to build a comprehensive training system. It builds on the theoretical base established by people like Thomas Gilbert and Geary Rummler and provides an application guide to using their principles. It provides a practical roadmap to the key elements of training as well as a tool chest for training management, and its applications focus means you can apply it to real-world situations. However, it is not a rigid, lock-step process but a guide that has great flexibility and application to a wide variety of settings. The tools and techniques described in the book can be customized to fit any size organization and many different sets of criteria and constraints. The information will work well for nonprofit and profit organizations and in public and private sectors. This book should be a great resource to anyone in any organization whether local, national, or global. It should also be of particular interest to organizations overseas and in the developing countries, such as Southeast Asia, Central America, and Eastern Europe, where there are currently no good models to follow.

In addition to providing a practical process to follow, this book will be a valuable ongoing reference tool in your training and management library. It is not a document you will read once and throw away. No matter where you are in your organizational development cycle, you will find yourself going back to it for further reference, information, and more in-depth understanding. Your training organization will develop in an iterative fashion, and I believe you will find yourself using the book that way, too.

In short, the book is a practical, systematic approach to institutional change using education and training as a platform to lead that change. It contains a wealth of information that today's organizational leader cannot afford to miss.

Bill Wiggenhorn
President, Motorola University

PREFACE

WHAT THIS BOOK CAN DO FOR YOU

In 1972 Ray Svenson was sent to the Bell System Center for Technical Education (BSCTE) in Lisle, Illinois to be the new Manager of Planning, Methods, and Results. BSCTE was organized in 1968 to serve the training needs of 50,000 technical professionals and engineers in the twenty-two Bell Operating Companies. As Manager of Planning, Methods, and Results, Ray's job was to design and implement the planning, instructional, and administrative systems and processes necessary to achieve the mission of the center. Ray was selected for the job because of his ten years experience across wide spectrum of telecommunications engineering functions and his specialized experience in technology planning, methods, and administrative systems development.

Most of the systems and processes described in this book were developed and implemented in one form or another during Ray's six years at BSCTE and have been refined and improved on over the last twelve years as we have applied them with the clients (primarily *Fortune* 100 companies) of our consulting business. Our methodology applies the disciplines of business planning, quantitative forecasting, systems design, and Total Quality Management to the training field, and links these disciplines to the specialized processes involved in training and education. This book is a documentation of all we have learned about building a successful world-class training organization since 1972, put into a how-to format so the methods can be used by readers. We have successfully applied these methods across a wide variety of industries, including

- Aerospace
- Automotive

- Chemicals
- Computers
- Electric power
- Electronics
- Financial
- Health care
- Insurance
- Metals
- Petroleum
- Public education
- Telecommunications.

The intended audience for this book includes

- Training directors
- Training managers
- Corporate executives
- Human resource executives
- Consultants
- Anyone assigned to develop a comprehensive training plan for an organization.

The purpose of the book is to provide you with the following:

- A comprehensive view of all the issues that are important in designing and managing a training system that supports business goals
- A systematic methodology for dealing with the issues
- Examples, worksheets, and checklists for your use in developing your own training system
- Specifications for the design of important training systems and processes
- A method for assessing your own training system against industry-best practices and pinpointing what parts of your system need the most improvement
- A method for linking training to Total Quality Management.
- Lots of ideas on the best practices that lead to superior performance, based on years of experience working with training departments. You will be able to try these ideas as you develop your own system.

HOW TO USE THIS BOOK

The following chart provides an overview of the structure of this book. As you can see, chapters 1 and 2 give a good overview of what constitutes a world-class training organization and how this book will help you develop one. The rest of the book provides

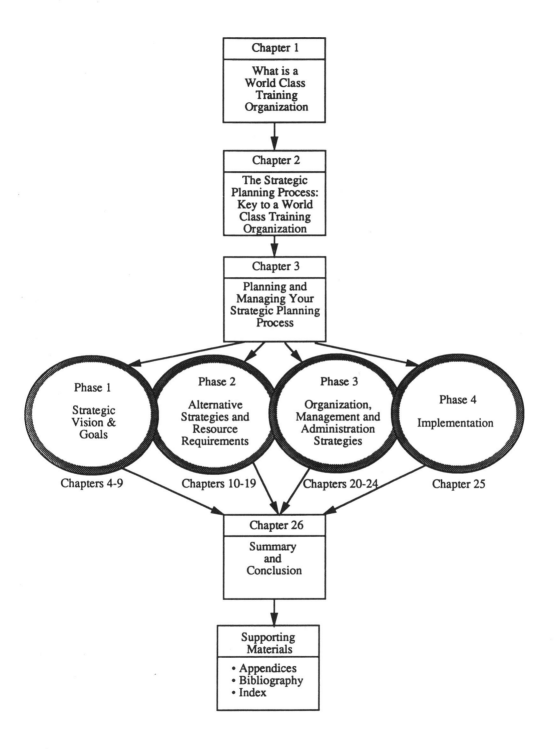

Chapter 1

What is a
World Class
Training
Organization

Chapter 2

The Strategic
Planning Process:
Key to a World
Class Training
Organization

Chapter 3

Planning and
Managing Your
Strategic Planning
Process

Phase 1

Strategic
Vision &
Goals

Phase 2

Alternative
Strategies and
Resource
Requirements

Phase 3

Organization,
Management and
Administration
Strategies

Phase 4

Implementation

Chapters 4-9   Chapters 10-19   Chapters 20-24   Chapter 25

Chapter 26

Summary
and
Conclusion

Supporting
Materials

• Appendices
• Bibliography
• Index

detailed information on all the phases of planning for a training system using a strategic business approach. You should first read through the whole book to get the overall picture. Later you will want to return to specific chapters to use them as resources and guides as you go through your own strategic planning processes.

We realize that at first glance this book appears very complex. As you work through the processes in your own organization, you will gain experience with the methods described and find that they are not as complicated as they look.

ACKNOWLEDGMENTS

Any book contains the input of hundreds of people who have touched the authors' lives. We would specifically like to thank the following people for their role in the development of this work. First, our thanks to Chuck Sener and Chuck Elmendorf, who sponsored the development of these systems while Ray was at BSCTE. We also thank Ray's many Bell System colleagues, who were heavily involved during the developmental period. They are too numerous to mention without leaving out someone who made an important contribution. Special thanks to Karen Wallace, Guy Wallace, and Mark Brown, our colleagues at Svenson & Wallace. Karen, Guy, and Mark have all contributed to the development and refinement of the methodology described and supported the preparation of the book. We also thank our clients, who have worked with us to apply and refine the methodology. We know it works because of their work in putting the systems in place. Several other people have had a hand in producing the book, critiquing our efforts, and providing support during the process. Our particular gratitude goes to Jeanie Mowrer, who shouldered the bulk of the word processing and put in many long and extra hours deciphering our nearly unintelligible script. Others who had a hand include Bernadette Adis, Barb Daly, Cindy Kirincic, Rob Prater, Debbie Purdy, Rachelle Salazar, Kim Smart, Dottie Soelke, Beth Svenson, and Rick Tuttle. We appreciate all of their efforts—we could not have done it without them. Finally, our thanks to Gerry Galbo, our editor at Prentice-Hall, for his patience, experienced help, and useful critiques of the material.

CONTENTS

PHASE 1: STRATEGIC VISION AND GOALS

PHASE 2: ALTERNATIVE STRATEGIES AND RESOURCE REQUIREMENTS

PHASE 3: ORGANIZATION, MANAGEMENT AND ADMINISTRATION STRATEGIES

PHASE 4: IMPLEMENTATION

LIST OF FIGURES

WORLD CLASS TRAINING: THE BEST PRACTICES IN THE INDUSTRY

THE QUEST FOR THE LEADING EDGE

Around the world today, organizations of all sizes in all fields are striving to be world class or best-in-class, striving for excellence, striving for total quality. This is true in all sectors of the global business community. It is also showing up in education, nonprofit, and government organizations. Everyone seems to be embarking on the quest for the high-performance organization. Organizations are learning that there is no resting place in this quest, no ultimate performance. There is only continuous improvement. Even the best are striving to be better, and if one organization stops to rest the others only get farther ahead. If those who are best stop to rest, they lose the lead. The race for peak performance is demanding and exhilarating; it has its price and its rewards, but it is one of the great worldwide movements of our time. Organizations, from General Motors to the government of Germany to Fred's Family Foods, join the race to improve their performance or they go out of business, get swallowed up or replaced.

As organizations become more sophisticated, their management begins to recognize that the most essential asset in this quest for peak organizational performance is human competence. Peters and Austin said in *A Passion for Excellence* (Random House; 1985, pg. 201), "To achieve distinction . . . requires not sleight of hand by geniuses but the commitment to excellence (quality, service, make it better/innovation) by everyone. In short, people are the unmistakable base." To create world-class companies and institutions, it is imperative to grow and support that base. Management is also beginning to recognize that competence itself is relative to the context and the competition. That is, the crew that was competent on yesterday's supertanker is not necessarily competent on today's supertanker. In addition, it means that if an orgainization is driven by the competition, it cannot stand still and stay on the leading edge. The fast pace of technological development and change makes this a constant fact of organizational life.

Therefore, even top performers must continually learn and improve if they are to stay at the top. This has been recognized in sports and the arts for a long time. Top athletes train regularly and hard with their coaches, and concert musicians take lessons and practice eight to ten hours per day throughout their performing lives. They do this both to keep their own skills honed and razor sharp and to stay on top of new developments, technologies, and rules of the game. People committed to organizational careers should be doing the same.

People have always recognized that acquiring competence requires training for certain jobs. For example, none of us would want to travel on a jet with a pilot who was not trained and certified. Yet airline management promotes people to supervise the individuals who build the planes without giving them supervisory training. But if an organization is going to be world class, in whatever field, management must support developing world-class employees at all levels in all units of the organization.

Sports teams, military units, artistic performers, and astronaut teams are noted for spending more time in training than in actual performance. These people are selected for their talent and then systematically trained and drilled to a high level of competence. Without training in specific skills and in coordinated team activity, even the finest talent performs incompetently as a group of undisciplined prima donnas. While the business world as a whole has not embraced training to the degree that these organizations have, there are some who have recognized its importance and established themselves as definite leaders in developing, maintaining, and improving human competence in their organizations—companies like IBM, Motorola, McDonald's, Arthur Andersen, the major airlines, and some of Ma Bell's offspring. None of these leaders are perfect. Most are looking for ways to improve. Some are slipping from their former leadership positions. But all of them can provide useful information and guidance for improving training systems.

In this chapter we describe the attributes of a world class training system for any organization, whether business, government, education, or nonprofit, based on the best practices of the training leaders in these fields. In the rest of the book we show you how to use a strategic planning process to plan and build your own world-class system and be on the leading edge with the best of the best. We want to help you answer the question, "What does a world-class training organization look like, and how do we build one?"

One note of caution: We are not offering you an instant prescription for world leadership in training. You have to crawl before walking, walk before running and so forth. Smaller organizations could conceivably achieve their goals in three to five years. Large organizations can expect five to ten years to get from ground zero to something approaching world class. Many of the things you would have to do to create your own high-performance training system inherently take time. Given top executive priority, lots of resources, and guided decision making, these time frames can be compressed. Remember the proverb, "The journey of a thousand miles starts with a single step." Read through this book and then begin the process described in it, one step at a time. Keep picking your feet up and setting them down in front of you, and you'll get there.

THE WCI STORY: A WORLD-CLASS EXAMPLE

This section paints a picture of a world-class training system in a typical mid-size corporation. We want you to be able to envision what your organization can become. We describe a fictitious corporation because no single company embodies all the characteristics we want to discuss. This picture, though idealized, is not based on future technologies we do not possess; it is based on the best practices already in place in the industry. Everything we describe can be found in place and working somewhere. That means that it can be in place and working for you, too.

Our fictitious company is called World Class, Inc. (WCI). WCI is one of the leading U.S. producers of optics. It manufactures a full line of binoculars, telescopes, microscopes, and photographic lenses and is rapidly gaining market share at the expense of the other U.S. manufacturers and the imports.

WCI has an Industry Division that makes optics for the high-end industrial market, a Sporting Division that makes binoculars, telescopes, and rifle scopes for the outdoor segment and a Photographic Division that makes camera, projector, and video lenses. All three of these divisions buy from the Clear-piece Division, which makes or acquires the actual glass and plastic lenses. WC Technology is the R&D unit responsible for keeping the corporation at the leading edge of optical technology. World Class Acceptance Corporation (WCAC) is a financing subsidiary providing the WCI Credit Card to potential customers and World Class Education Systems (WCES) is the education and training subsidiary. This structure is shown in Figure 1-1.

Ten years ago, WCI began implementing a Total Quality Management (TQM) culture. It realized that you cannot have a world-class organization without a TQM culture which includes

- Leadership defining and communicating vision and values

- Leadership managing the business in a way that supports the vision and values

- A strategic plan, annual plans, and a budget supporting the vision and values

- Requirements established for products and services, processes and suppliers, based on systematic analysis of customer needs and wants

- Design, control, and continual improvement of products and services, processes, suppliers, and training system

- Human resources systems, including organization and team structures, job designs, performance improvement systems, and training and education system supporting the vision and values

- Results achievement, especially regarding customer satisfaction and internal specifications.

This TQM culture resulted in WCI being the first optics company to win the

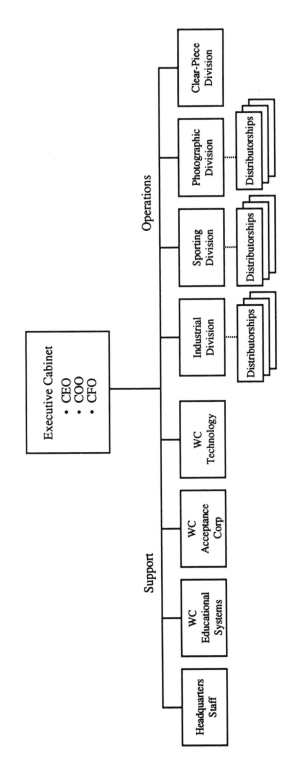

Figure 1-1 World Class, Inc. (WCI) Organization Structure

Malcolm Baldrige National Quality Award. A major part of the WCI commitment to TQM is the Total Learning Culture (TLC), which embodies the twin philosophies that everyone in the system (employees, distributors, and suppliers) must master all the competencies required for peak performance at their assigned tasks and that continuous learning is a way of life necessary to keep the entire workforce at the cutting edge. Every employee in all WCI divisions, subsidiaries, headquarters departments, and distributor-ships has an Individual Learning Plan (ILP) and is accountable for achieving annual learning objectives. This is a part of the training and education system requirement for supporting the overall organizational vision and values.

To get an idea of how this training and education system works, let's visit some of the WCI divisions, subsidiaries, and headquarters units to look at the education and training from the vantage point of the employees. We go first to the Sporting Division assembly plant in Deep Springs, Michigan (a union plant).

John Temple is an assembly worker on the robotized bifocal assembly line. He has been with WCI for twenty-five years and has seen dramatic changes. Let's let John tell his own story.

> I spent most of my life hand-assembling binoculars on the old body assembly lines. I did the same thing day after day, year after year. It was boring, but it didn't take much skill, which was good because I couldn't read very well and could barely add and subtract. Eight years ago the company announced it was going to modernize its assembly process and go to a high level of automation. Our jobs were going to require retraining, but nobody would be laid off. I was scared because I knew I couldn't handle the training program. I was assured that I wouldn't lose my job but I would have to commit to a learning program that included catching up on basic skills in a program supported by a special WCI/union fund.
>
> I was given a bunch of tests for getting a place in the program and promised a $400 bonus when I could pass eligibility tests for automated assembly training. I spent four months off work, at full pay and benefits, attending Deep Springs Community College (DSCC) classes in which I learned reading, English, and basic math. Most of the instruction was done at the computerized learning center, where I also learned basic keyboarding skills. When I graduated, not only was I ready to enter automated assembly training, but I could read the Detroit papers, help my kids with their school work, and help my wife with the family budget. During the day I then entered automated assembly basic training and at night I continued in a voluntary evening program at DSCC, paid for by the fund, and got my GED in two more years.
>
> In the new automated body line there are fifteen separate operations to learn. I am now trained and certified on twelve of those operations, and my Individual Learning Plan says I should be able to do the other three in the next twelve months. This will bring me to the top pay grade in a five-step program based on being good at these assembly skills. Most of this training is hands-on learning on the line with an experienced worker as my tutor. Some of it is in the classroom to get oriented to the manuals. My next goal is to qualify for the robotics technician training program.

Our next visit is with Leslie Erickson, the Training Director at the Deep Springs Assembly plant. Leslie has a staff of twenty instructional designers and facilitators. All in-plant instruction is done by members of the line organizations after they have received thorough trainer training. Leslie gives us an overview of training at the Deep Springs plant.

We have job specifications which specify responsibilities, tasks, and skill and knowledge requirements for every job in the plant. There is a curriculum plan for each group of jobs that links into a master curriculum coordinated by WCES. We have ILPs on file for every employee, and we track completions and skills certification.

We get 60 percent of our training materials from WCES, including everything from supervisory skills to programmable logic controllers. The other 40 percent is developed locally by our instructional designers working with experts from the line organizations. We only develop material that is unique to the Deep Springs plant. Everything else we buy.

The plant has a Plant Training Council co-chaired by the plant manager and the union leadership with subordinate training committees in operations, maintenance, and engineering. The plant manager sits on the WCES Manufacturing Curriculum Advisory Council. Our supervisors, managers, engineers, and other professionals spend time every year at WCES training programs, and we have an NTU (National Technological University) television classroom for fifteen engineers who are working on advanced degree programs.

Our training results system shows that we meet 93 percent of our training needs at an annual cost of about $4 million. Our estimated value-added right now is about $40 million for a ten-to-one return on investment.

Our facilitators play a critical role in supporting the self-directed work teams at the production centers and the corrective action teams which are part of our TQM system. The facilitators also are responsible for training and coaching all of the part-time instructors in our technical programs from the line organizations.

A joint management and union committee administers our participation in the WCI/union retraining fund.

Ian McAllistair has been the plant manager at Deep Springs for the past fifteen years. Previously he was plant manager for one of the smaller clear-piece plants, where he had started as a mechanical engineer almost forty years ago.

Our whole way of life has changed in the last ten years. We used to be a traditional, bureaucratic, authoritarian operation with adversarial labor relations. When the company announced its intention to move into TQM, its intention to change our values and organizational culture, I didn't believe it would fly. I'd seen all kind of programs come and go over the years. But they've convinced me. Now I'm a total enthusiast!

The Total Learning Culture concept and the education and training system the company put in place were the critical mechanisms that helped it happen. Of course, it didn't hurt that our bonuses got tied to quality and learning results along with production and profitability. We put our money where our mouth was.

Before we got into all this, I spent almost no time on education and training issues. Now I spend at least two weeks a year at WCES and University Executive education programs and an additional 20 percent of my time helping direct our own training program and serving on the WCI Manufacturing Curriculum Advisory Council.

You said Leslie Erickson quoted you a ten-to-one return on investment for training activity. I believe this is too conservative. The intangibles such as improved morale and feeling proud of being part of a winning high-performance team are hard to measure, but I'm convinced that they are just as important to our success as the measurable results. Labor relations used to give me ulcers. Now it's almost a pleasure.

Now to José Ruiz, head of the local union at the Deep Springs plant.

My main job is making sure that our members get fair treatment and making sure that they get opportunities and help to advance. Ten years ago, our backs were to the wall. We were afraid of losing our jobs to a combination of automation and overseas competition. When the company approached us and asked us to partner with them to beat the competition and save jobs, we felt skeptical but knew that we had nothing to lose. We fought hard for job security, increased pay for more skills, and paid retraining. In exchange we gave up a lot of our traditional rules. Looking back, we made the right moves. WCI and our plant have been so successful that we now have more jobs and our average pay is 15 percent above the local competition, counting the incentive bonuses. I believe we have the highest skilled workforce in the industry. The word is out, and we have at least ten qualified applicants for every new job opening.

Let's go now to a WC industrial distributorship and showroom in the suburbs of Chicago. John Pym is a salesman who has been in this distributorship for ten years.

Sales training has come a long way in my years of selling for WCI. Every year now when new equipment comes out, we get a library of interactive videodisc training that explains features and options, performance characteristics, new technologies and what they do for the customer, comparison to competitive products, demonstration of all the controls, and selling tactics. This system is menu driven, so I can review any aspect at will whenever I have the need. I can also use it to demonstrate operator features to customers.

The advanced selling skills training I received at the WC sales academy really put the polish on after all my years of homegrown experience. Besides my being much better equipped to sell, everybody else knows their job and does it well. Service and customer satisfaction are so good that selling is easier. Another thing I love is the products we sell. I'm really proud of the quality, materials, design, and workmanship.

Sun Chang is the service manager at the same distributorship.

Every one of my service technicians is factory certified. The factory runs a regional service training center which also serves as a recruitment screening center. Here's how it works. They maintain a list of qualified candidates. They qualify applicants by putting them through a battery of tests, including performance tests on basic optical repair skills in the shop.

When I need a new service tech, I notify the factory and they send me two or three qualified candidates. The one I hire goes to eight weeks of advanced training on WC optics, tools, and maintenance procedures and starts with me as a factory-certified service technician. We pay what seems like a big fee, but it's really cheaper than trying to do it ourselves, not to mention the savings we get from higher productivity, good workmanship, and very low customer returns and complaints.

We have an interactive videodisc training system in the shop with discs for all optical products for the last three years. These discs have sophisticated question-and-answer troubleshooting aids and demonstrations of all the common repairs. When new products and equipment come out, we all watch an introductory segment that explains the differences from previous versions and watch the demos of features and uses. The first time we do something new, we do it in pairs to check each other. The factory school has a hotline and a representative on wheels.

I attended a four-week school two years ago at the WC Service Academy to learn all the basics of being a service manager, and I get a videodisc each year with advanced service management techniques. Our shop scores an average of 96 percent on the WC Service Quality and Productivity Index.

Jim Lang has been the owner of the distributorship for the past thirty years. His father owned it before him.

When WCI announced its intention to install a distributor certification program as part of its new TQM philosophy, I was ready to rebel. I had been used to running my own business my own way for a lot of years. When the chain of quality concept was introduced, though, it made all kinds of sense. It starts with figuring out what the customer wants and designing equipment to those specs, building them defect free, and then providing high-quality sales, financing, and service at the distributorship. We are the human face of the company to the customer.

As a part of this program, everyone in my organization went back to school, including me. It's a very expensive program, but the results speak for themselves. We sell a lot of optical instruments and make excellent profits. This outfit used to be full of stresses and strains because there were many things we didn't know how to do well. WCI has a model of the high-performance distributorship that its education and training programs are built on. The goal is to help all of us achieve superior performance, and it's definitely working.

Obviously, WCI is doing something right with its education and training system to get all these rave reviews. Let's take a look now at the elements of this system.

WCI EDUCATION AND TRAINING

The elements of WCI education and training organization are shown in Figure 1-2. In the next few pages, we briefly describe each of the elements in WCI's organizational system. These elements are explained in greater detail later in this book. We're not suggesting that this is the only way to organize a world class educational system. It

- **Training Departments**
  - World Class Education Systems, Inc. (WCES)
  - Division Training Departments
  - Local Training Departments (Plants and other major locations)

- **Advisory Structure**
  - Executive Education Board
  - Curriculum Advisory Councils
  - Training Administration Council
  - Divisional Training Councils
  - Local Training Committees

- **Learning Facilities**
  - Corporate Education Center
  - WC Technical Education Center
  - Divisional Training Facilities
  - Local training facilities

- **Administrative Network**
  - Online database, information system, ILP system, and registration and scheduling
  - WCES customer service department
  - Divisional training coordinators
  - Local training coordinators
  - Distributorship supplier training coordinators

Figure 1-2   WCI Education and Training Infrastructure

is simply one example of a complete system that is linked closely to business performance requirements.

Training Departments

WCES   WCES is headed by Bill Wagner, who is Vice President and General Manager of WCES and a corporate officer in WCI reporting to the President and Chief Operating Officer. He has bottom-line responsibility for WCES operations and leadership and coordination responsibility for all education and training across the corporation and in support of distributorships and preferred suppliers.

WCES is responsible for the operations of the Corporate Education Center, which includes the Executive Education Institute, Management Institutes, and the Sales Academy; and for the operations of the WC Technical Education Center, which includes research, development, and manufacturing technology training as well as the Service Academy. WCES is also responsible for

- Coordinating corporate strategic training plans

- Conducting needs analyses and developing curriculum architecture designs across the corporation

- Centralizing courseware development and delivering centralized instruction

- Designing and operating common administrative systems

- Measuring education and training results

- Establishing education and training process standards

- Providing training and education consulting support.

Division Training Departments   Division training departments are headed by a Division Training Director, who reports to the Vice President, Human Resources, and is responsible for leadership and coordination of Education and Training across the division. Division training departments are responsible for

- Coordinating division strategic and operational training plans

- Conducting division needs analysis and developing curriculum architecture

- Developing division-specific courseware

- Centralizing delivery of training to division target audiences

- Providing consulting support to line organizations

- Overseeing training departments within the division.

Local Training Departments   Local training departments exist in most business locations with more than 100 employees. They are headed by a Local Training

Manager who is responsible for leadership and coordination of education and training at the location and usually reports to the plant or location manager or location human resources (HR) manager. Local training departments are responsible for

- Developing location training plans
- Conducting local needs analyses
- Developing location-specific courseware
- Delivering training at the location
- Coordinating procurement of training from the division training department and WCES.

Advisory Structure

The education and training advisory structure (shown in Figure 1-3) is the formal system of partnership between the training departments and the organizations they serve. This structure provides the mechanism for evaluating and prioritizing needs, making planning decisions, allocating resources, communicating information, and accounting for results.

Executive Education Board   The Executive Education Board is responsible for sponsoring and managing the investment in education and training across the corporation and supporting distributorships and preferred suppliers. In addition, it serves as the Board of Directors for the WCES subsidiary. It is chaired by the President and Chief Operating Officer and includes the Divisional Vice President/General Manager and several corporate vice presidents.

Curriculum Advisory Councils   The curriculum advisory councils are cor-poration-wide councils that oversee education and training activities in the following curriculum areas:

Management skills

Executive education

Quality

Research, design, development, and engineering

Marketing

Manufacturing

Distributorship support

Preferred supplier support

Materials and logistics

Product management.

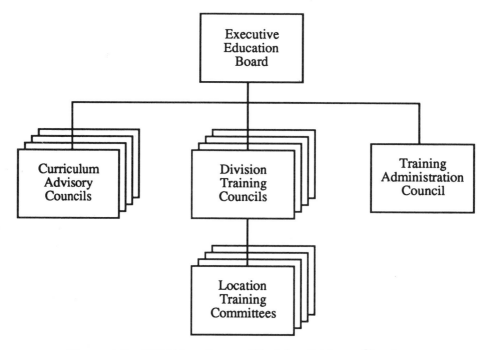

Figure 1-3 WC Education and Training Advisory Structure

These groups are generally chaired by a director-level manager from a corporate staff with same-level membership from the division. The Distributorship Support Council includes six dealers, two representing each division. The Preferred Supplier Support Council includes six representatives from supplier companies. The curriculum advisory councils are accountable to the Executive Education Board.

Training Administration Council   The Training Administration Council is chaired by the Vice President/General Manager of WCES and includes the training directors of all the divisions. This council is responsible for administrative coordination of education and training across the corporation and includes planning and administrative systems. It is also responsible for coordinating

- Recruiting
- Training
- Career development of training staffs across the corporation.

This council is accountable to the Executive Education Board.

Division Training Councils   The division training councils are chaired by a top division executive and include heads of the major divisional departments. They are responsible for sponsorship and investment management for all education and training activities within their division. They review and approve the Division strategic and operational training plans and review annual results against plans. They are accountable to the Executive Education Board.

Local Training Committees   Local training committees are chaired by the location manager and include the heads of significant location departments. They are responsible for sponsorship and support for location training activities, plans, and budgets. They are accountable to the division training councils.

Learning Facilities

WCI has a complete spectrum of high-quality learning facilities. The Corporate Education Center on the WCI headquarters campus has classroom and other learning facilities for executive, management, sales, and other functional and professional training that does not require expensive laboratories.

The WC Technology Education Center is located on the main campus of WC Technologies and has optical technology laboratories of all kinds including the service academy shops.

The divisions all have learning facilities that enable them to deliver training effectively at the division level. The locations, particularly the larger plants, have complete facilities including classrooms, laboratories, and computerized learning centers.

The distributorships have all installed interactive videodisc learning centers for both service and sales as a part of the Distributor Certification Program. Each region has a service training center where service technicians are screened and trained.

Engineers and technicians anywhere in WCI who have compatible workstations can access a wide variety of computer based instructional programs via the WC Information Network. They can also participate in National Technological University (NTU) credit and non credit programs at the locations across the Corporation that have satellite downlinks and video classrooms. A video teleconferencing network is available to most locations for informational training that is needed quickly by groups in many locations.

The general principle behind the WCI training facilities strategy is to keep the actual training as close to the employee's work location as is economically and instructionally feasible. This reduces all sorts of barriers to learning and fosters the philosophy that learning is an important and regular part of everyone's job.

Bringing people together occasionally for certain types of programs at the corporate education centers has another strategic benefit. It helps foster a feeling that WCI is one large team all working together under a common set of values toward common ends. It also helps people establish networks of peers throughout the company with whom they feel comfortable seeking and sharing ideas and information. It is one of the ways employees obtain synergy from being a part of a diverse corporation.

It is expected that as learning technologies develop and evolve, the facility mix will evolve to take maximum advantage of them.

Administrative Network

There are two important aspects of the WC educational administrative network: the computer and communications network, and the human network. These, of course, are not independent of each other but form a vital people-and-information support team that helps the entire education and training operation to run smoothly.

Computer and Communications Network The computer and communications network gives training coordinators, supervisors, managers, and individual employees all over WCI on-line access to training information and the means to send information into the system. Individual employees can

- Look up their own training records
- Access their Individual Learning Plan
- Build their Individual Learning Plan online
- Look up available programs
- Request registration in a program
- Provide evaluation data on programs they have already participated in.

Supervisors and managers access the system to

- Review and approve employees' individual learning plans
- Approve registration for learning programs
- Track progress against employees' individual learning programs
- Build a training plan for their group
- Monitor progress against their group training plan
- Provide evaluation data on employees' transfer of skills from training to the job and value of the learning to the business.

Training coordinators in the Divisions, in WCES, and at Locations use the system for a wide variety of purposes including:

- Forecasting demand
- Scheduling classes and registering of trainees
- Scheduling training facilities and instructors
- Reporting status of programs under development
- Identifying and analyzing backlogs for training.

Training Directors and Training Managers in the Divisions, WCES and at locations use the system for

- Building their training plans
- Building plans for projects
- Tracking progress against plans and budgets
- Reviewing and analyzing results.

The training results measurement system is online and can be accessed by training managers, line managers, and members of the executive support structure to review and analyze results at the corporate, division, or location level as well as to evaluate data for individual courses or training programs. The results reporting system is menu driven and allows the user to look at the data in many different ways to obtain whatever analysis is of interest.

The Human Coordination Network   Every organizational entity has a designated training coordinator. This includes all the distributorships and preferred suppliers. For smaller groups this is a part-time job, but for the large plants and division office there is a full-time coordinator. The hub of this coordination network is the WCES Customer Service Department.

The people in this network are responsible for keeping the education and training system running smoothly, for anticipating and responding to problems, and for contributing ideas for continuous improvement of the system. They are the human face of education and training to employees throughout the system. Their performance is measured in terms of the quality of service they provide.

In addition, the people in this network are heavy users of the computer and communications network and they can communicate with each other over the network in a variety of ways, including electronic mail and electronic calendar access. There is also regular telephone and fax communication around the network.

Twice each year, WCES hosts a Training Coordinator Conference in which plans and information are shared, issues raised and worked on, and ideas for improvement developed.

The philosophy behind the administrative network is that information is essential to effective decision making, and since every employee is expected to make appropriate learning decisions and choices, management is committed to providing everyone with the information they need. Access codes are used to safeguard privileged information. For example, only the individual employee, the supervisor, and the training coordinator have access to the employee's training record and Individual Learning Plan.

WCI IMPLEMENTATION HISTORY

All of this sounds a bit overwhelming. But remember, the world class system we have just described was not put in place all at once. It took nearly ten years moving one step at a time to become fully implemented, and this was quick work. WCI's first strategic plan was developed over eight years ago.

This first strategic training plan took six months to complete. Annual updates to the plan take two to three months. However, the time invested has been worthwhile. This strategic training plan, backed by WCI executives, has been the driving force behind the impressive system that has been built. It has provided the vision and helped to make the resources and talent available to achieve it. Figure 1-4 provides an overview of how the plan was developed and implemented over the years.

EARMARKS OF A WORLD CLASS LEARNING SYSTEM

We have already told you that your organization does not have to match WCI's in form or structure to be world class. But what must it have? For any training organization to be world class, it has to exhibit certain characteristics or earmarks. Next we outline the earmarks of a learning system that make it world class. WCI's system exhibits these earmarks, but it could just as easily have taken a number of other forms and still be world class. Whatever form your system takes, it needs to exhibit these earmarks, too.

Cultural Values Support Full Competency Development and Lifelong Learning

The organization exhibits, in both words and deeds,

- Commitment to providing everyone with skills and knowledge needed to perform assigned tasks
- Commitment to lifelong learning to enhance performance, stay at the cutting edge, and develop career potential
- Recognition of the link between learning and quality, productivity and profitability.

There Is Strong Executive Leadership and Participation

- Top executives have a vision for the role they expect education and training to play in achieving their goals and objectives.

Year 1	Year 2	Year 3	Year 4	Year 5	Year 6	Year 7

• First Strategic Training Plan Developed (first six months)
• WCES Subsidiary formed; begins operations with existing available programs
• Executive Support Structure established
  – Executive Education Board
  – Curriculum Advisory Councils
  -- Distributor
  -- Manufacturing
  -- Product
  -- Management
  -- Quality
	• Additional Curriculum Councils
	  – Engineering and Technology
	  – Design
	  – Marketing
	  – Materials and Logistics
	  – Financing
	  – Management Skills
	• Basic Skills/Literacy Program designed; WCI/Union Fund established
	• Curriculum Architectures designed
	  – Distribution
	  – Manufacturing
	  – Product Manufacturing
	  – Quality
	• Sales Academy, Service Academy Technical Education; and the Corporate Education center approved
	• Courseware Development Group produces top five priority courses
		• Basic Skills/Literacy Program piloted in one plant as one Community College Technical Education Center
		• Sales and Service Academies open doors in temporary quarters
		• Curriculum Architectures designed in four more areas
		• Courseware Development produces 25 more courses
		• Distributor certification system implemented
		• Division Education and Training model implemented in all four Product Divisions, WC Technologies, and WCAC
			• Basic Skills/Literacy Program implemented across WCI
			• Corporate Education Center opens; Sales and Service Academies move in
			• Executive Development Program established
			• NTU brought in to all plants and Engineering and Technology locations
			• Interactive videodisc training system for sales and service implemented
			• Curriculum Architectures designed for three more areas
			• Courseware Development produces 100 more courses
				• Results system measures 35 percent of training needs met
				• WCES takes on performance consulting role
				• Courseware development produces 125 products
				• Video conference instruction textbook implemented at all major locations
				• Addition approved for Corporate Education Center
				• WC Technical Education Center opens
					• 50 percent of training needs met
					• WC Education and Training Information System goes on line; provides real-time access to training information and ILP aids
					• 30 percent of employees have ILPs on file
						• 65 percent of training needs met
						• 90 percent of employees with ILPs on file

Figure 1-4 WCI Strategic Training Plan Implementation Time Line

- Executives play a direct role in linking education and training to business goals through participation in executive education boards, approval of strategic training plans, approval of resource budgets, and review of results.

- Executives play a key role in establishing expectations, monitoring performance, and providing rewards and consequences regarding implementation of comprehensive learning systems and culture.

- Executive action matches rhetoric.

- Executives are aware of the level of annual investment in education and training and manage this investment as carefully as they manage capital investments.

The System is Characterized by Total Participation across All Levels of the Organization

- Everyone recognizes the important role learning plays in their working lives and in the success of the organization.

- Everyone has an Individual Learning Plan.

- Every organizational unit has an education and training plan.

- Employees take responsibility for their own learning.

- Supervisors and managers are important players in the learning system, establishing expectations, monitoring and coaching application of new knowledge, and providing rewards and recognition for learning results.

- Formal training is recognized to be only a part of the learning process; work assignments and coaching play significant, planned roles.

- Managers and executives act as role models by spending time in education and training and talking about what they have learned.

The Learning System is Driven by Business Performance Goals and is Competency Based

- Functional curricula are in place based on definition and analysis of functional tasks to be performed to achieve business goals.

- New systems and products are implemented with a supporting curriculum based on analysis of new tasks and skills and knowledge required by all populations affected.

- Corporate initiatives, such as implementation of TQM, have the support of a performance-based curriculum.

- Training and education programs develop measurable competencies based on business performance needs.

- Training priorities are set based on expected return on investment (ROI).

There are Tight Linkages between Training Departments and the Users of Their Services

- Curriculum advisory councils help define and prioritize training needs.

- The user community participates in developing courseware by providing field expertise and field testing the materials.

- The user community provides its best performers for part-time or full-time assignments as instructors.

- The training departments maintain a strong customer service orientation.

- Providers and users work together to devise and implement strategies for effective transfer of learning to the job.

Resources are Matched to Need and Objectives

- Training needs are quantitatively estimated.

- Plans and objectives are built based on quantitative needs and estimated ROI.

- Resource allocations are sufficient to achieve committed objectives.

Training Staffs are Competent and Include a Balanced Mix of Expertise

- The training staffs themselves are selected and trained to a high standard of competence.

- Training staffs include an appropriate mix of career professionals in instructional design, performance analysis, and other specialties as well as subject-matter experts drawn from the field and from outside sources of expertise.

- Training staffs have a strong sense of their contribution to business success.

- Sufficient clerical and administrative support resources are provided to leverage the time of high cost professional and managerial talent.

A Balanced Array of Strategies is Employed

- Training strategies have been implemented which provide the best balance of learning effectiveness, cost, administrative convenience, least disruption of the work environment, and timeliness.

- Training is provided at the most appropriate location whether centralized, onsite or on the job.

- An appropriate mix of delivery technologies such as classroom, laboratory, computer based, videodisc, video teleconference, expert systems, job aids, and training embedded in mechanized systems are deployed.

- The training departments are aware of emerging training technologies, and they experiment with applications and transfer mature technologies into service.

- Selection of media considers qualitative effectiveness and total cost of ownership.

There Is Strong Administrative Coordination of Education and Training

- The end user of training can go to a single source to find available training opportunities to meet his or her needs.

- There is a common information system and database to keep track of training information and make it widely available.

- There are common process standards and performance measures for needs analysis, curriculum architecture, courseware development, delivery, and maintenance and evaluation.

- There is a common results measurement system for education and training.

- There is a common registration and scheduling system.

- There is a common system for developing individual learning plans and organization unit plans for education and training.

- Curriculum architectures are linked across the organization to minimize duplication and maximize benefits from expensive courseware development.

- The mission and roles of training departments and line organizational units are coordinated to care for all the education and training needs with minimum overlap and to avoid internal competition.

- Strategic and operational training plans are coordinated across the entire organization and linked to the business planning calendar.

Internal Education and Training Resources Are Leveraged through Appropriate Use of Outside Resources

- Universities, colleges, and other academic institutions provide basic skills, degree programs, and advanced specialized education.

- Contractors provide courseware development resources to handle peak loads and special requirements.

- Contract instructors with specialized expertise augment expert instructors drawn from the field.

- Training and education consultants provide specialized expertise to training departments.

WHERE TO BEGIN

As you can see, there is a lot of ground to cover to build a system that exhibits all these characteristics. Where do you start to plan, design, and implement a high-performance education and training system for your organization? A strategic training plan should be your first step. The rest of this book gives you the planning and design ideas, procedures, and tools to develop your strategic plan and begin to implement your own world-class training system. Your part is to provide the time, effort, resources, and energy needed to make it a reality. In the words of the Russian ballet dancer Anna Pavlova, "success depends in a very large measure upon individual initiative and exertion, and cannot be achieved except by dint of hard work." (*The MacMillan Dictionary of Quotations*, MacMillan, NY 1989, pg. 550)

Of course, education and training alone will not give you world class business performance. It is only one of the essential ingredients. Other important systems that need to be in place for a world class business include

- Management systems
- TQM system
- Human resources systems
- Technology
- Financial and physical resources.

The education and training system interacts with all these other systems to help provide the competencies needed, but it can not make up for inadequacies in these other systems. However, as you begin to develop and model the characteristics of a world-class training organization, these other systems should begin to take note and start to emulate your success. Become a champion for this effort—there are great rewards and results to be achieved.

2

THE STRATEGIC TRAINING PLAN

Chapter 1 painted a picture of the world class training system. It sounds like a big task. How do you get there? We suggested in chapter 1 that the strategic training plan is the starting place for getting there. This chapter provides an overview of the strategic training plan and answers the what, why, how, who, and when questions for developing a strategic training plan. The remaining chapters provide detailed examples and procedures for developing the plan.

We begin with a definition of the strategic training plan and a description of its typical contents. This is followed by a description of a four-phase planning process for developing the plan. We then present a rationale for the plan, describe the roles of key players in the planning process, and finally tie the plan to the business planning cycle.

WHAT IS A STRATEGIC TRAINING PLAN?

A strategic training plan defines the training needed to achieve the goals of the business and lays out a comprehensive roadmap for meeting these needs. In the words of James L. Pierce, "Planning is but another word for the vision that sees a creative achievement before it is manifest." (from Kurian, George Thomas *Handbook of Business Quotations*, Prentice Hall, Inc., Englewood Cliffs, NJ, 1987, pg. 124). Your strategic training plan provides the vision that sees your world class training organization before it is manifest. The plan answers these questions:

1. What are the challenges facing our organization and our strategies and goals for dealing with these challenges?

2. What skills, knowledge, and competencies do we need in the organization to achieve our goals?

3. How can we make sure that our employees, suppliers, and customers know what to do and how to do it; what is training's role?

4. How adequate is our present training system to address these needs successfully?

5. What kind of a training system do we need? What should it look like three to five years from now?

6. What strategic goals shall we establish for training?

7. What training strategies will most effectively and efficiently achieve these goals?

8. What is the estimated training workload to execute these strategies?

9. How many resources should we commit, and what is the expected return on investment?

10. What organizational, management, and administrative systems do we need to deploy the resources effectively and get the job done?

11. How shall we implement the plan?

Strategic training plans can and often should be developed at a number of different levels. For example, you have a plan for

- An entire corporation
- A business unit or division
- A function such as research and development
- A major work location or plant.

The questions are the same, the scope and complexity is obviously different. For the purposes of this book, we assume the plan is for an entire organization or corporation or a major business unit. If you intend to develop a plan with a smaller scope, simply scale everything to the scope you have selected. The principles and procedures we give you will work for any scope.

Strategic Training Plan Contents

At the conclusion of the strategic planning process, all outputs are documented in a strategic training plan. Figures 2-1 and 2-2 provide example outlines of strategic training plans for two radically different organizations. The first organization (Figure 2-1) is a small pizza chain with plans to grow from four stores to thirty stores in five years. Its strategic training plan lays out the training approach to supporting this growth. This plan is a relatively simple document compared to our second example, which is for a fictitious giant auto maker doing $30 billion a year in sales (Figure 2-2). You can see that there is

I. Overview

   A. Training implications of business plan
- Growth goals
- Quality control
- Cost control

   B. Major training strategies
- Manager training
- Cook training
- Counter training

   C. Cost/benefit analysis
- Training costs
- Cost of not training
- Expected Return on Investment

   D. Implementation
- Outside resources to develop systems and materials
- Our managers to execute the training

II. Development of Systems and Materials

   A. Analysis of tasks and skills
- Timing
- Resource requirements

   B. Development of training materials
- Timing
- Resource requirements

   C. Develop "Training Store" concept
- Timing
- Resource requirements

   D. Develop evaluation system
- Timing
- Resource requirements

III. Implementation

   A. Training the managers for implementation
   B. Implementation support
   C. Evaluation method
   D. Management feedback and control process

Figure 2-1 ABC Pizza Company Strategic Training Plan Outline

I. Executive Summary

    A. The Strategic Role of Training in WCI
        1. Where our business is going
        2. Skills and knowledge as a strategic asset
        3. Training and education as a means
        4. A proposed WCI training and education policy

    B. A Vision of WCI Training in 1994

    C. Where We Are Today

    D. How We Compare to Our Competition

    E. How We Compare in the World

    F. What We Have to Do to Achieve Our Vision
        1. Strategic goals
        2. Estimated cost to achieve
        3. Estimated business cost of status quo solution

    G. Required Executive Support

II. A Strategic Vision of WCI Training

    A. Analysis of Training Requirements to Achieve Business Goals

        1. Training required to bring new employees and existing employees to skill level required for peak performance

        2. Additional training required to support key business initiatives/goals
            • Quality initiative
            • Improved asset utilization
            • Two new plants
            • Restructuring of Marketing, Sales, Product Management functions
            • Deployment of modern manufacturing technology and methods
            • Pay-for-skills provision in new labor contract

        3. Summary of estimated training requirements
            • By function
            • By location

Figure 2-2   Giant Auto Corporation Strategic Training Plan Outline

B. Assessment of Existing Training
    1. Amount compared to needs
    2. Quality
    3. Cost
    4. Systems in place
        • Needs analysis
        • Training materials development
        • Delivery
        • Results measurement
        • Planning
        • Linkage to line and staff management
        • Facilities and equipment
    5. Barriers to achieving 1994 requirements

C. Assessment of Our Competition

D. Benchmark Analyses of Other Top Companies

E. Overall Conclusions from the Analysis Data
    1. Implications for competitive position, profitability, quality, customer satisfaction, and employee needs satisfaction
    2. The size and scope of the challenge
    3. Major issues to be faced

F. Proposed WCI Training and Education Policy
    1. Rationale
    2. Policy statement
    3. Implementation approach

G. A vision of WCI training in five years

H. Strategic Training Goals
    1. Amounts and kinds of training to meet business goals
    2. Training system improvement goals
    3. Executive and line management involvement

III. Quantitative Plan for Training to be Provided

A. Development/Acquisition of Training Material
    1. Forecast of materials to be developed (1990-94)
    2. Materials and development strategies to be used
    3. Unit cost of development
    4. Maintenance cost-estimating formula
    5. Forecast of development resource requirements and cost, various scenarios

Figure 2-2   (continued)

B. Delivery of Training
  1. Personnel forecast (1990-94), force size and inward movement
     • By function and level
     • By location

  2. Training Requirements per Person
     • By function and level
     • By location
     • By type of training

  3. Delivery Strategies to be Used

  4. Delivery Requirements Forecast (1990-94)

  5. Unit Cost of Delivery, by Delivery Strategy, Location, and Type of Training

  6. Delivery plan, resource requirements and cost, various scenarios

C. Additional Resource Requirements
  1. Needs analysis and curriculum architecture design
  2. Results measurement
  3. Instructional technology surveillance, assessment, transfer, development
  4. Training staff development and training
  5. Training information system

IV. Training Systems Development and Implementation

  A. Governance of Training
     1. Overall philosophy
     2. Executive training advisory board
     3. Functional curriculum councils (middle management)
     4. Location training committees
     5. Training administration council (training directors)
     6. Planning, priorities, and accountability process

  B. Results Measurement System
     1. Measurement philosophy
     2. Key performance measures and measurement hierarchy
     3. Specifications for results measurement system
     4. System development plan
        • Activities
        • Schedule
        • Resource requirements

Figure 2-2 (continued)

C. Organization of Training
   1. Organization issues addressed
   2. Alternative structures and comparative analysis
   3. Target organization, year 5
   4. Evolution of the organization, years 1-5
   5. Subunit mission, responsibilities
   6. Process flow
      • Needs analysis and Curriculum Architecture Design
      • Training materials development
      • Delivery
      • Planning
   7. Resources required to complete detailed organization design

D. Staffing Strategy
   1. Staffing issues
   2. Alternatives and comparative analysis
   3. Staffing strategies
   4. Recruiting strategies
   5. Recognition/retention strategies
   6. Resources required to implement staffing strategy

E. Financing and Financial Accountability
   1. Issues addressed
   2. Alternatives and comparative analysis
   3. Financing strategies
      • Training needs analysis, curriculum design
      • Materials development
      • Delivery
      • Allocation of overhead
   4. Approvals and accountability

F. Supervisor/Manager Support System
   1. Overall philosophy
   2. System specification
   3. System development plan
      • Activities
      • Schedule
      • Resource requirements

G. Training Facilities
   1. Requirements forecast
   2. Existing inventory
   3. Issues addressed
   4. Facility plan
      • New facilities to be added
      • Abandonment of some existing facilities
   5. Anticipated costs
   6. Resources required to implement the plan

Figure 2-2   (continued)

V. Summary Resource Requirements (Years 1-5)

A. Staff Requirements
   1. Training Materials Development
   2. Delivery
   3. Needs analysis and curriculum design
   4. Results measurement, etc.
   5. Instructional technology support
   6. Operation and maintenance of facilities and equipment
   7. Support staff
   8. Management
   9. Development of administrative systems

B. Capital Requirements
   1. Facilities
   2. Equipment
   3. Furnishings

C. Expense Budget
   1. Personnel
   2. Procured materials
   3. Procured services
   4. Facilities operation

Figure 2-2   (continued)

a much greater level of detail and information required in a strategic training plan for a broader scope or larger organization. As you get further into this book, you will begin to be able to determine the outline for your own strategic plan.

FOUR-PHASE PLANNING PROCESS

Whatever the size of your business, if you are developing a strategic training plan for the first time, it is to your advantage to divide the planning process and planning outputs into major phases. The first strategic training plan for an organization can be a complex undertaking. Breaking the project into phases with key milestone review points at the end of each phase helps make it more manageable and less overwhelming. The four phase process outlined in Figure 2-3 is one convenient and logical way to do this, but there is nothing sacred about four phases or the specific ingredients of each phase. For instance, you might count the project plan as a separate phase and have a five-phase process. (Note that the process for doing future annual updates is usually much simpler and may not have all of these phases.)

In the following sections we provide you with a brief overview of the outputs from each of these phases. In subsequent chapters we provide detailed examples and step-by-step procedures for completing each phase.

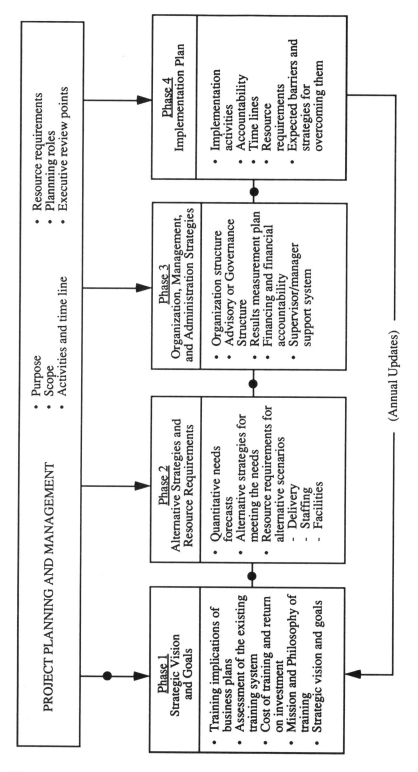

Figure 2-3 Four-Phase Strategic Planning Process

● = Executive Review Point

Project Plan

Doing a strategic training plan is a big project in its own right. As with any big project, one of the keys to success is managing the project well. Managing a project well starts with a good project plan, which keeps you from losing your way or failing to allow enough time and resources to do a good job on the project. We prefer to develop an overall project plan at the beginning of the strategic planning process which provides project purpose and scope, a detailed plan for phase 1, and general plans for phases 2 through 4. Detailed plans for phases 2 through 4 will be completed at the conclusion of the previous phase.

For your first time using the strategic planning process, we recommend allowing ten months to complete the strategic plan. Figure 2-4 shows how you might divide that time down for each phase of the planning process. For annual updates to the plan, allow three months minimum.

Chapter 3 provides more detail on project planning and project management, including a sample project plan that you can use for a model when building your own project plan.

Phase 1: Strategic Vision and Goals

The purpose of this phase is to develop the broad view of training needed to ensure the success of the business plan and to establish the vision and goals for providing this training. The outputs of this phase include

- Training implications of business plans
- Assessment of the existing training system
- Mission, philosophy, and roles of the training organization
- Strategic vision and goals.

Project plan and approval	1 month
Phase 1 and review	3 months
Phase 2 and review	3 months
Phase 3 and review	2 months
Phase 4	<u>1 month</u>
	10 months

Figure 2-4 Time to Complete Strategic Training Plan

Training Implications of Business Plans   The chart identifying training implications of business goals and challenges is one of the most important aspects of the strategic training plan. This is where training activities are linked to business results. For example, assume that a franchised pizza business is planning to double its number of stores over the next two years. What are the training implications associated with this growth? Or, what are the training implications of a major quality initiative in a manufacturing company? What are the training implications of implementing a major new office automation system?

Most businesses and other organizations today are deeply involved in making fundamental and pervasive changes on a continuing basis to their products, processes, operations, methods and technologies. All of these changes have significant training implications. If the training implications are not identified and addressed, businesses or business units can fail or fall short of expected results.

Your business plan should provide the following:

1. A list of specific challenges facing the business, and the strategies and goals that have been established for dealing with these challenges
2. Training implication of each challenge

- Who is affected?
- What new skills and knowledge will those people need, and when will they need them?
- How much will it cost to provide this training?
- How much will it cost if you do not provide this training?
- What is the expected return on the training investment?

Doing this part of the strategic training plan is addressed in more detail in chapter 4.

Assessment of the Existing Training System   The assessment of the existing training system should be done against four sets of criteria:

1. Your internal assessment of what is versus what ought to be in your training organization (more details in chapter 5)
2. Your assessment of what is in your training organization versus what your competition is doing (more details in chapter 6)
3. Your assessment of what is in your organization versus what the best-in-class organizations are doing (This is known as benchmarking, more details in chapter 6.)
4. Your calculation of training costs today (see chapter 7).

The assessment of the present training system requires a hard-nosed look at the training implications of your company's current business plans. The purpose of this assessment is to give you a measure of the gap between what is and what ought to be. The assessment may tell you that continuing business as usual will provide all the training that the organization needs, or it may tell you that fundamental restructuring of the training system and major changes in training resources are required. More likely, it will tell you something between these two.

The assessment of your competition should tell you what competitors are doing about training. Is their training system positioned to give them a competitive edge? How serious is this threat? Are you ahead of your competition? What do you need to do to maintain your edge? What specific competitive advantages accrue from training?

The assessment of your organization against the best-in-class (benchmarking) should give you a more objective picture of what else could be done to bring your organization to superior performance in its chosen field. Looking at the gap between your training system and that of the leaders shows you what you need to do if you truly want to become leaders, or world class. If you do not do this, you may keep improving your training organization according to internal or competition-based criteria, but may not improve enough to become leading edge yourself.

Your assessment of your training system should provide the following:

1. An assessment of the capability of your overall training system and its subsystems and processes to do what is needed, efficiently and effectively

2. An assessment of the adequacy of basic curricula to train people who are entering new jobs

3. An assessment of the adequacy of training resources to carry the basic training load and address all the specific business challenges that have been identified

4. An assessment of your relative position with respect to competitors

5. A benchmark assessment of your position relative to best-in-class organizations (optional)

6. An estimate of the total cost of training today and the return on investment.

Mission and Philosophy Statements The mission statement of the training organization is a clear statement of the expected contribution of training to the business. This statement should include mission, scope, and roles for the overall training organization. Mission, scope, and roles for individual training departments and roles for managers, supervisors, and others in the training system can then be built from this overall mission.

The training plan must identify the roles of line and staff management in carrying out training responsibilities. Without this clear definition of roles and responsibilities, important training needs can go unaddressed, or conversely more than one organization can attempt to address the same needs, resulting in internal competition and conflict or simply unnecessary redundancy.

The strategic training plan should also include a well developed philosophy statement for the training organization. This training philosophy statement provides a list of principles and values which the organization should use as a basis for making training decisions. This collection of principles and values may include statements such as the following:

- The role of our training organization is to improve job performance for all employees.

- Employees are responsible for their own competencies and careers.

- The organization is responsible for providing the means for employees to develop their skills and knowledge.

- All training should be based on an analysis of job performance requirements.

The development of the philosophy statements helps clarify the fundamental values and guidelines that will be used to make planning and tactical decisions for the training function.

Your mission and philosophy statements should provide the following:

1. A clear sense of the mission of all training within your organizational scope
2. A set of guiding values and philosophies about training
3. Purpose and roles for each individual training department
4. A set of training roles for line and staff management.

Developing mission and philosophy statements is addressed in detail in chapter 8.

Strategic Vision and Goals for Training Many training organizations have found it helpful to develop a picture of what training will be like in the organization three to five years down the road. This vision of future of training should include not only what the training department will be doing but what line managers will do and what individual employees will do with respect to training. It should describe the impact of training on business results and the roles that will be played by executive management, middle management, and line supervision in the training function. The vision should be clear enough and comprehensive enough so everyone involved can see where they are going and develop a sense of ownership, commitment, and drive to actualize the vision. A good strategic vision can be a powerful and exciting motivator to help get people behind the process of building a world class training organization. It helps them understand what that organization is going to look like.

The strategic goals for training outline the major accomplishments required to make the vision a reality. These goals should not be narrowly defined, such as the delivery of a specific training course, but should be much more broadly responsive to business needs. Examples of such broad goals might include

- Create a new system to develop and deliver training to the company's customers on the operation and maintenance of our products.

- Create a high-quality performance-based research and development curriculum to support the R&D plans of the business.

- Establish a training department in each of the major business units of the company with responsibility for functional and technical training.

Your strategic vision and goals for training should provide the following:

1. A clear vision of the training system needed to support business goals
2. A short list of strategic goals to achieve the vision
3. A one-page description of each of these goals.

Developing this vision and set of goals is explained further in chapter 9.

Executive Review, Phase 1   Once you have completed the training implications of business plans; assessment of existing training system; mission, philosophy, and roles of the training organization; and strategic vision and goals, you have completed phase I of the strategic planning process. The end of phase 1 is a good time for executive review. We recommend reviewing the outputs of phase 1 with a panel of top executives in a two- to four-hour session. The executives should consider the following questions:

1. Did we get all the significant business challenges, strategies, and goals?
2. Is our assessment of the training implications believable?
3. Is our assessment of the present training system believable?
4. Are our statements of mission, roles, and philosophy acceptable? What can we do to make them stronger?
5. What do you like about the vision and goals? What don't you like? Where can these be improved?

You should overview what will be done in phases 2 through 4 of the strategic planning process and obtain executive commitment for support. These executive reviews are important not only for getting your questions answered, but also for obtaining the buy-in and support of the power players in your company. This support is a key ingredient for the future success of your training organization. If possible, you want to come away from this meeting with some real champions for your effort.

Phase 2: Methods and Resource Requirements

Assuming you have the support of the executive review board and do not need to revisit phase 1 in any significant way, you can then go ahead with phase 2 of the process.

The purpose of phase 2 is to investigate alternative strategies for achieving the vision and strategic goals, to estimate their associated resource requirements, and then to select a strategy mix and adopt a three- to five-year resource plan. The outputs of this phase include

- Quantitative needs forecast
- Alternative strategies for meeting the needs
- Resource requirements for alternative scenarios.

Quantitative Needs Forecast   The needs forecast is completed to develop a quantitative picture of all the work that must be done to achieve the vision, mission, and goals. This work can be divided into needs analysis, curriculum architecture design, training materials development, delivery of training, and development and deployment of administrative systems. Your quantitative needs forecast should provide the following:

1. A three- to five-year staffing requirements forecast
2. Needs analyses for major functions or job groups, for new systems, and for other initiatives
3. Curriculum architectures for functions, systems, and major initiatives
4. A three- to five-year forecast of training needs
5. A three- to five-year forecast of training materials to be developed and maintained
6. A three- to five-year forecast of training delivery requirements.

This sounds easier than it is. In fact, it is a complex process that requires some real effort and time. The analysis must be completed for all major segments of the training population. The results must then be combined to make a complete picture of the needs. The process for doing the six steps listed above is explained in chapters 10 through 12.

Alternative Strategies for Meeting the Needs   Based on the numbers and types of requirements identified in the needs forecasts and the logistics involved, alternative strategies must be explored, particularly for developing materials and delivering training. For example, centralized training delivery at a single location is much more feasible for a utility whose employees are all within a 75-mile radius than it is for a business unit with locations all over the United States or the world. In addition, interactive computer-based instruction at the worksite is much more feasible where thousands of widespread employees must be trained on common administrative procedures than it is for training corrective action teams in a single manufacturing plant. The strategy mix chosen has major implications for the effectiveness, timeliness and cost of training.

Your definition of alternative strategies should provide the following:

1. A list of development strategies
2. A list of delivery strategies
3. Criteria for using these strategies
4. Unit costs for each strategy.

Resource Requirements for Alternative Scenarios Now we come to one of the most important bottom-line questions: How much can be done at what cost? Usually, when the data are in, what is being done today is far less than what is needed to address fully the challenges of the business. This means that a stiff price, usually not apparent, is paid in lost business performance, one of the "costs of nonconformance," to borrow a phrase from quality guru Philip Crosby.

There are two obvious scenarios for which resource costs should be calculated:

Scenario 1: What can be accomplished by optimally deploying the level of resources we are spending today?

Scenario 2: How much would it cost to come close to meeting the important needs of the business within three to five years?

A common outcome of this analysis is that scenario 1 gives us far too little, and scenario 2 requires so much that even if the training departments were given blank checks, they could not gear up fast enough to spend the resources productively. Most of the large, high quality training and education systems that come within shouting distance of fully meeting needs have been built up over a decade or more. Examples include Arthur Andersen, Motorola, AT&T, and IBM. If this is the case, then we need to run some scenarios between scenarios 1 and 2 and finally settle in on one that becomes the plan.

Your analysis of resource requirements should provide the following:

1. An analysis of the resource requirements implicit in several different three- to five-year scenarios for meeting various fractions of the total estimated need
2. Resource implications of varying the development and delivery strategy mix
3. A workable three- to five-year game plan to present for executive approval.

Staffing Strategy When Ray started his career as an engineer at Bell Laboratories, Chuck Elmendorf, the Executive Director for the unit, was chairman of the Education Committee. He hand picked the other members of the committee. They hand picked the instructors from among the top talent in the organization. Consequently, anyone who had any ambition wanted to be appointed as an instructor. The recognition value from management and peers was terrific. In addition, employees all usually enrolled in several courses each year because they knew there was valuable knowledge to be obtained. At the end of Ray's first three years on the job, he felt like he had received a second master's degree in Telecommunications Transmission Technology taught by some of the world's leading practitioners.

We tell this story because we see too many counterexamples. Training departments staffed with people who do not carry the respect of the trainees or the management will fail no matter how many resources they have or how good the plan or the organization. Training is one area that should only be staffed with high-quality talent. The leverage is just too great to do otherwise.

In the modern training organization, the staff consists of more than just instructors. There are instructors, designers, developers, writers, analysts, specialists in computer-based instruction and more.

Your staffing strategy should provide the following:

1. A definition of the needed mix of talents to staff the jobs in the organization structure
2. Sources for these talents (line organizations, consultants, college hires, etc.)
3. Policies for recruiting, selection, retention, and career management.

Facility Strategy   The training facilities strategy can be a big deal or a little deal depending on your situation and the strategy you select. If you elect to use rented hotel space for most of your training, it's a little deal. If you elect to build a corporate education center and regional technical training schools, it's a big deal.

For some types of training there really is no choice. For example, hands-on skill development on expensive equipment requires laboratory or simulator training because structured on-the-job training (OJT) would be unsafe or jeopardize operations. Nuclear power plant operators are trained in basic operations on simulators and drilled to handle contingencies on the same simulators. Pilots are trained on various levels of simulators before they fly the real thing. There are powerful advantages to corporate education centers if management has a desire to forge a common corporate culture and develop communication networks and synergy among far flung managers, professionals, and technicians.

Your facility strategy should provide the following:

1. What kinds of training facilities you need
2. Where they should be located
3. What the capacity requirements are over a five- to ten-year forecast period
4. How much it will cost
5. What the risk of obsolescence is with changing training technologies.

Refer to chapters 13 through 18 for more information on alternative strategies, scenarios, and resource requirements for development, delivery, staffing, and facilities.

Executive Review, Phase 2   Once you have completed your three- to five-year training action plan you have completed phase 2 of the strategic planning process. At this point, you should have another executive review. The executive review at the end of phase 2 is really truth time. You are asking for commitment to a three- to five-year plan that probably falls short of fully addressing all the foreseen needs and yet costs a lot more than the organization has been accustomed to spending on education and training. There is no point in building an action plan without executive support for the level of resources required to execute it.

We have seen situations in which, when presented with all the evidence and alternatives, the executives have decided to increase the resources devoted to training at the same time they are forcing an overall downsizing of the company. We have also been part of a situation in which already large training commitments were doubled every three years over more than a decade with strong executive backing based on this type of strategic analysis.

Your executive review of phase 2 should provide the following:

1. Executive commitment to a three- to five-year game plan and the resources to execute it

2. Recognition that the homework has been done well and that executive decision making, though requiring tough choices, was well informed.

Phase 3: Organization, Management, and Administrative Strategies

With executive commitment and resources behind you, you can now proceed with phase 3 of the strategic planning process.

The purpose of phase 3 is to figure out what you have to do organizationally and administratively to execute the game plan committed to in phase 2. Questions to be answered in this phase include the following:

1. How will training be organized?
2. How will it be governed?
3. How will the training effort be staffed?
4. Where will it be housed?
5. How will it be paid for?
6. How will its performance be measured?
7. What systems are needed to support supervisors and managers in performing their training roles?
8. What other administrative systems need to be built or modified?

All these elements are part of the design of the training infrastructure.

Administrative Systems   There are a number of administrative systems that must be planned. We do not usually think of most of these as falling within the strategic plan, but there are always exceptions, and it is important to the success of your organization that they be addressed with care. Failing in any of these areas can seriously affect the success of the overall effort. Some of these systems include

- Registration and scheduling
- Training information/record keeping
- Communications (newsletters, announcements)
- Materials management
- Personnel administration
- Procurement.

Chapter 19 explains administrative systems further.

Organization Structure   There is no single best organization structure for training. What is required is a structure that will work to achieve the goals that have been established within the culture and framework of the larger organization. The same game plan can usually be executed successfully by a number of alternative organization structures. These options are dealt with more fully in chapter 20.

An analysis of your orgainization structure should provide the following:

1. How many training departments you will have
2. What their missions, roles, and scope of responsibility are
3. How they will coordinate to achieve the overall game plan
4. How they will be structured internally
5. How you will evolve to this new structure from what you have today.

Governing or Advisory Structure   One of the most important administrative issues in training is the governance or advisory linkage between the training departments and the internal and external departments they serve (i.e., the customers of training). The governing or advisory structure is the means of forging a true working partnership between the suppliers and customers of training services. The better this partnership mechanism is, the tighter will be the relationship between training activities and the real needs of the business. When this partnership arrangement is working well, training activities are a result of demand from the organizations that are the training customers. When there is no governance system, the training departments make their own determination of what their customer needs and then proceed to try to sell it or find themselves reacting to the real or fancied needs of individual managers.

The most successful training systems have formalized this linkage and tuned it to work like a well-oiled machine. Common components of the advisory structure include

- Executive advisory board
- Functional curriculum councils (marketing, manufacturing, etc,)
- Administrative council (directors of training)
- Location training committees (sales district, plant, etc.).

Setting up a working advisory structure should provide the following:

1. An overall governance system
2. Mission, roles, and membership rules for each advisory group
3. A plan for linkage to the training departments
4. A plan for creating or evolving the structure.

Chapter 21 explains the workings of the advisory structure in more depth.

Supervisor or Manager Support System   Training departments can be perfectly organized, staffed, financed, housed, managed, and play their role flawlessly, and still you will have a marginally performing system overall if managers and supervisors in the customer departments who use your training are not making appropriate decisions and taking effective action. You must start from the premise that most managers and supervisors do not know how to make effective use of a world class training system, and even if they do, they can not if they lack the information they need.

Managers and supervisors should be asking and answering these questions:

- What training is needed by each person in my organization?
- When is it needed?
- What is the best source?
- How can I manage my workload with people out for training?
- How do I pay for training?
- What do I need to do to prepare people for training and to make sure it pays off when they get back?
- How can I track my performance in maintaining the competence of my workforce?

The training system must have a strategy for providing managers and supervisors with the skills, knowledge, information, tools, and incentives for asking and answering these questions competently.

Your design of a supervisor or manager support system should include specifications for the following:

1. Information systems and communication channels
2. Job aids and procedures
3. Training for supervisors and managers.

See chapter 22 for more information on this topic.

Financing Strategy and Financial Accountability   How is the organization going to pay for the cost of training, and how will the training department account for its use of financial resources? There are a number of ways to do this, including

- Overhead staff budgets
- Charge-back systems
- Payroll tax
- The training subsidiary.

All have their advantages and disadvantages. You will have to pick a strategy that is a good fit for your organizational culture and that has the best chance of succeeding.

Financial controls and accountability are equally important. Without good controls, training budgets are commonly overrun and there is inadequately detailed historical data on which to project realistic budgets. The need for financial accountability is axiomatic, but to whom will you account and for what?

Your financing strategy should provide the following:

1. Financing strategy for
   - Development budget
   - Operations budget
   - Capital budget
2. A system for data collection and financial control
3. A policy on financial accountability to whom and for what
4. A plan to develop and implement the system.

Chapter 23 provides more information on financing strategies.

Results Measurement Plan   The results measurement plan defines how you will measure and account for training results. These results can include categories such as

- Percent of needs met

- Cost of training
- Customer organization and trainee satisfaction
- Mastery of learning within training
- Transfer of skills and knowledge to job performance
- Payoff in terms of business performance
- Return on investment (ROI).

The managers of training, the governance structure, and the customer organizations should use these measures as tools to identify and correct weaknesses and to support and monitor continuous improvement.

Your results measurement plan should provide the following:

1. A hierarchy of measures to be used
2. A strategy for collecting and storing the data
3. A plan for a system of regular reports to stakeholders
4. A plan for developing and implementing the system.

Chapter 24 deals with measuring results.

Executive Review, Phase 3   Some of the plans and decisions of phase 3 require executive review and some do not. If you propose to build a $50 million corporate education center, you will require executive review. Your plans to provide a first class supervisor or manager support system probably do not require executive review. Your executive review time is scarce, so be careful how you spend it. Another point to consider is that some executives will get drawn into whatever level of detail you present to them, so keep their attention on the big issues where you need their decisions and/or support.

Phase 4: Implementation Plan

If your strategic training plan is at all complex, it will not be actualized by just having made and documented all the planning decisions and gaining executive support. You have to lay out a list of implementation activities on a time line, assign accountabilities, provide resources, and follow up on results. For some activities such as the detailed planning and implementation of a new corporate education center, you may need one or more full time people and a planning committee.

Your implementation plan should provide the following:

1. Implementation activities lists
2. Milestones to monitor progress

3. Assignments of accountability
4. Resource allocations for implementation tasks
5. Progress tracking and reporting system.

Annual Updates to the Strategic Training Plan

In today's environment, conditions are constantly changing. The three- to five-year plan we draw up today starts obsolescing even before it is completed. Part of your implementation activities should include updating your strategic training plan. We recommend an annual update unless your environment is very stable. You do not need to go to the same amount of trouble for the annual update as you did for the initial plan. You should, however, revisit all the basic questions, collect and analyze new data, rerun your options, and cut new plans extending three to five years into the future. Major unpredicted events such as corporate restructuring could cause you to go back and revise your plan even in midyear. When AT&T was going through its divestiture planning, they revised their training plans several times during one year.

Dividing the project into the four phases with executive reviews between phases is usually overkill for the annual update. It is more practical to do it all in one phase and present the results for one executive review using last year's plan as the platform unless you are doing a major overhaul to the plan.

Chapters 25 and 26 deal with implementation and updating the strategic plan.

WHY SHOULD YOU GO TO ALL THIS WORK?

There are several major reasons for developing a strategic training plan:

- To support the business in its quest for quality and productivity
- To figure out the important training requirements of the business
- To get participation and support from executive management
- To have a roadmap or game plan for building the infrastructure and getting the important training done
- To provide a framework for measuring training effectiveness.

Without a strategic training plan, many of the important training requirements of the business may go unrecognized and may not be addressed at all or poorly addressed at the last minute. The strategic training plan can help identify the consequences of not addressing important training needs and help mobilize resources to avoid these negative consequences. Figuring out the important training requirements of the business in a proactive, forward-looking way provides enough advanced planning so training can be ready when needed for critical requirements and not treated as an afterthought, providing too little too late.

Executive management is accountable for business results. In today's rapidly changing environment, business results can be seriously affected by ineffective training. A strategic training plan is the tool for executive management to ensure that business results will not be hampered by lack of effective training. Management should participate and actually make all the key decisions. If executive management is properly involved in the planning process, it will provide the leadership and resources to execute its decisions. Stimulating executive leadership in the training arena is as important as obtaining management support for resources; if the leadership is there, the resources will automatically follow. The planning process provides a structured mechanism for dialog with executives on all the important training issues of the organization.

The strategic training plan provides the necessary vision and a roadmap for achieving that vision by mobilizing all the players in the process. It provides expectations and direction for everyone involved and eliminates routine contention over what to do and in what order.

Finally, the strategic training plan provides a framework for measuring training effectiveness. Measuring training effectiveness without a strategic training plan is like evaluating the size and shape of a suit without putting it on the body of the person who expects to wear it. In the context of a strategic training plan we can ask

- Did we accomplish the important goals?
- What was the benefit to the business?
- Was the benefit worth the cost?
- What did we miss?
- What was the cost to the business of the misses?

HOW TO PREPARE THE STRATEGIC TRAINING PLAN

The specific sequence of steps required to prepare a strategic training plan will vary depending on the size and nature of the organization, the presence or absence of a significant existing training organization or organizations, the planning skills of employees, and time and resource constraints. The suggestions offered here, however, are valid in any of these circumstances. They include

- Following a structured planning process
- Building in decision points along the way
- Documenting the plan
- Using computerized spreadsheets for the quantitative part of the plan.

Following a Structured Planning Process

Regardless of the specific approach you use, you should follow a structured, step-by-step planning process designed to address the key planning questions and issues and systematically complete the planning decisions.

It is a good idea to start by writing the outline for the final strategic training plan, and then design the process to make sure that everything you want in the final plan is created during that process. Your process should be tailored to your own needs and follow a logical flow that provides answers to all the important questions and issues you have outlined in the final plan.

As we stated earlier, a major strategic training plan could take six to ten months and a great deal of effort. It can save much time and anguish at the end if decision points are established along the way which will guide successive planning efforts. For example, if you can get executive management to agree on the training implications of key business goals and strategies and a vision for training to meet the needs of the business, then it is easier to spend the necessary effort to quantify what it will take to accomplish that vision. If you get all the way to the end of the planning process and the executives say "Well, we didn't really want you to do all of that," you have wasted a great deal of effort.

Document the Plan

The planning process and planning decisions are much more important than planning reports and documents; however, it is important to document the plans for several reasons:

- Documented plans record what was done and the rationale for what was done.

- A report provides a communications vehicle to others who were not part of the planning process.

- A formal planning document forces you to think through all the issues.

- A report will provide you or your successor with a roadmap for updating the plan next year and the year after.

Many managers sneer at planning reports that lie gathering dust on shelves. This is not the fault of those who wrote the report, but of a lack of implementation commitment on the part of management. The report is an essential archive of the planning process and a resource for those who must execute the plan.

Computer Spreadsheets and Databases for Quantitative Planning

Some parts of the plan will require quantitative forecasts of training requirements, training materials requirements, resource requirements, and the like. Even in a fairly small organization, the quantitative part of this plan can get involved, with many different options presenting themselves. It is a good idea to use computer spreadsheets and database programs from the beginning to do the quantitative part of the plan.

With computerized spreadsheets and databases, it is easy to keep track of:

- Changing assumptions
- Different scenarios
- Different constraints.

With a computer you can ask all the what-if questions without spending many hours tediously recalculating everything for every change that you want to examine.

WHO SHOULD BE INVOLVED IN DEVELOPING THE STRATEGIC TRAINING PLAN?

The key players in the strategic planning process include

- Executive management
- Top management of the training function
- A project leader or planning manager
- A planning team
- Outside consultants (optional).

The following paragraphs describe the roles of each of these key players.

If executive management is to use the strategic training plan as its tool for assuring that training is positioned to support the needs of the business, it should own the plan. The roles of executive management in the planning process include

- Making all strategic decisions
- Providing leadership and resources
- Holding training and line management accountable for implementing the plan and reporting results.

The top management of the training function obviously has a large stake in the strategic training plan and should share ownership of the plan with executive management. The roles of the top management of the training function include

- Organizing the planning effort
- Assigning planning resources
- Performing many of the planning tasks
- Making technical decisions
- Executing the plan
- Accounting to executive management for results against the plan.

A project leader or planning manager is needed in most cases to lead the planning process. The planning manager's roles include

- Developing the project plan
- Assembling the planning team
- Assigning planning tasks
- Facilitating planning meetings
- Writing the reports.

In most cases, the planning project will be more extensive than can be completed by an individual person. Therefore, a project team is required. This team could include only training personnel, or it could include members of line management. The roles of the planning team include

- Collecting data
- Framing decisions
- Organizing and evaluating options
- Framing recommendations to upper management
- Computing resource implications of various planning options
- Designing the infrastructure.

The planning process can be a high stakes process. If you have not been through the development of a strategic training plan, or if you have insufficient time or resources in house to accomplish the plan by the needed schedule, an outside consultant can be a significant help. The consultant's roles may include

- Consulting on the planning process
- Coaching the planning manager and project team through the process

- Facilitating planning meetings
- Performing some of the planning tasks, such as data collection
- Preparing the planning reports
- Supporting the planning team in presenting the plan to top management
- Serving as an expert resource to the planning team.

TIMING ISSUES

Strategic training plans should be tied to business planning cycles. Ideally, the strategic training plan should be part of the strategic business plan. This means that you must find out about the strategic business planning process and calendar and determine how best to integrate the strategic training plan.

The strategic training plan should be updated every year and become a routine part of the strategic business plan of the organization. The first time such a plan is developed, the effort will be much greater than required for the annual updates.

Conversely, the first time through you should limit the scope. Do not try to answer all questions completely and definitively the first time through. You can fill in details and add nuances in succeeding years. If you get too complex the first time, the result can be mind-boggling and you will never implement it.

The strategic training plan should be used as a framework to establish the annual plan and budget for training. The annual plan and budget is easier to sell if it is based on a strategic training plan that has executive management ownership and commitment. The annual plan and budget spells out for the coming year

- Needs analysis and curriculum design projects to be undertaken
- What new training programs or materials will be developed or acquired
- How much training will be delivered and by what means
- Specific training organization or administrative systems improvements to be undertaken
- The resource costs in people, budget, equipment, and facilities.

Figure 2-5 shows a typical organizational planning calendar and where the strategic training plan and annual training plan and budget fit into this calendar.

We hope that at this point you are convinced that you need a strategic training plan to become a world-class (or at least a much better) training organization. As we stated earlier, your first task is to develop a detailed project plan. Chapter 3 provides the guidelines you need to do this.

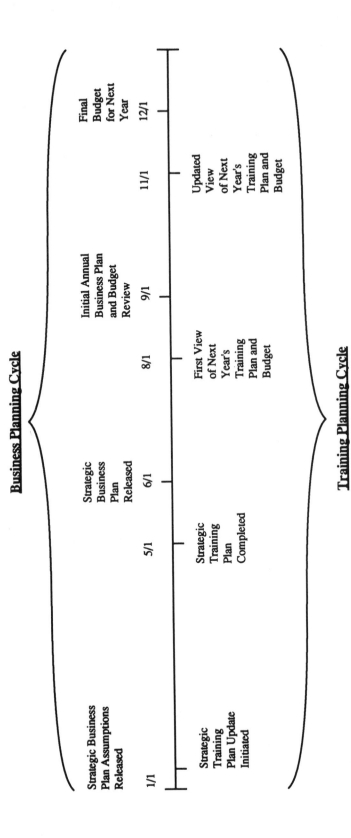

Figure 2-5 Planning Calendar

3

HOW TO ORGANIZE AND MANAGE THE PLANNING PROJECT

As you set out to develop your strategic training plan and build your world class training organization, a major key to success or failure will be the way you organize and manage the planning project. Without effective organization and management of the planning project, you run the risk of failing to complete a quality plan, failing to obtain political support for the plan, and stumbling over organizational roadblocks to implementing the plan. A good project plan, complemented by commitment and follow through on the part of the players involved, can prevent many of these problems. Some of the essential issues to consider in organizing and managing your planning project include

- Selecting or defining the purpose, scope, objectives, deliverables, and deadline for the plan
- Selecting the planning teams
- Developing a project plan
- Keeping the project moving and on schedule
- Collecting and managing data
- Building consensus.

SCOPING THE PLANNING PROJECT: AN ELEPHANT OR A BREADBOX

One of your first problems is the scope of the project. This may be handed to you by executive order or you may have to determine it yourself. Figure 3-1 presents possible scoping dimensions and sample project boundaries. As you can see, the scope you select

51

will determine the size and complexity of your planning project and should influence the way you staff the project and even your detailed planning process.

How you select the scope of your planning project will be influenced by several factors:

- Executive decree
- Budget
- Number of people available to work on project

SCOPING DIMENSIONS	SAMPLE PROJECT BOUNDARIES
Customers of training	• Entire corporation • One business unit • One department (e.g., Engineering) • Employees at all levels • Customers of the company • Suppliers of the company • Employees in exempt positions only • Worldwide • North America only
Types of education and training	• Job skills • Generic management and personal skills • Advanced degree programs • Remedial basic skills/literacy
Other roles performed by the training department	• Performance consulting • Assessment center operations • Screening of new hires
Time horizon	• Three-year plan • Five-year plan • Three-year plan with ten-year outlook
Issues to be excluded	• Training requirements of individual business units or plant locations • Centralization of training • Executive education

Figure 3-1 Scoping Dimensions and Project Boundaries

- Needs of various departments and business units
- Level of cooperation among departments and business units
- Business requirements
- Time limitations
- Experience with the planning process.

In general, if you want to do a large project but are having trouble getting buy-in, you can do a project with a smaller scope as a test project and get buy-in to expand the project later as a result of your success. It is better to start small and expand later than to start too big and not be able to carry it out. Starting with a single department or business unit can be a good way to prove the value of the methodology.

As we pointed out in chapters 1 and 2, this training effort will take time. Allow yourself a time horizon far enough away to facilitate implementation of your plan with a reasonable degree of success. But remember, people will want to see some results in a reasonable amount of time as well. Your time horizon should be neither too close nor too far.

Who determines the scope of your project as well as the time frame depends in large part on the structure and politics of your company. It should be someone or some group of people with enough clout in the organization to get support and approval for the scope of the project selected (as well as budget and cooperation among players).

In the process of doing the planning project, some individual issues can become large enough to make separate projects or side studies of them. Examples of the types of side studies we have been involved with include the following:

- Examine the strategic potential for computer-based instruction as a major corporate training delivery system (you could substitute video teleconferencing, expert systems, or any other major technology).

- Develop a training facilities plan for four metropolitan areas in the U.S. where the company has major concentrations of employees.

- Develop a plan to combine five separate training departments into one newly formed corporate education department.

- Develop a specification for a new corporate education center on the company's headquarters campus.

Each of these studies was strategic in nature but complex and difficult enough to bog down a broader strategic training planning effort. They required a separate planning team, schedule, budget, etc. You may find it necessary to develop some side projects in your planning project as well. These types of studies should not be done in a void however. They should be tightly tied to and interactive with the broader strategic training plan.

Another example of a scoping decision involves a corporation with four business units. The overall planning project is broken down into related subprojects:

- Corporate-wide training strategy
- Business unit training strategies for each of the four units.

These projects have separate planning teams but are coordinated by an overall steering committee.

It is a good idea during the scoping phase to define the specific objectives and deliverables to be produced. Writing a draft of the table of contents for the final report is an excellent way to do this (see sample outlines in Figures 2-1 and 2-2, chapter 2).

SELECTING THE PLANNING TEAM

Before you go any further with your project, you need to put together a workable planning team. It is important to have the participation of several people if this effort is going to succeed. The planning team selection will greatly influence the quality of your plan and the organizational acceptance of the plan. A successful team strategy we have used is composed of a three tier planning team:

- Steering committee
- Working committee
- Planning staff.

The steering committee is a group of executives who will help with scoping, framing major policy issues, and selling the plan to the organization. The executives on this committee should be at a high enough level to make decisions and set policy. They may meet only at critical milestone review points during the planning project and be available as individuals for guidance and counsel during the entire project.

The working committee is composed of senior managers of training and/or representatives of the customer organizations. The working committee members typically spend a considerable amount of time engaged in various planning tasks.

The planning staff may be one or more people who are devoted full time or nearly full time to the project. They will do much of the detailed data analysis, computation, report writing, and preparation of presentation materials. It is important that someone with strong quantitative skill, be on the planning staff, as you will see as you progress through this book.

The project team must be selected with attention to the following criteria:

- Representation of important constituencies (e.g., training departments and their client departments)

- Knowledge of the broader business and the issues associated with training

- People whose opinions will be respected by the decision makers

- People who are known for providing wise counsel

- People who are visionaries

- People who are skeptics

- Planning skills

- Interpersonal and team skills

- Availability to schedule the necessary time to participate fully.

One person, usually a key figure on the working committee, should be designated as the project leader. Sometimes there is an obvious choice for this position, such as the planning manager for corporate education and training. In other situations there is no obvious choice. The project leader is responsible for

- Negotiating the project scope with the steering committee

- Suggesting membership in working committee and planning staff

- Assembling and orienting the planning team

- Designing the planning process with support from the planning team

- Facilitating the preparation of the project plan

- Coordinating and tracking all project activities

- Facilitating meetings of the planning team

- Directing the planning staff

- Acting as a liaison with the steering committee.

In short, the project leader is the one who must make it all happen, usually through leadership and persuasion and without direct authority over the other members of the planning team.

HOW TO DEVELOP THE PROJECT PLAN

Once a project leader has been identified and members of the project team have been selected, a project plan should be drafted to present to these groups for their input and approval. The project plan is a written document that spells out the following information:

- Background of the project (i.e., why we decided to do this)
- Purpose of the project
- Scope of the project
- Objectives to be achieved
- Deliverables to be produced
- Planning process that will be followed
- Detailed tasks and activities
- Activity assignments and resource requirements
- Schedules
- Planning team organization and roles.

A project plan can vary in length from a couple of pages to as many as fifty or more pages, depending on the scope, complexity, number of people involved, time frame, etc. We suggest the following sequence for developing the project plan:

1. Select a project leader
2. Develop a written draft of the background, purpose, scope, objectives, and deliverables
3. Recruit or appoint steering committee members
4. With the steering committee
   - Review draft of scope, etc.
   - Discuss membership in the working committee
   - Establish a schedule
   - Recruit working committee and appoint planning staff
5. Develop an overview of the planning process (see the four-phase process, discussed chapter 2)
   - Process phases
   - Outputs for each phase
   - General approach to developing the outputs
6. Assemble the working committee
   - Review background, scope, etc.

- Present roles of the steering committee, working committee, planning staff, and project leader

- Present proposed planning process

- Facilitate development of detailed activity list, flow chart, assignments, and schedule

7. Document the completed project plan.

PROJECT PLAN CONTENTS

In this section we give you an overview of what your project plan contents might look like. Appendix A contains an example project plan from one of the projects we participated in recently. (Names and labels have been changed, but the body of the plan is intact.) This sample can serve as a guideline for you in developing your own plan and is a good example of the content of a multiphase project. As we mentioned in chapter 2, if you are planning a multiphase project, you should develop a detailed project plan for the first phase and general plans for later phases. Then develop detailed plans before entering each phase. This can save you the trouble of redoing lots of detail later as things change and unexpected developments occur. It also allows you to learn as you go through the process and change your methodology as you learn more about what you are doing.

Purpose and Background

This section of the project plan should describe succinctly what this project is about (purpose) and why you decided to do it (background). The purpose statement should be only two or three sentences long. For example, the purpose statement might be something like the following.

> The purpose of this project is to develop a three- to five-year strategic plan. This plan defines and directs a training system to help employees develop the skills, knowledge, and attitudes to perform at a level needed for the company to achieve its business goals.

The background section of the project plan is optional. Our example in Appendix A does not include one. Generally, it is a good idea to include one for people who may not be familiar with the history and rationale behind the decision to do this project.

Background statements will include information about

- Cultural and business trends affecting the company or business unit

- Internal changes that have influenced the decision to do this project

- Who commissioned the project

 • Why the project is needed.

Figure 3-2 provides a sample background statement.

Scope

The scope section of the project plan is a simple statement of the boundaries and size of the project defined in the purpose statement. A scope statement might say something like

> This project is limited to engineers and researchers in the R&D groups at ACME.
>
> or
>
> This project includes all employees of the Timbuktu plant of Genius Manufacturing, Inc.

Background

XTelco, along with the entire telecommunications industry, is facing an era of challenge and change. Some of the challenges include

 • Implementation of new technology
   - ISDN
   - Digital switching
   - Fiber optics
   - Etc.
 • New sources of revenue
 • Implementation of critical business systems
 • Competition/deregulation
 • Customer service
 • Quality process
 • Aging of the workforce
 • College recruitment
 • Organizational changes resulting in restructured jobs
 • Implementation of a participative management culture.

These and other challenges facing the business have important training implications. If these training implications are not addressed, the critical skills needed for success in the business may not be acquired, resulting in high risk to business results.

For this reason, our CEO, Mr. High Roller, commissioned the Training and Development department to develop a plan for training all employees to be able to meet the challenge of the future for our business.

Figure 3-2   Sample Background Statement

Objectives

The objectives section of the project plan describes what you hope to achieve with this project. For example, objectives for a strategic training plan might include

- To develop a system that meets the training needs of the company and all present and future employees over the next five to ten years
- To implement a training system that provides a training Return on Investment (ROI) of at least 10 to 1 over the next five years.

Deliverables

The deliverable list specifies the outputs that are to be produced in carrying out this project. Figure 3-3 provides a sample list of deliverables for a strategic training plan project.

Planning Process

The purpose of this section of the project plan is to provide the reader with an overview of the process that will be followed in carrying out the project. For example, you may want to tell the reader that your strategic training project will be carried out in four phases, tell them the names and purpose of each of the phases, and inform them of the executive review points between phases. Our example project plan in Appendix A includes a detailed description of a strategic training plan process. Note that in this example, objectives and deliverables are folded into the planning process. You may find that it is desirable to combine sections, or add or delete sections that are different from the ones shown here. These examples are meant as guides, not rules.

Activities, Resources, and Schedules

Your detailed activity list, resource requirements, and schedules can all be combined in a useful chart format, as shown in Figure 3-4. Charts like this will form the basis of your project management and tracking as you carry out the project, so it is helpful to put in as much detail as you can. On a complex project, your project plan may include several pages of charts and may have columns for a large number of project team members.

When you have completed all these sections, you should have a workable project plan ready for steering committee review.

Planning Team and Roles

In this section of the project plan it is helpful to describe the structure of your

DELIVERABLES

Phase 1: Strategic Training Plan

The outputs to be produced in this phase include

- A list of challenges facing the business
- A list of significant business plans
- Training implications of the challenges and business plans
- An inventory of existing training from both internal and external sources
- A personnel forecast for the next three years
- A broad quantitative estimate of the amount of course development required over the next three years
- A broad quantitative estimate of the amount of training delivery required over the next three years
- A broad estimate of the resources required to meet the training requirements over the next three years
  - People
  - Financial
  - Facilities.

Phase 2: Detailed Development and Delivery Plans

The deliverables of this phase are detailed quantitative plans for course development and training delivery. Specifically, this phase will produce

- Training development requirements and priorities for each major function
- Training delivery requirements and priorities for each major function
- Strategies for carrying out the development and delivery requirements
- Allocation of resources for carrying out the development and delivery requirements.

Phase 3: Training Organization and Administration

The purpose of this phase is to determine organization, staffing, and administration requirements for carrying out the training plans. Specifically included in this phase will be

- Organization structure
- Staffing strategy
- Training advisory structure
- Financing strategy
- Other administration systems for training.

Figure 3-3 Sample List of Deliverables

	Estimated Resources (Days)					Schedule	
	Consultant		XTelco/ACME				
Tasks	CS	PS	PT	PL	SC	Start	End
Phase 1							
1. Meet with Steering Committee to review Project Plan	2.0	2.0	–	1.0	1.0	1/1	1/6
2. Orientation of Project Team	2.0	2.0	1.0	1.0	–	1/9	1/13
3. Interview executives and training department	–	–	3.0	3.0	–	1/13	1/20
4. Planning meeting to assimilate the data and	5.0	1.0	4.0	4.0	–		

Figure 3-4 Activity and Schedule Chart Format

planning team and its roles. For example, you may want to specify the various committees, who is on each committee (if you know that), what is the role of each committee, and who is the project leader. This provides readers with people they can contact if they have questions or suggestions about the project.

We cannot stress enough the importance of a good project plan. The project plan is the working tool of the project leader. With a complete project plan everyone involved knows what is to be done, by whom, and when. Nothing is left to the imagination for later disputes over what it was you intended to do. We never do any project, even a very small one, without at least a brief project plan containing all the essential elements.

HOW TO KEEP THE PROJECT MOVING AND ON SCHEDULE

Project management and control is an important topic that warrants a book all by itself. There are several good books available on this topic (we mention some of them in our bibliography), and we do not intend to repeat their contents here. However, we would like to share with you some tips we have gleaned from our years of managing projects of all sizes and watching clients do good and bad jobs of managing their projects. Pay attention to these practices and put some effort in learning to be a good project manager. If your projects are not managed well, they cannot succeed.

Keeping a strategic training plan moving is likely to be tough because the members of your planning team probably will not be pulled completely off their regular jobs to devote themselves exclusively to your planning project. Here are ten tips for keeping things moving and on schedule:

1. Negotiate the detailed activity list, assignments, and schedule with the planning team in a group session so the team members are making commitments to each other as well as to you.

2. Let the team know that dates have been set for milestone reviews with the executive-level steering committee and that planning team members will be present at the steering committee meetings to be accountable for their task commitments. This will add an important additional incentive to get the tasks done.

3. Develop your own system for staying on top of all dates, tasks, resources, etc., and use it. For a complex project, a computerized project management program can be very helpful.

4. Plan regular team meetings to work together on interim tasks and issues. This puts the monkey on everyone's back to do the preparatory steps on schedule. Infrequent team meetings encourage team members to procrastinate, leaving too much until too late.

5. Do careful advance preparation for all meetings of the planning staff, working committee, and steering committee. This should include

   - Scheduling meetings as far ahead as possible

   - Obtaining members' commitments to attend

   - Sending agendas and relevant information for the meeting ahead of time

   - Reserving a room with enough seating and tables

   - Providing refreshments for lengthy meetings

   - Having flip charts, overhead projectors, markers, etc., in the room

   - Reminding people of any commitments for presentations, accountability, etc.

6. Stay in close communication with all team members throughout the project to monitor progress, help clear roadblocks, and solve problems.

7. Ask team members to provide regular written progress reports on their responsibilities, which are compiled and reported to the steering committee on a regular basis.

8. Develop a large milestone chart for the wall of the meeting room or some other visible place and mark off progress on it so everyone has feedback about how well things are going.

9. If, for whatever reason, someone is unable to pull their weight, thank them for their help and ask them to permit you to obtain a replacement.

10. As a last resort, if some of the work is still not getting done, diplomatically reassign it, if possible.

One last issue in keeping the project moving is how much time to allow for reviews of drafts. It is unrealistic to expect people to give you overnight turnaround on reviewing a major report. On the other hand, too much time for reviews will slow you down to a crawl. Our best results here have been to let people know in advance when they will be receiving a major report for review and get their commitment for a two- to three-day turnaround or one week at most. Then be sure to meet your delivery date and follow up with all the reviewers.

In summary, the keys to keeping a project moving and on schedule are

- Preparation
- Commitment
- Follow-through
- Accountability
- Follow-up
- Feedback.

Dedicate yourselves to making the project a success by following these simple practices.

COLLECTING AND MANAGING DATA

For a large planning project, there will be masses of data to collect, organize, and manage. As you go through the rest of this book, you will become more aware of some of the types of data collection you will need to undertake. Our brief suggestions for managing this data include the following:

1. It is helpful to assign one member of the planning staff to be the manager of the files, databases, and spreadsheets. This way you always know who to contact when you need some information, and everyone knows who is responsible for obtaining and keeping the data.

2. Make sure that original copies of important documents do not leave the central file. We cannot emphasize enough the importance of this. We have witnessed too many situations where important information is needed and it has disappeared from the files. Results of this can be disastrous. Only give out duplicates—never the originals.

3. As we mentioned before, use computerized databases and spreadsheets wherever possible to permit easy access, sorting, computation and reworking of data. We have been in the computer age for more than twenty years now. If your systems are not current or you are not using computers, you cannot hope to be world class now or in the future. Make the investment in hardware, software, and training personnel now, because each day it gets harder to catch up.

4. Make sure everyone on the planning team knows how to access and use the data

that is needed to carry out assigned responsibilities. Do not let your project fail because people could not get or were not given access to the information they need.

5.   Do not burden people with unimportant data—give them what they need when they need it, but do not give them more than they need. If you give them more than they need, valuable time is spent sorting through the unimportant to find the important.

As Alvin Toffler points out in *Powershift*, knowledge is power. Obtain, manage and use data and information to build your knowledge base and help you develop a powerful strategic training program.

BUILDING CONSENSUS

The strategic planning process often reveals issues that are difficult to resolve. The very reason for doing the plan is to get the major issues out on the table where they can be looked at and dealt with, but this does not automatically make for easy consensus and decisions. Some decisions are difficult because they inherently entail tough choices; some are difficult because one or more of the players has a personal stake in the outcome; and some are difficult because the wrong players are involved.

Almost every major planning project reveals a few sticky issues. For example, if there is an opportunity to combine several smaller training departments into one larger department for increased efficiency and a higher standard of quality, there will only be one training director left after the merger. This can be threatening to several people and make for a tough choice. Or, if it makes sense economically to shift a large fraction of training from centralized classroom style to structured on-the-job training, what do you do with the corporate training center? What happens to the training staff?

One method that helps resolve some of these cases is to go through a formal decision analysis with the planning team. Some of the steps in a formal decision process include

1.   Define the decision purpose.
2.   Develop a list of criteria for comparing the alternatives.
3.   Weight the criteria.
4.   Define the alternatives.
5.   Evaluate each alternative against each of the criteria.
6.   Compute the weighted sum value of each alternative.
7.   Identify and assess risks.
8.   Decide.

If you are unacquainted with formal decision making processes, it can be helpful to make a good seminar or workshop in decision making a priority in your own professional development program. There are several good programs available. One that we are familiar with and have seen achieve positive results is the "Process Management Skills" workshop from Alamo Learning Systems. It includes a helpful unit on decision making. The steps we just listed parallel those in the Alamo program.

The formal decision analysis method may yield a clear winner, and it may not. If there is a clearly superior alternative, the objectors may accept it in the face of evidence from the decision analysis. If there is no consensus in the working committee, a decision may have to be referred upward to the steering committee or to someone in the organization hierarchy who has the power to decide. Remember, though, that diplomacy and negotiation are preferable to force.

Some alternatives are foreclosed because one or more people with sufficient power are opposed to them. This is a fact of life. Accept these constraints and plan around them. There is some validity in the old saying "You can't fight City Hall." You could win that battle and end up losing the war.

SUMMARY

Project planning and management is the backbone of success in your strategic planning effort. This process involves the following steps:

☐ Scope the project
☐ Select the planning team
- Steering committee
- Working committee
- Planning staff
☐ Select the project leader
☐ Draft the project plan
- Purpose
- Background
- Scope
- Objectives
- Deliverables
- Planning team and roles
- Planning process
- Activities
- Resources
- Schedule

☐ Review the project plan and get commitments with all members of the planning team

☐ Keep the project moving and on schedule

- Prepare
- Commit
- Follow through
- Be accountable
- Follow up
- Provide feedback

☐ Assign a data manager

☐ Collect, manage, and disseminate data, information, and knowledge (provide power)

☐ Participate in the computer age

☐ Build consensus

- Inform
- Negotiate
- Decide
  - Work around.

Follow these guidelines and you will be well on your way to a successful strategic training plan and implementation. A side benefit is that these skills will be helpful to you in all parts of your job, wherever you go. They make you a valuable commodity!

Once you have a complete and approved project plan in hand you are ready to begin phase 1 of the strategic planning process. This phase consists of two basic thrusts:

1. Looking back, in the form of

   - Analysis of business challenges, strategic goals, and their training implications (chapter 4)
   - Analysis of the existing training situation
     - Internal (chapter 5)
     - Compared to competitors (chapter 5)
     - Compared to best-in-class (chapter 6)

2. Looking ahead, in the form of

   - Determining the future mission and philosophy of your organization (chapter 8)
   - Setting your strategic vision and goals (chapter 9).

TRAINING IMPLICATIONS OF BUSINESS CHALLENGES, STRATEGIES, AND GOALS

If a training organization is to be successful in the eyes of the overall organization and its executives, and hence continue to receive budget and resources to operate, it must be able to show that its training activities are linked to business results.

If training is to support business strategies and goals, then you must find out what these goals are for your company and understand their implications for training.

There are basically two ways to find out about business challenges and what is being planned for the business:

- Read business plans (if they exist)

- Talk to people, primarily the executives involved in developing the plans. Most executives will be glad to give you an hour and a half of their time.

As you read and interview, you will be looking for challenges, strategies, and goals in the following areas:

- Markets

- Competition

- Technology

- Products and services

- Customer/supplier relationships

- External regulations

- Management and workforce issues.

COMMON BUSINESS CHALLENGES

For each of the areas you will be researching, there are many common themes. Some of the themes common to many organizations today include

- Markets
  - Many companies are expanding into global marketplaces.
  - Customer expectations for high-quality products and services are increasing.
  - Many markets for traditional bread-and-butter products are shrinking.
  - Markets for products and services embodying new features, new technologies, and specialties are expanding.
  - Customers want convenience, they want things to work right, they expect a reasonable price, and they want courteous, efficient, and timely service.
- Competition
  - Competition is tougher than it used to be.
  - The best competitors have embarked on the path of continuous improvement and will become continually tougher.
  - Competitive position based on new technology requires a high level of investment in product development and rapid cycle time from conception to marketplace introduction.
  - As a technology matures, there is usually a major shakeout in the industry; the weaker players will drop out and a few will be left to dominate.
  - In mature technologies, the ability to provide high quality at a low price with good service determines market share.
- Technology
  - Information and communications technology is having a major impact on the way everyone works across all organizations, all functions, all levels.
  - Integration and automation technologies are having a major impact on manufacturing.
  - Each industry has a long list of technologies, evolving at various speeds with varying impacts on markets, products and services, the inner work processes, and competition.
  - It is estimated that over half of all the scientists, engineers, and mathematicians who have ever lived are working today.
- Products and services
  - New product and service introductions are increasingly important to competitive success.
  - Existing products are being weeded out more forcefully.
  - Rapid response to desired feature and price options is a major factor in some markets.

- Many organizations are planning or selling complete systems, not just individual products; these systems often integrate products produced by others.
- Customer/supplier relationship
  - Many organizations are forming strategic alliances or partnerships with suppliers and customers doing business in radically different ways.
  - Suppliers and customers are also often competitors.
- External regulations
  - Many industries have recently been or will be deregulated, forcing new ways of doing business.
  - Trade restrictions are generally being reduced worldwide.
  - Environmental, safety, and health regulations are expected to get tougher continually.
  - Equal opportunity and equal access laws and regulations will be getting stricter.
- Management practices
  - Many if not most major organizations have embarked on a path toward major shifts in values, organizational culture, and management style; but old habits die hard.
  - Layers of middle managers and overhead staffs are being trimmed in downsizing programs; sometimes bone and muscle are accidentally trimmed along with the fat.
  - Most organizations are implementing or seriously considering implementing Total Quality Management (TQM) as a new and permanent way of life.
  - Incentive pay programs are extending from the executive suite to the hourly workforce.
  - Rigid organization structures are being replaced by more flexible organizations with teams that cut across organizational lines.
  - Self-directed teams are becoming ever more popular on the production floor.
  - There is a growing recognition that internal strife and adversarial relationships between management and labor serve no one's interest except the competition.
- Workforce issues
  - Functional illiteracy is gaining recognition as a serious problem for recruiting qualified workers and for retraining the in-place workforce.
  - There is a growing recognition that America is facing a skilled worker shortage in the next five to ten years; this is already apparent in some sectors.
  - The workforce will increasingly be made up of a multicultural mix.
  - The number of women in the workforce will continue to grow, and they will continue to move into higher-level and nontraditional positions.
  - The average age of the workforce will be increasing.
  - The use of nontraditional expedients to entice people into the workforce, including flextime, job sharing, part time, contract labor, and others, is increasing.

- People with highly marketable technical and professional skills will be more selective about the organizations they choose to work for and the assignments they are willing to accept.
- Increased use is being made of consultants, contractors, and freelancers to carry specialized or irregular workloads that formerly would have been staffed by employees.

All of these challenges have major training implications. This is far from a complete list. There are many good books and articles documenting and commenting on these trends and their impact on organizational life. We have listed several in our bibliography. We particularly recommend the following (see bibliography for complete references):

When Giants Learn to Dance, Rosabeth Moss Kanter

Workforce 2000, Hudson Institute

American Renaissance, Marvin Cetron

Powershift, Alvin Toffler

Every organization and industry or sector has its own special trends and challenges. The challenge for you in developing your strategic training plan is to figure out

- What are the challenges for your organization?
- Which ones have the major training implications?
- What is the appropriate training response?

ANALYSIS PROCESS

There are five major steps in carrying out your analysis process:

1. Analyze written business plans, executive speeches, annual reports, and other relevant literature.
2. Interview executives.
3. Segment the training population.
4. Compile the data and develop a complete map of training implications and probable business consequences.
5. Perform cost/benefit analysis.

This is usually best done by a planning team made up of top managers of the training departments, perhaps with a consultant for guidance and/or facilitation. We'll take a look at each of these steps in turn.

Analyzing Written Business Plans

Reading the business plans is important. Before you talk to executives and other key managers, you should at least read what they have written. We have seen companies where business plans were guarded like state secrets, ostensibly to keep the information out of competitors' hands. However, this is like refusing to feed your dog because the neighbor's dog might get some of it. Sooner or later, your dog is not going to have enough resources to guard your house properly. Assuming you have access to these plans, however, you want to look for the following items:

1. Business challenges
2. Strategies responding to the challenge
3. Goals established to implement the strategies.

Figure 4-1 provides an example of written business plans for a waste removal company.

Remember as you read that you are looking for challenges, strategies, and goals in all of the following areas:

- Markets

- Competition

- Technology

- Products and services

- Customer/supplier relationships

- External regulations

- Management and workforce issues.

---

1. Business challenge: landfills are reaching capacity, and there is a great social resistance to opening new ones and to building incinerators.

2. Strategy: move aggressively into the recycling business.

3. Goal: annual capacity targets for the next five years for recycling aluminum, paper, plastic, and glass.

Figure 4-1 Example from a Business Plan for a Waste Removal Company

You can use a worksheet like the one in Figure 4-2 to catalog your findings as you go through the business plan.

Interviewing Executives

Written business plans, annual reports, and outside analysts' reports will all give clues, but chances are they will not tell the whole story. To get the whole story, you will have to go to the executives.

Interviewing executives is one of the single most important activities in developing your strategic plan. There are two major reasons for interviewing top executives:

1. To fill out your profile of business challenges, strategies, and goals
2. To involve them in creating the organization's training strategy.

Involving top executives is at least as important as the information you get. There will be many times in the future of your planning and implementation project when you will want their support. If they had a hand in setting direction and are part of the process, they will be much more likely to give it. We usually suggest an interview of one and a half hours each with

- Top officers
- Heads of divisions or business units
- Heads of the functional units.

If an executive's thoughts are extremely well organized, you might be done in forty-five to sixty minutes, but thirty minutes is never enough. In our experience you will get better, more candid information if you interview individuals rather than an executive with his or her staff.

The number of people to be interviewed may range from a few to twenty-five or more depending on the size of the organization. You will want to make up your interview list to include everyone who has significant input and whose political support you need. A checklist format like the one shown in Figure 4-3 is a good way to track your interview progress. A good way to lay the groundwork for your interview process is to send each of your prospective interviewees a letter like the one in Figure 4-4.

Some executives may suggest that they do not know enough about training to spend an hour and a half with you on the subject. Emphasize that what you really need is their input on business goals, which they do know a great deal about, and that you want to start them thinking with you about training issues from a strategic perspective.

Here are some helpful questions to ask in the interview:

1. What are the most significant challenges facing the business and/or your part of the business?

CATEGORY: MARKETS

1. Challenge: _____

   _____

   _____

   Strategy: _____

   _____

   _____

   Goals: _____

   _____

   _____

2. Challenge: _____

   _____

   _____

   Strategy: _____

   _____

   _____

   Goals: _____

   _____

   _____

3. Challenge: _____

   _____

   _____

   Strategy: _____

   _____

   _____

   Goals: _____

   _____

   _____

Figure 4-2   Business Plan Analysis Worksheet

Last Name, First Name	Title	Phone	Date of Interview	Time	Location	Interview Complete

Note: A checklist like this can easily be set up on a computer spreadsheet, which will then allow you to sort it by last name or date.

Figure 4-3 Interview Checklist

- Markets
- Competition
- Technology
- Products and services
- Supplier/customer relationships
- External regulations
- Management and workforce issues

2. What strategies and goals have been established to address these challenges?

February 13, 1990

John S. Percy
Corporate Director of Training
619 W. Main Street
Detroit, MI

Ms. J. H. Armistead
General Manager, Midwest Region
1325 E. Madison Street
Chicago, IL

Dear Jeanette:

The corporate training department is in the process of developing an integrated corporate training strategy. We need your assistance in aligning our training strategy with important business goals.

Specifically, we would like 1-1/2 hours of your time to interview you on the following issues:

1. Challenges facing the business
2. Business strategies and goals
3. Training implications of the strategies and goals
4. Ways of handling the training implications.

Someone from my department will call you within the next week to ask for an appointment. Thanks for your help.

Regards,

John

Figure 4-4 Sample Interview Preparation Letter

3. What groups of people will need new skills or knowledge for these goals to be achieved?

4. What is the downside business risk if we do not have or develop people with these new skills and knowledge? (Be as quantitative as possible.)

5. Are you willing to provide support in the form of:

   - Training budget to meet these needs?

   - Your time and the time of your subordinate managers to help establish priorities and provide overall guidance?

Encourage executives to expand on each topic as much as possible and to provide "war stories" if it helps explain a point. Do not ask yes or no questions—ask open-ended questions if you want to get more information.

It is a good idea to have two people conduct the interview. Unless you are a very skilled interviewer, it is difficult to ask questions, listen carefully to the responses, probe deeper, and keep notes all at the same time. If there are two of you, it is much easier. One person can take notes while the other is the primary interviewer, and you can compare notes afterward.

In our experience (we have conducted hundreds of these interviews), most executives give thoughtful answers to these questions. The thought process involved raises their interest in the strategic importance of training, and they usually promise their support.

A typical comment at the conclusion of the interview is, "I'm very glad we had this conversation. I can't remember the last time I systematically looked at our training requirements. I want to be involved in supporting an effective training system."

COMPILING THE DATA

You must now compile all the data you obtained from reading reports and interviewing executives. If there were a number of people involved in collecting the data, a good way to do this is in a group meeting. Have someone facilitate the group and summarize their comments on a flip chart or electronic whiteboard using the format shown in Figure 4-5, or one you devise that meets your needs better.

Depending on the size and complexity of the organization, this procedure should take from one to five days. It goes better if each interviewer has documented the interview data and analysis of reports, with copies provided to members of the group.

An alternative is to have one person read all the material, integrate it, and then review it with the group. By doing it this way, you will miss the flavor and nuances. For example, the major challenges are usually seen by all the executives. They may, however, see different implications because they look at the challenge from the viewpoint of their own roles, responsibilities, experience, and knowledge. A facilitated group data compilation brings out the richness of these various viewpoints.

Business Challenge:		
Strengths	Weaknesses	Goals

Figure 4-5 Data Collection Format

Appendix B provides sample outputs of this type of data compilation. You may want to refer to these formats when developing your own compilation system.

ANALYZING TRAINING IMPLICATIONS OF BUSINESS CHALLENGES

There are three basic questions to answer in analyzing the training implications of business challenges.

1. Who is affected, and what is the timing of the impacts?
2. What new or changed tasks must they perform and what is changing in their required repertoire of skills and knowledge?
3. How important is it to the business that these new competencies are developed quickly and effectively (i.e., what is the priority of each of these skills)?

Determining Who is Affected: Segmenting the Training Population

Everyone in an organization will not be affected the same way by every challenge or change. Therefore, you must find a scheme for dividing up the organization into cells or segments in which people are likely to have common needs. Marketeers call this market segmentation. You are segmenting the internal training "market."

We have found the following dimensions useful for grouping or segmenting the training audience:

- Functional

- Hierarchical

- Organizational

- Geographical

- Customers

- Suppliers.

Figures 4-6 and 4-7 show example training audience segmentations for an electronics manufacturing company and for a retail chain. You do not want to do a more detailed segmentation than this for strategic planning purposes or you will lose the forest for the trees.

New Tasks and Their Priorities

Once you have completed the training market segmentation, you can take the data from your reading and interviews and match it to each market segment for each business challenge to determine training implication and priorities. For example, in Figure 4-8 the business challenge is for an electronics manufacturing firm to expand into global markets. The three training market segments addressed in this example are executives, marketing executives and professionals, and product management executives and professionals. Training implications are identified in each, and the year the training is needed identifies the priority of the particular type of training.

Figure 4-9 provides a second example, the implementation of a Total Quality Management system for a retail chain business. In this example, diagnosing the training implications would be easier if the TQM strategic plan has already been developed. Ideally, the strategic TQM plan would contain a training strategy. Be careful, however, we have seen many TQM training plans that are naive and leave out critical audiences such as middle management.

Functional

- Research and Development
- Marketing
- Manufacturing
- Distribution
- Sales
- Customer Services
- Procurement
- Product Management
- Human Resources
- Management Information
  Systems
- Accounting
- Legal

Hierarchical

- Executives
- Middle Management
- Supervisors
- Professionals
- Exempt
- Nonexempt

Business Units

- Consumer Electronics
  Group
- Automotive Electronics
  Group
- Medical Electronics
  Group
- Airborne Electronics
  Group

Geographical

- U.S.
  - Eastern
  - Central
  - Western
- Europe
- Asia

Customers

- Engineers
- Operators
- Maintenance personnel
- Managers

Suppliers

- Engineers
- Production Management
- Quality Assurance

Figure 4-6   Electronics Manufacturing Segmentation

Functional

- Marketing
- Purchasing
- Distribution
- Retail operations
- Catalog sales
- Information Systems
- Accounting
- Legal
- Human Resources

Business Units

- Headquarters

- Divisions
  - Northeast
  - Southeast
  - Midwest
  - Northwest
  - Southwest
  - Alaska

- Districts

Hierarchical

- Executives
- Middle management
- Supervisors
- Exempt
- Nonexempt

Figure 4-7   Retail Chain Segmentation

Segment	Training Implications	Training
Executives	Learn enough about global markets to pick target markets and develop a strategy	Year 1
Marketing: Executive through professional (select group)	Learn enough to analyze target markets and develop marketing plans including product modification requirements, sales strategy, etc.	Year 2
Product Management: Executive through professional (all affected product lines)	Learn enough to develop detailed product plans for target markets • Features • Regulatory requirements • Distribution • Sales support • Service • Profitability analysis	Year 2
(Continue this exercise through all affected segments.)		

Figure 4-8 Expansion into Global Markets, Electronic Manufacturing

Segment	Training Implications	Training
Executive	Learn enough about TQM to develop a vision, values, and TQM strategic plan	Year 1
Quality: New VP and staff	Learn enough about TQM to develop the system structure and implementation plan	Year 2
Business Units: Executives and Middle Managers	Learn enough to develop business unit strategic quality plans with help from quality staff	Years 2-3
Business Units: All levels, all functions	Orientation to TQM vision, values, strategic plan, and their expected role	Year 3
Business Units: Supervisors exempt and nonexempt, line functions	Corrective action team skills	Years 3-4
	Quality tools	Years 3-4
(Continue analysis through all segments, as appropriate.)		

Figure 4-9 Implement TQM, Retail Chain

Perform Cost/Benefit Analysis, and Estimate Return on Investment

You only have enough data at this stage to do a rough estimate of a cost/benefit analysis. Later on in the process you will greatly refine it, but this quick analysis will tell you where your big targets of opportunity lie and will help you to formulate your vision, mission, and strategic goals.

For this purpose we define the cost/benefit ratio as the cost of nonconformance divided by the cost of conformance for meeting the training needs associated with each of the business challenges. That is,

$$\text{Cost/benefit ratio} = \frac{\text{cost of nonconformance}}{\text{cost of conformance}} = \frac{\text{cost of not training}}{\text{cost of training}}$$

For any specific business challenge, the cost of conformance is the cost of fulfilling all the training needs it generates. The cost of nonconformance is the cost to the business of not fulfilling the training needs. The return on investment formula is similar.

$$\text{ROI} = \frac{(\text{cost of nonconformance} - \text{cost of conformance})}{\text{Cost of conformance}}$$

$$= \frac{(\text{cost of not training} - \text{cost of training})}{\text{cost of training}}$$

Let's try an example application. Suppose the electronics company identified in Figure 4-8 has made a strategic decision to implement a new CAD/CAM technology at a total capital cost of $300 million. It expects in return for this investment to achieve

- 30 percent reduction in time to bring new products to market

- Reduced product development cost and manufacturing cost

- Improved product quality

- Reduced materials cost through implementation of group technology embedded in the CAD/CAM system.

Total expected payoff is in excess of $1 billion per year.
The roll-out schedule is as follows:

- Airborne group, year 1

- Consumer group, year 2

- Automotive group, year 3

- Medical group, year 3.

Figure 4-10 shows the impacted functions and their associated costs. You can see that the population segmentation scheme assisted materially in estimating the training requirements associated with the new technology. Since none of these functions exist outside the United States, Europe and Asia are not involved. The training cost per person is determined by looking at historical data. The total cost of conformance to the standard of excellence (everyone trained for peak performance) is about $5.3 million, or about 1.8 percent of the capital investment and 0.5 percent of the expected annual benefit.

Now let's estimate the cost of nonconformance. Experience of other companies suggests that implementation without full training lengthens the time to bring this type of technology up to full performance. Therefore, as shown in Figure 4-11 the cost/benefit ratio = 94 and the return on the training investment is 93 to 1, an extremely good bargain.

You can then compile a table, like the one shown in Figure 4-12 summarizing this analysis for the top business challenges. An important subtlety here is that the cost of compliance is cumulative across all these challenges, but the cost of noncompliance is

Functions	Number of People Affected	Training Cost per Person	Total Cost of Training
Research and Development	600	2,000	$1,200,000
Manufacturing	4,000	1,000	$4,000,000
Procurement	150	500	$75,000
Product Management	60	500	$30,000
Management Information Systems	20	500	$10,000
Accounting	30	500	$15,000
TOTAL	4,860	----	$5,330,000

Figure 4-10 Costs for Affected Functions

	Year 1	Year 2	Year 3	3 Year Total
A. Without Training	50%	75%	90%	
B. With Training	80%	90%	95%	
C. Penalty for Non-conformance (B minus A)	30%	15%	5%	
D. Cost of Non-conformance	$300 million (30% of $1 billion)	$150 million (15% of $1 billion	$50 million (5% of $1 billion)	$500 million
E. Cost of Non-conformance/ Cost of Conformance				500/5.3=94

Figure 4-11 Percent of Benefits Achieved

not since failure to train in any one of these areas could result in loss of sales, higher cost, etc. In other words, there may be several things we could do wrong to lose the same benefits. This is why we cut the gross cost of noncompliance by a factor of 2 to get a more realistic estimate.

SUMMARY

Analyzing the training implications of business challenges, strategies, and goals consists of the following steps.

☐ Read business plans and interview executives to identify challenges, strategies, and goals in the following areas:

Business Challenge	Cost of Conformance with Training Need	Cost of Non-Conformance	Return on Investment - ROI
1. Implement CAD/CAM.	5.3 million	0.5 billion	94.34
2. Implement TQM.	7.2 million	1.2 billion	166.67
3. Systematically select, train, and qualify all employees entering new jobs.	80 million	2.0 billion	25.00
4. Global market expansion	1.2 million	0.8 billion	666.67
5. Fully support new product introduction.	3.0 million	1.0 billion	333.34
6. Implement customer training system.	6.0 million	1.5 billion	250.00
	Total Cost of Compliance = 103 million	Gross = 7 billion Derating factor = 2:1* Estimated = 3.5 billion	Total Return on Investment = 33:1

*Note: We used a derating factor of 2 to 1 because some of the $7 billion gross is estimated, and some of the amounts going into that total are not mutually exclusive. Therefore, the derating factor makes the assumption that the total is only half real.

Figure 4-12   Electronics Manufacturing Company, Business Challenge ROI

- Markets
- Competition
- Technology
- Products and services

- • Customer/supplier relationships
- • External regulation
- • Management and workforce issues

☐ Segment the training population according to the following dimensions:

- • Functional
- • Hierarchical
- • Organizational
- • Geographical
- • Customers
- • Suppliers

☐ Compile the data and develop a complete map of training implications and probable business consequences.

☐ Complete a rough estimate of

- • Total cost of training
- • Cost of conformance
- • Cost of nonconformance
- • Return on investment

Once you have completed these steps you will have a good overview of where the organization is going, training will have to do to support that, and the costs and benefits of training.

5

Evaluating Strengths and Weaknesses of Existing Training

Before you begin to develop your plan for the future, you should have some idea of what is good about what you are currently doing and what could be better. You should evaluate the strengths and weaknesses of your existing training system. This may seem like a good idea, but the question that often arises is, "strengths and weaknesses compared to what?" There are several frames of reference you could use:

- An ideal model

- The practices of leading companies

- What your competition is doing

- What you need to accomplish your strategic goals and vision.

All of these are important and useful in providing you with good ideas and information that will help sell your plan to executive management.

In this chapter, we provide you with a system for evaluating yourself against an ideal model that contains just about everything a perfect training system would have. No real-world organization has all the attributes of this ideal, though they all exist somewhere. The leading companies are leading because they have more of the pieces in place than other companies.

To find out what the leading companies practice, read Jack Bowsher's book, *Educating America* (John Wiley & Sons, 1989). Jack recently retired as head of IBM's Education function. The first half of his excellent book overviews the training and education practices of leading American companies.

In addition to reading, we heartily recommend that you research what is being done by the leaders in industry and by your competition through phone calls and visits. First-hand exposure carries an emotional impact you will not get by reading. Chapter 6 provides information on how to adapt the system described in this chapter to do that.

This chapter contains four steps for analyzing your own strengths and weaknesses as a training organization:

Step 1. Self-rating against the characteristics (earmarks) of a world-class training system

Step 2. Understanding the ideal training system

Step 3. Identifying systems and processes of the ideal training system that affect the earmarks in Step 1

Step 4. Self-rating against the systems and processes of the ideal training system.

By the time you complete this chapter, you should have an objective and comprehensive view of the strengths and weaknesses of your training organization.

SELF-RATING SYSTEM

The following questionnaire provides you with a simple way to rate your own organization training system by rating your position against each characteristic on a five-point scale. We suggest that you make copies of the questionnaire and have the members of your planning team complete it. Compile the results for a broader view of how your organization is doing. You may be surprised at the results.

	Very Weak		Good		Out-standing
Cultural Values Support Full Competency Development and Lifelong Learning.					
The organization exhibits in both words and deeds:					
• Commitment to providing everyone with skills and knowledge needed to perform assigned tasks	❑	❑	❑	❑	❑
• Commitment to lifelong learning to enhance performance, stay at the cutting edge, and develop career potential	❑	❑	❑	❑	❑
• Recognition of the link between learning and quality, productivity and profitability.	❑	❑	❑	❑	❑

	Very Weak		Good		Out-standing

Total Participation

- Everyone recognizes the important role learning plays in their working lives and in the success of the organization.   ❑ ❑ ❑ ❑ ❑
- Everyone has an individual learning plan.   ❑ ❑ ❑ ❑ ❑
- Every organizational unit has an education and training plan.   ❑ ❑ ❑ ❑ ❑
- Employees take responsibility for their own learning.   ❑ ❑ ❑ ❑ ❑
- Supervisors and managers are important players in the learning system, establishing expectations, monitoring and coaching application of new knowledge, and providing reward and recognition for learning results.   ❑ ❑ ❑ ❑ ❑
- Formal training is recognized to be only a part of the learning process; work assignments and coaching play significant, planned roles.   ❑ ❑ ❑ ❑ ❑
- Managers and executives act as role models by spending time in education and training and talking about what they have learned.   ❑ ❑ ❑ ❑ ❑

The Learning System is Driven by Business Performance Goals and is Competency Based.

- Functional curricula are in place based on definition and analysis of functional tasks to be performed to achieve business goals.   ❑ ❑ ❑ ❑ ❑
- New systems and products are implemented with a supporting curriculum based on analysis of new tasks, skills, and knowledge required by all populations affected.   ❑ ❑ ❑ ❑ ❑
- Corporate initiatives such as implementation of TQM are carried out with the support of a performance-based curriculum.   ❑ ❑ ❑ ❑ ❑
- Training and education programs develop measurable competencies based on business performance needs.   ❑ ❑ ❑ ❑ ❑
- Training priorities are set based on expected return on investment.   ❑ ❑ ❑ ❑ ❑

	Very Weak		Good		Out- standing

There are Tight Linkages between Training Departments and the Users of Their Services.

- Curriculum advisory councils help define and prioritize training needs. ❏ ❏ ❏ ❏ ❏
- The user community participates in developing courseware by providing field expertise and field testing the materials. ❏ ❏ ❏ ❏ ❏
- The user community provides its best performers for part-time or full-time assignments as instructors. ❏ ❏ ❏ ❏ ❏
- The training departments maintain a strong customer-service orientation. ❏ ❏ ❏ ❏ ❏
- Providers and users work together to devise and implement strategies for effective transfer of learning to the job. ❏ ❏ ❏ ❏ ❏

There is Strong Executive Leadership and Participation.

- Top executives have a vision for the role they expect education and training to play in achieving their goals and objectives. ❏ ❏ ❏ ❏ ❏
- Executives play a direct role in linking education and training to business goals through participation in executive education boards, approval of strategic training plans, approval of resource budgets, and review of results. ❏ ❏ ❏ ❏ ❏
- Executives play a key role in establishing expectations, monitoring performance, and providing rewards and consequences regarding implementation of comprehensive learning systems and culture. ❏ ❏ ❏ ❏ ❏
- Executive action matches rhetoric. ❏ ❏ ❏ ❏ ❏
- Executives are aware of the level of annual investment in education and training and manage this investment as carefully as they manage capital investments. ❏ ❏ ❏ ❏ ❏

Resources are Matched to Need and Objectives

- Training needs are quantitatively estimated. ❏ ❏ ❏ ❏ ❏
- Plans and objectives are built based on quantitative needs and estimated return on investment. ❏ ❏ ❏ ❏ ❏
- Resource allocations are sufficient to achieve committed objectives. ❏ ❏ ❏ ❏ ❏

	Very Weak		Good		Out-standing

Training Staffs are Competent and Include a Balanced Mix of Expertise.

- Training staffs are selected and trained to a high standard of competence. ❑ ❑ ❑ ❑ ❑
- Training staffs include an appropriate mix of career professionals in instructional design, performance analysis and other specialties as well as subject matter experts drawn from the field and from outside sources of expertise. ❑ ❑ ❑ ❑ ❑
- Training staffs have a strong sense of their contribution to business success. ❑ ❑ ❑ ❑ ❑
- Sufficient clerical and administrative support resources are provided to leverage the time of high cost professional and managerial talent. ❑ ❑ ❑ ❑ ❑
- Training is provided at the most appropriate location whether centralized, on site, or on the job. ❑ ❑ ❑ ❑ ❑
- An appropriate mix of delivery technologies such as classroom, laboratory, computer based, videodisc, video teleconference, expert systems, and embedded training in mechanized systems are deployed. ❑ ❑ ❑ ❑ ❑
- The training departments are aware of emerging training technologies, experimenting with applications and transferring mature technologies into service. ❑ ❑ ❑ ❑ ❑

There is Strong Administrative Coordination of Education and Training.

- The end user of training can go to a single source to find available training opportunities to meet his/her needs. ❑ ❑ ❑ ❑ ❑
- There is a common information system and database to keep track of training information and make it widely available. ❑ ❑ ❑ ❑ ❑
- There are common process standards and performance measures for needs analysis, curriculum architecture, courseware development, delivery, and maintenance and evaluation. ❑ ❑ ❑ ❑ ❑
- There is a common results measurement system for education and training. ❑ ❑ ❑ ❑ ❑
- There is a common registration and scheduling system. ❑ ❑ ❑ ❑ ❑

	Very Weak		Good		Out- standing

- There is a common system for developing individual learning plans and organization unit plans for education and training. ❑ ❑ ❑ ❑ ❑
- Curriculum architectures are linked across the organization to minimize duplication and maximize benefits from expensive courseware development. ❑ ❑ ❑ ❑ ❑
- The mission and roles of training departments and line organizational units are coordinated to care for all the education and training needs with minimum overlap and to avoid internal competition. ❑ ❑ ❑ ❑ ❑

Internal Education and Training Resources are Leveraged through Appropriate Use of Outside Resources.

- Universities, colleges, and other academic institutions provide basic skills, degree programs, and advanced specialized education. ❑ ❑ ❑ ❑ ❑
- Contractors provide courseware development resources to handle peak loads and special requirements. ❑ ❑ ❑ ❑ ❑
- Contract instructors with specialized expertise augment expert instructors drawn from the field. ❑ ❑ ❑ ❑ ❑
- Training and education consultants provide specialized expertise to training departments. ❑ ❑ ❑ ❑ ❑

WHAT AN IDEAL TRAINING SYSTEM LOOKS LIKE AND HOW IT WORKS

Now that you have looked at your own training system, we will show you the structure of an ideal training system (see figure 5-1.) This model is intended to serve as a reference for you as you continue to assess the strengths and weaknesses of your own training system. It shows the training system as an integrated set of systems and processes which interact to produce results.

As you can see, the ideal training system is composed of five major systems, including

- Governance—The overall structure of committees and councils that oversees the work of the training organization

GOVERNANCE				
Executive Board of Education	Functional Curriculum Councils	Training Administration Council	Project Committees	Organizational Unit Training Committees

PLANNING					
Strategic Training Plans	Annual Training Plan and Budget	Organizational Unit Training Plans	Individual Training Plans	Project Plans	Delivery Plans and Schedules

OPERATIONS					
Needs Analysis	Curriculum Architecture	Instructional Design/ Development	Delivery	On-the-Job Application	Maintenance

RESULTS					
Overall Performance	Trainee Opinions	Mastery Testing	Transfer of Learning to Job Performance	Impact on Business Results	Financial Results

SUPPORT					
Information System	Registration and Scheduling	Communications	Production Support	Facilities	Technologies
Specialists Support	Administrative Manuals	Organization Structure	Financial Systems	External Resources	Supervisor/ Manager	Staffing

Figure 5-1   The Training System

- Planning—The hierarchy of planning at all levels that drives the work of the training organization forward

- Operations—That part of the training system that is most often meant when we think of training

- Results—The system that tells us how well we are doing

- Support—The system that provides all the backup processes.

Each major system has a number of processes as shown in Figure 5-1. The names we have given the systems and processes are not important; what they represent is. Detailed descriptions of each system and process are included in Appendix C for your reference and future use. We suggest that you take time out to review this appendix carefully before proceeding with the next section. We have defined the following for each system and process:

- Purpose
- Responsibilities
- Outputs
- Participants
- Performance measures.

SYSTEMS AND PROCESSES' AFFECT ON EARMARKS

Now that you have become familiar with the earmarks of a world-class training organization and the systems and processes that make up an ideal training system, look at the way these two affect each other. The following matrices show the relationship of each of the five major systems in the attributes of a world class training organization. The purpose of these charts is to give you a guide for determining which system you may need to work on or beef up according to your self-rating on the attributes in Step 1 (see p. 88).

USING THE IDEAL MODEL TO ASSESS STRENGTHS AND WEAKNESSES

Now you know how you rate against the earmarks, and what training systems affect those earmarks. It is time to rate yourself against the systems and processes to determine how you will improve them.

For each process you will assess

1. Performance
2. Quantity and quality of resources
3. Other strengths and weaknesses
4. Impact of weaknesses on ability to meet training needs of the business
5. Priority for change.

Figure 5-2 provides a form for carrying out your assessment. Complete this form for every system and its processes that affect attributes in which you rated yourself less than good.

Finally, you need to make a summary assessment of the overall training system. The same general questions apply. Use the form in Figure 5-3, "Overall Assessment of the Training System." List as major strengths those good features of the present system

System or Process: _____

Assessment of Present Performance:_____

_____

_____

Assessment of Ability to Meet Future Needs: _____

_____

_____

Enough Resources?   _____

Quality of Resources?   _____

                         _____

                         _____

                         _____

Other Strengths: _____

                         _____

                         _____

                         _____

Other Weaknesses: _____

                         _____

                         _____

                         _____

Assessment of impact   _____
of weaknesses on   _____
ability to meet   _____
training needs of   _____
the business   _____

                         _____

Priority for change: _____

Figure 5-2 Training System Strengths and Weaknesses

you feel sure you need to keep to meet future requirements. List as major weaknesses only those features of the present system that must be corrected to meet future requirements of the business.

SUMMARY

To evaluate the strengths and weaknesses of your existing training organization, you should have completed the following:

Assessment of Present Performance:

Training needs met: _____
_____
_____

Training needs not
met or met
incompletely: _____
_____
_____
_____

Areas where training
is effective: _____
_____
_____
_____

Areas where training
is less effective
than needed: _____
_____
_____
_____

Overall cost of
training provided: _____
_____

Estimated cost to
business of
abandoning: _____
_____
_____

Estimated cost to
business of training
deficiencies: _____
_____
_____

Assessment of ability
to meet future needs: _____
_____
_____

Quantity of Resources _____
_____

Quality of Resources: _____
_____

Major Strengths _____
_____
_____
_____

Major Weaknesses _____
_____
_____
_____

Figure 5-3   Overall Assessment of Training Systems

☐ A self-evaluation filled out by the members of your planning team on how you compare to the attributes of a world class training organization

☐ A review of the structure of the ideal training system shown in Figure 5-2 and its systems and processes, as developed in Appendix C

☐ An identification of the system and processes that affect attributes on which you do not rate well

☐ An evaluation of your existing strengths and weaknesses in those systems and processes.

Doing this well can be a lengthy and difficult exercise, but it can be important and enlightening if it is done thoughtfully and comprehensively.

Attributes/System Matrix

Systems Attributes	Governance	Planning	Operations	Results	Support					
1. Cultural Values										
• Commitment to providing everyone with skills and knowledge needed to perform assigned tasks	• Executive Board • Curriculum Councils	All	All	• Overall Performance						
• Commitment to lifelong learning to enhance performance, stay at the cutting edge, and develop career potential	• Executive Board									
• Recognition of the link between learning and quality, productivity and profitability	• Executive Board			• Impact on Business Results	• Communications					

Attributes/System Matrix

Attributes \ Systems	Governance	Planning	Operations	Results	Support
2. Total Participation					
• Everyone recognizes the important role learning plays in their working lives and in the success of the organization.		• Individual Training Plans		• Impact on Business Results	
• Everyone has an individual learning plan.		• Individual Training Plans			
• Every organizational unit has an education and training plan.		• Organization Unit Training Plans			
• Employees take responsibility for their own learning.		• Individual Training Plans • Delivery Plans and Schedules			• Communications • Registrations & Scheduling
• Supervisors and managers are important players in the learning system, establishing expectations, monitoring and coaching application of new knowledge, and providing reward and recognition for learning results.			• On-the-job Application		• Supervisor/Manager Support System
• Formal training is recognized to be only a part of the learning process; work assignments and coaching play significant, planned roles.			• On-the-job Application • Curriculum Architecture		• Supervisor/Manager Support System
• Managers and executives act as role models by spending time in education and training and talking about what they have learned.		• Individual Training Plans	All		

Attributes/System Matrix

Systems / Attributes	Governance	Planning	Operations	Results	Support
3. The learning system is driven by business performance goals and is competency based.					
• Functional curricula are in place based on definition and analysis of functional tasks to be performed to achieve business goals.		• Strategic Training Plans	• Needs Analysis • Curriculum Architecture		
• New systems and products are implemented with a supporting curriculum based on analysis of new tasks, skills, and knowledge required by all populations affected.		• Strategic Training Plans	• Needs Analysis • Curriculum Architecture		
• Corporate initiatives such as implementation of TQM are carried out with the support of a performance-based curriculum.		• Strategic Training Plans	• Needs Analysis • Curriculum Architecture		
• Training and education programs develop measurable competencies based on business performance needs.			• Needs Analysis • Curriculum Architecture • Instructional Design/Development • Delivery	• Mastery Testing	
• Training priorities are set based on expected return on investment.	• Executive Board • Curriculum Councils	• Strategic Training Plans • Annual Training Plan and Budget	• Needs Analysis • Curriculum Architecture		• Information Systems

Attributes/System Matrix

Attributes / Systems	Governance	Planning	Operations	Results	Support
4. There are tight linkages between training departments and the users of their services.					
• Curriculum Advisory Councils help define and prioritize training needs.	• Curriculum Councils	• Annual Training Plan and Budget	• Needs Analysis • Curriculum Architecture		
• The user community participates in developing courseware by providing field expertise and field testing the materials.	• Project Committees		• Instructional Design/ Development		• Staffing
• The user community provides its best performers for part-time or full-time assignments as instructors.	• Curriculum Councils • Project Committees		• Delivery		• Staffing
• The training departments maintain a strong customer-service orientation.	• Executive Board • Curriculum Councils • Project Committees				• Registration & Scheduling • Communications • Organization Structure
• Providers and users work together to devise and implement strategies for effective transfer of learning to the job.			• Curriculum Architecture • On-the-job Application • Instructional Design/ Development		

Attributes/System Matrix

Systems / Attributes	Governance	Planning	Operations	Results	Support
5. There is strong executive leadership and participation; executive action matches rhetoric.					
• Top executives have a vision for the role they expect education and training to play in achieving their goals and objectives.	• Executive Board	• Strategic Training Plans			
• Executives play a direct role in linking education and training to business goals through participation in executive education boards, approval of strategic training plans, approval of resource budgets, and review of results.	• Executive Board	• Strategic Training Plans • Annual Training Plan and Budget		All	
• Executives play a key role in establishing expectations, monitoring performance, and providing rewards and consequences regarding implementation of comprehensive learning systems and culture.	• Executive Board	• Strategic Training Plans	• On-the-job Application	All	• Supervisor/Manager
• Executives are aware of the level of annual investment in education and training and manage this investment as carefully as they manage capital investments.	• Executive Board	• Strategic Training Plans		All	• Financial Systems

Attributes/System Matrix

Attributes \ Systems	Governance	Planning	Operations	Results	Support
6. Resources are matched to aneed and objectives. • Training needs are quantitatively estimated.		• Strategic Training Plans • Annual Training Plan and Budget • Org.anization Unit Training Plans			
• Plans and objectives are built based on quantiative needs and estimated return on investment.		• Strategic Training Plans • Annual Training Plan and Budget • Organization Unit Training Plans		• Impact on Business Results • Financial Results	• Information Systems
• Resource allocations are sufficient to achieve committed objectives.		• Strategic Training Plans • Annual Training Plan and Budget • Organization Unit Training Plans			• Information Systems • Financial Systems

Attributes/System Matrix

Systems / Attributes	Governance	Planning	Operations	Results	Support
7. Training staffs are competent and include a balanced mix of expertise.					
• The training staffs themselves are selected and trained to a high standard of competence.					• Staffing • Specialist Support
• Training staffs include an appropriate mix of career professionals in instructional design, performance analysis, and other specialties as well as subject-matter experts drawn from the field and from outside sources of expertise.					• Staffing • Specialist Support • Organization Structure
• Training staffs have a strong sense of their contribution to business success.	All			All	• Communications
• Sufficient clerical and administrative support resources are provided to leverage the time of high-cost professional and managerial talent.					• Staffing • Organization Structure • Production Support

Attributes/System Matrix

Attributes \ Systems	Governance	Planning	Operations	Results	Support
8. A balanced array of strategies is employed.					
• Training strategies have been implemented which provide the best balance of learning effectiveness, cost, administrative convenience, least disruption of the work environment, and timeliness.		• Strategic Training Plans • Delivery Plans and Schedules	All		• Facilities • Organization Structure • Staffing
• Training is provided at the most appropriate location whether centralized, on site, or on the job.		• Strategic Training Plans	• Delivery		• Facilities • Organization Structure • Staffing
• An appropriate mix of delivery technologies such as classroom, laboratory, computer based, videodisc, video teleconference, expert systems, and embedded training in mechanized systems are deployed.		• Strategic Training Plans	• Curriculum Architecture • Instructional Design/ Development • Delivery		• Technologies • Facilities
• The training departments are aware of emerging training technologies, experimenting with applications, and transferring mature technologies into service.					• Technologies

Attributes/System Matrix

Systems / Attributes	Governance	Planning	Operations	Results	Support
9. There is strong administrative coordination of education and training.					
• The end user of training can go to a single source to find available training opportunities to meet his/her needs.	• Training Administration Council				• Communications
• There is a common information system and database to keep track of training information and make it widely available.	• Training Administration Council				• Information Systems
• There are common process standards and performance measures for needs analysis, curriculum architecture, courseware development, delivery, and maintenance and evaluation.	• Training Administration Council		All	All	• Administrative Manuals
• There is a common results measurement system for education and training.	• Training Administration Council			All	
• There is a common registration and scheduling system.	• Training Administration Council				• Registration & Scheduling
• There is a common system for developing individual learning plans and organization unit plans for education and training.	• Training Administration Council • Organizational Unit Training Committees	• Organization Unit Training Plans • Individual Training Plans			• Administrative Manuals

Attributes/System Matrix

Systems / Attributes	Governance	Planning	Operations	Results	Support
9. There is strong administrative coordination of education and training (continued).					
• Curriculum architectures are linked across the organization to minimize duplication and maximize benefits from expensive courseware development.	• Training Administration Council		• Curriculum Architecture		
• The mission and roles of training departments and line organizational units are coordinated to care for all the education and training needs with minimum overlap and to avoid internal competition.	• Training Administration Council	• Strategic Training Plans			• Administrative Manuals
• Strategic and operational training plans are coordinated across the entire organization and linked to the business planning calendar.	• Training Administration Council • Organizational Unit Training Committees				• Administrative Manuals

Attributes/System Matrix

Systems / Attributes	Governance	Planning	Operations	Results	Support
10. Internal education and training resources are leveraged through appropriate use of outside resources.					
• Universities, colleges, and other academic institutions provide basic skills, degree programs, and advanced specialized education.		• Strategic Training Plans	• Curriculum Architecture • Delivery		• External Resources
• Contractors provide courseware development resources to handle peak loads and special requirements.		• Strategic Training Plans	• Instructional Design/Development		• External Resources
• Contract instructors with specialized expertise augment expert instructors drawn from the field.		• Strategic Training Plans	• Delivery		• External Resources
• Training and education consultants provide specialized expertise to training departments.					• External Resources • Specialist Support

6

BENCHMARKING

In chapter 5 you took a look at the strengths and weaknesses of your existing training organization. You did what we refer to as an internal evaluation. That is, you took a look at what you felt the strengths and weaknesses of your organization are, but you did not compare them against any external standard. But to do a thorough analysis of your training system you also need to do an external evaluation. That external evaluation should be in two major areas:

- What is being done by your competition and how do you compare?

- What is being done by the best-in-class and how do you compare?

The idea is similar to what athletes do when they want to become Olympic champions. They scout the competition and try to figure out what the competition does well, in order to emulate it, as well as what the competition does poorly, to determine how to beat them. In addition, they look at the best-in-class: What are the world records? How did the record-holders achieve them? What do they have to do to set a new world record?

The method that is used by business and industry to do this kind of external comparison has been around for a long time. It was popularized by the Japanese as part of their approach to quality improvement. They started looking at their competitors' products and taking them apart to see what was good about them and what could be done better. This technique has now been formalized into a process known in the world of Total Quality Management tools as benchmarking. Benchmarking has been defined by Robert C. Camp in his book *Benchmarking: The Search for Industry Best Practices That Lead to Superior Performance* (Milwaukee, WI: Quality Press, American Society for

Quality Control) as "the search for industry best practices that lead to superior performance."

Carrying out such an external evaluation, or benchmarking, is a project in itself. If you decide to carry out a benchmarking project (and we highly recommend that you do), you should develop a project team and project plan specifically for doing the benchmarking project. The results of that project will then be rolled up into your overall strategic plan.

The purpose of carrying out a benchmarking project is to be able to attain a leadership position in training and thus enable your company to meet its overall business goals. The only way to be sure you are a leader is to see what others are doing and determine if you are doing it better. The basic question behind all this is, Who is getting the best performance, what practices are they following to get that performance, and are these practices adaptable to your situation? This process is so important that it has become one of the criteria for winning the Malcolm Baldrige National Quality Award. Several companies (including NCR and IBM) are now developing their own internal guidelines for benchmarking within the training organization. This will become a growing trend as more and more companies realize the importance of training to their overall quality improvement efforts and the importance of applying the methods of quality improvement to the training function itself. In addition, benchmarking provides the added incentive that external comparisons often provide a much stronger stimulus to action than an internal desire for continuous improvement. It is a strong selling tool to your management.

The remainder of this chapter provides an overview of a process you can use to carry out your own benchmarking project. For additional information on this process, refer to Robert Camp's book, referenced earlier and in the bibliography.

THE BENCHMARKING PROCESS

The benchmarking process we advocate is basically a four-step process, as shown in Figure 6-1.

The purpose of Step 1, Scoping the Benchmarking Project, is to determine how much of the total training system you are going to investigate. Step 2, Selecting the Benchmarking Partners, addresses the question of who you are going to look at and compare your company to. The purpose of Step 3, Collecting and Analyzing the Data, is to develop a data collection plan, collect the data, and analyze it to identify present and future gaps and best practices. Step 4, Developing Action Plans, is the process of developing plans to improve performance in the areas you identified as needing improvement in Step 3. Note that this is an ongoing process. You may be doing benchmarking projects at many different levels at many different times. In addition, you will be revisiting previous benchmarking projects every three to five years to determine whether someone else has become a top performer that you might want to look at, as well as how you and the benchmarking partners are doing against the best practices now.

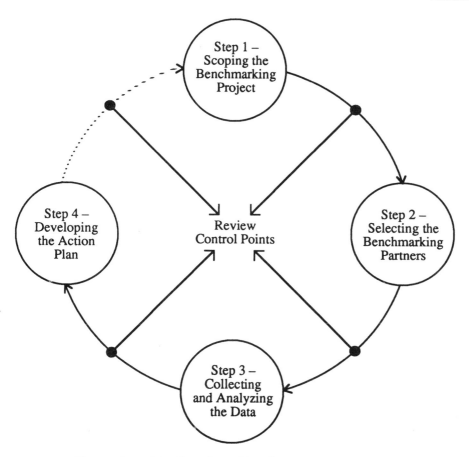

Figure 6-1   The Benchmarking Process

Step 1. Scoping the Benchmarking Project

The first step when doing a benchmarking project is to decide how much of the total training system you are going to investigate. This can be done at several different levels. For example, you can investigate

- The whole training system in a major corporation
- A single curriculum area such as engineering or marketing
- One of the major training systems, such as production systems (including needs analysis, curriculum architectures, and course development processes)
- One individual process, such as registration and scheduling or results measurement

- Applications of an individual instructional Technology, such as Interactive Videodisc or Expert Systems.

Figure 6-2 shows possible scope options. You can deal with a functional slice, a training process slice, a piece of either, a training process in a single function, or the entire training system for a business unit or the corporation.

Your scope decision should be based on what you are trying to accomplish. For example, if you want to compare yourself to a competitor, you should probably look at the whole training system for your company and theirs. Or, if the self-rating you did in chapter 5 pointed out some specific areas of weakness, such as inadequate course maintenance processes, you might want to do a benchmarking project on those particular areas. If there are people out there touting superior performance in some area by using some special technique, that would also be worth a look. You need to figure out what you want to get out of this project and then base your scoping decision on that.

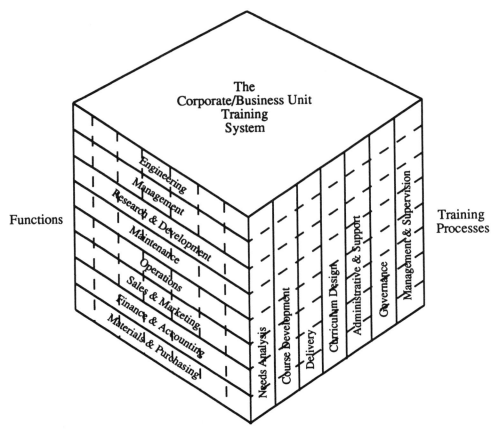

Figure 6-2 Benchmarking Scope Options

Step 2. Selecting Benchmarking Partners

Once you have identified the scope of your project you need to decide who you want to compare yourself to. These organizations will be your benchmarking partners. For a normal benchmarking project, you will probably want three to five partners, possibly two or three competitors and one or two other organizations. To select your benchmarking partners, you should

- Identify who your most serious competitors are in your major product or service area. Choose several of these as possible benchmarking targets.

- Identify the best-in-class organizations in training by
  - Reviewing the training literature
  - Attending training conferences
  - Networking with other training directors and training managers.

Once you have a list of several possible candidates, rank them in priority order. You may not get all of them to cooperate, so you want to have some as possible backups. Remember, too, that you must be willing to share your own data with the companies you choose and let them benchmark themselves against you—that is why we call them benchmarking partners.

The best way to approach your potential partners is to write a brief letter to the training directors of the organizations you are interested in. Explain your interest in the project, what they will get out of doing the project with you (theoretically the same things you will get out of doing the project with them), how much time and how many resources it will take, and when you expect the project to be finished. Close your letter by giving them a time frame in which you will make a follow-up call to determine their level of interest. If they are interested when you call, then offer to come to their location and meet with them to discuss the project further.

Step 3. Collecting and Analyzing Data

The purpose of this step is to gather all the data needed for you and your benchmarking partners to compare yourselves with each other to determine the best practices in the industry. There are several possible sources of data you will want to consider, including

- Published literature in the form of
  - Books
  - Magazines
  - Professional journals
  - Electronic databases
- Data collected directly from benchmarking partners

- Tours and on-site visits
- Interviews on the phone and in person
- Surveys and questionnaires
- Focus groups.

Data collected directly from benchmarking partners is by far the best source. However, much can be gleaned from the literature, and assigning someone to do some research in this area can pay off very well. We recommend that you use as many of these sources and means as you have time and resources for.

Once you have determined the sources of data you are going to use, you need to develop your data collection instrument(s). These may be in the form of interview guides, surveys, focus group agendas, literature search forms, etc. To develop your data collection instruments, decide what are the critical performance measures you want to look at. The problem is that the performance measures for training are not recognized and standard across the world as they are in sports, where you can measure the time for a 400-meter race, or in production, where you can measure feet of aluminum coil produced per day. In training there are fewer performance areas that are recognized by everyone and measured by all companies. As a starting point use the earmarks of a world-class training organization, discussed in chapter 1. For example, if you want to compare an entire training system or business unit, you can use the self-rating questionnaire in chapter 5, which is based on those earmarks, to develop a quantitative scale on which to compare your performance against your benchmarking partners'. It is possible to take this questionnaire and assign it a 1,000-point total score, and spread points out across all the earmarks. You can complete it for your company, and all your benchmarking partners can complete it as well. You can then compare yourselves against each other. Granted, there is some subjectivity in such a system, but it will give you a starting point.

Regardless of which performance measures you use (see chapter 24 and Appendix C for more information on performance measures for training), you need to develop a scale for assigning values to these measures. Figure 6-3 shows an example based on the questionnaire from chapter 5.

Another possible data collection instrument could be made using the systems and process analysis sheets from chapter 5 (Figures 5-2 and 5-3). Your benchmarking partner can complete these as well, and then you can get together and talk about the differences and the results.

You then must develop the actual instruments for collecting the data as well as a method for determining what practices the partners are following that lead to superior performance. You also need a way to predict future performance, because you will always be shooting at a moving target as you try to become a leader in the training field.

Regardless of what methods you use, you want to end up with a chart like the one shown in Figure 6-4 for *each* of the performance measures you have decided to benchmark on. This chart shows your current rating on the measure (in this case, percent of training needs met in the sales offices), Company A's past and current performance on the measure, Company B's past and current performance on the measure, and the projected five year target for you, for Company A and Company B. This allows you to

	Very Weak		Good		Out- standing	Total Points

Total Participation

- Everyone recognizes the important role learning plays in their working lives and in the success of the organization.

  ☐ 0 ☐ 5 ■ 10 ☐ 15 ☐ 20   <u>10</u>

- Everyone has an Individual Learning Plan.

  ☐ 0 ■ 5 ☐ 10 ☐ 15 ☐ 20   <u>5</u>

- Every organizational unit has an education and training plan.

  ☐ 0 ☐ 5 ☐ 10 ■ 15 ☐ 20   <u>15</u>

- Employees take responsibility for their own learning.

  ☐ 0 ■ 5 ☐ 10 ☐ 15 ☐ 20   <u>5</u>

Figure 6-3 Example Rating Scale

deal with the question, "What do we have to do to follow our projected curve and become the best in the next five years?"

Using all this information from the rating forms, the systems and process analysis charts and the gap analysis, you now should be able to find a correlation between your overall performance indicators and the supporting systems and processes. Basically, you will take all your forms and gap analysis charts (like Figure 6-4) and sit down with your benchmarking partners in a focus group to discuss the issues. For example, using the discrepancy shown in Figure 6-4, sit down with Company A and Company B and ask them what they are doing now and what they intend to be doing in the future that will get them to their projected performance. In this case, Company A may tell you they are doing something like the following:

- We have individual training plans for all employees at all levels in every sales office.

- We have computer-based product training at each sales office site.

- All of our sales managers are compensated for their training results. They are used to being compensated for sales results, and this fits in very well with their mode of operation.

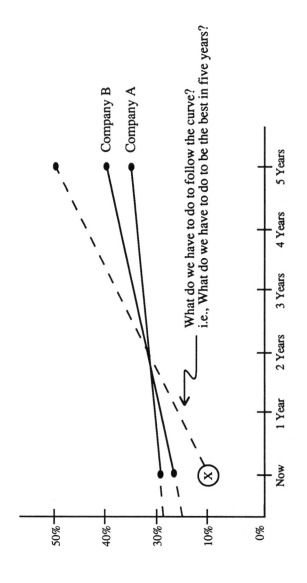

Performance Measure: % of Training Needs Met in Sales Offices

Figure 6-4 Sample Gap Analysis

- We have a comprehensive performance-based sales curriculum.

- We have a sales academy in which we do our training for core sales competencies.

These may or may not be things you are doing or doing well enough—you will be able to determine that in the course of your discussion. All of this information will lead you to developing your action plans in Step 4.

Before you go on, note that this process of collecting and analyzing data for benchmarking is no different than any other data collection and analysis methodology used for results measurement or needs analysis or other areas you might be familiar with. The important thing is to know what information you want to get and to design a system that will allow you to get it systematically, comprehensively, and efficiently.

Step 4. Developing Action Plans

When you have completed your collection and analysis and group debriefing, you can then set about comparing your results to your partners' results, your practices to their practices, and select those areas to work on where they have a better idea or better performance than you. These are the areas for which you will establish action plans for changing your practices and improving your performance. For example, you may decide in sales office training to adopt the following three practices:

- Compensate sales managers for training results.

- Establish a sales academy.

- Institute Computer Based Training (CBT) product training at the sales office sites.

Possible action plans for each of these items might be

- Assign one member of your staff to work with the national sales manager and human resources compensation manager to work on the compensation issue.

- Establish a task force to develop a proposal for a national sales academy.

- Establish a small task force to develop a proposal for implementing computer-based training for sales office site product training.

A project plan would be developed for each of these action plans using the formats described in chapter 3.

Review Points

Notice that Figure 6-1 indicates several review points along the way. It is always a good idea to have a specific time to stop and take a look at the benchmarking project and determine whether to proceed, to go back and gather more data, or to stop the project.

SUMMARY

Benchmarking is an important process used to help you identify better practices than the ones you have been using and to improve your performance as a training organization. You cannot claim to be world class unless you have actually gone out and evaluated yourself against the best and found that you are right up there with them. The steps in the benchmarking process are as follows:

☐ Step 1: Scope the benchmarking project.

☐ Step 2: Select your benchmarking partners.

☐ Step 3: Collect and analyze data.

☐ Step 4: Develop action plans.

☐ Review periodically for go ahead, go back, and stop decisions.

ACCOUNTING
FOR TRAINING COST

As you go through the strategic planning process, you will have to answer questions about cost every step of the way. At the beginning, at least as early as the review of the project plan, management will want information on what the training is going to cost the company. If management is not asking, you need to tell them anyway. One of the purposes of the strategic planning effort is to put management in the driver's seat regarding training investments. Management needs to understand that training expenditures are for developing the human assets of the business. These human assets, as mentioned in chapter 1, are the business's most important assets. Top management is responsible for directing and controlling expenditures to develop the business's assets. Management cannot do this intelligently if you do not provide accurate and comprehensive data on the expenditures and returns associated with training efforts and programs.

You must be able to determine present expenditures and estimate future expenditures. This is not as simple as it sounds. It is our experience that few organizations have a true and accurate measure of their cost of training. In fact, in many organizations, well over half of all expenditures for training go unaccounted for. Some training organizations are afraid to find out—they think that if management knows what they are really spending, budgets or resources could be cut.

More frequently, though, the training department has insufficient resources to get the job done. This results in individual managers resorting to expedient means to get their necessary (and in some cases not so necessary) training done. These expedients are often more expensive and less effective than adequately resourcing the training department in the first place. An accurate and believable picture of costs can be helpful in getting resources allocated in a much better way.

To be world class or best-in-class requires managing intelligently and allocating our resources accordingly. Accurate and up-to-date information about all aspects of the program, including the costs associated with it, is essential. Without it, you are operating on uneducated guesses, and ultimately that is a prescription for disaster. In some areas, precise measurement of cost will be impossible. In those areas, you will have to obtain as much data as possible to make a believable estimate.

The purpose of this chapter is to provide you with a framework and methodology for determining what costs you need to measure and how to do so. It is to your advantage to set up these cost systems on computer spreadsheets. The extra time required up front will more than pay for itself over the course of the next ten years, as you use the system over and over to recalculate costs as things change in your program.

The steps we recommend in estimating present and future costs are as follows:

1. Design your cost breakdown structure.

2. Use the worksheet formats provided in this chapter to develop computerized spreadsheets for cost calculation.

3. Use your spreadsheets to calculate present costs for each category of your cost breakdown structure.

4. Based on current costs, future trends, rate of inflation, etc., estimate future costs for each category of your cost breakdown structure.

5. Update the worksheets on a regular schedule as required by your steering committee.

The result of these efforts will form an integral part of and play a critical role in your strategic planning project.

HOW TO DESIGN YOUR COST BREAKDOWN STRUCTURE

You need a cost breakdown structure to be certain you have accounted for all relevant costs, so you are not one of those organizations accounting for less than half of the costs associated with training. Your cost breakdown structure should be designed to be helpful and useful when you must make planning decisions regarding the allocation of training resources to meet future needs. We suggest that you break down costs into the major categories of the training system structure (previously presented in chapter 5):

- Governance
- Planning
- Operations
- Results
- Support.

For a large organization, you may also want breakdowns by organizational unit and/or by major function. In each category, you should keep separate estimates of costs that fall within the training department budget and those that fall in other budgets. You will always have training costs that do not fall within the training department budget. We do not advocate putting all the training resources in the training department. Some training tasks are best done by line organizations (e.g., structured on-the-job-training or OJT, can be a most effective system if properly managed). We advocate that you deliberately plan what roles should be assigned to the training departments and what roles should be assigned to the line organization. The resources required to do both should be accounted for and managed in such a way that both organizations can fully accomplish their assigned roles. As you will see later in this chapter, you should also separate capital expenditures from expenses. (It is easier to calculate labor costs in person days rather than actual dollars. However, you can convert to dollars by multiplying person days by weighted average salaries for the positions involved, and at some point it is likely that you will need to do this.) In the end, you should be able to roll up estimates for each category into a simple expense chart such as the one shown in Figure 7-1.

As always, these categories are only guidelines. Ultimately, you will need to design a structure that fits your own context and situation. The next section provides breakdowns and worksheets for each of the categories we suggest. You may wish to modify these as well. They are provided to teach you the concept and give you a checklist of items to consider for each category.

GOVERNANCE SYSTEM COSTS

As you learned in chapter 5, the governance system is composed of five categories of governance:

Year _____

Category	Training Budget	Other Budgets	TOTAL
Goverance Costs Planning Costs Operations Costs Results Costs Support Costs			
TOTAL COSTS			

Figure 7-1   Training Expense Roll-Up

- Executive board of education
- Functional curriculum councils
- Training administrative council
- Organizational unit training committees
- Project committees.

Each of these categories becomes an expense category when calculating governance system costs. Within each category there are three cost lines.

- Preparing for and attending meetings
- Purchased services
  - Catering
  - Consultants
  - Etc.
- Materials production.

For each cost item, in each category, you must calculate the following costs.

- Number of person days expended by training staff
- Number of person days expended by other staff
- Estimated training department budget
- Other budgets.

All of these items should be estimated using a spreadsheet similar to the one shown in Figure 7-2. In the future, historical data will allow you to calculate these numbers more precisely.

PLANNING SYSTEM COSTS

The second system that must be addressed when estimating training costs is the planning system. As we saw in chapter 5, the planning system is composed of the following processes.

- Strategic training plans
- Annual training plan and budget
- Organizational unit training plans

EXPENSE ITEM	# OF PERSON DAYS EXPENDED		EXPENSE ESTIMATES		TOTAL
	TRNG STAFF	OTHERS	TRNG DPT BUDGET	OTHER BUDGETS	
• EXECUTIVE BOARD OF					
EDUCATION					
- MEETINGS					
- PURCH. SVCS.					
- MATLS.					
SUBTOTAL					
• FUNCTIONAL CURRICULUM					
COUNCILS					
- MEETINGS					
- PURCH. SVCS.					
- MATLS.					
SUBTOTAL					
• TRAINING ADMINISTRATION					
COUNCIL					
- MEETINGS					
- PURCH. SVCS.					
- MATLS.					
SUBTOTAL					
• PROJECT COMMITTEE					
- MEETINGS					
- PURCH. SVCS.					
- MATLS.					
SUBTOTAL					
• ORGANIZATIONAL UNIT					
TRAINING COMMITTEE					
- MEETINGS					
- PURCH. SVCS.					
- MATLS.					
SUBTOTAL					
• TOTAL COST OF					
GOVERNANCE					
- MEETINGS					
- PURCH. SVCS.					
- MATLS.					
TOTAL					

Figure 7-2 Governance System Costs Spreadsheet

- Individual training plans
- Project plans
- Delivery plans and schedules

Expense line items for each of these processes include

- Employee time
- Purchased services
- Travel and living expenses
- Other miscellaneous expenses.

For each cost item, in each category, you must estimate the following costs:

- Number of person days expended by training staff
- Number of person days expended by other staff
- Estimated training department budget
- Other budgets.

All of these items should be estimated using a spreadsheet like the one in Figure 7-3.

OPERATIONS SYSTEMS COSTS

Operations, which forms the bulk of training systems work, is understandably the most complicated system for which to estimate costs. The operations system processes that must be accounted for in addressing training system costs are

- Needs analysis
- Curriculum architecture
- Instructional design and development
- Delivery
- Courseware maintenance.

Needs Analysis and Curriculum Architecture

Expense line items for needs analysis and curriculum architecture are the same and include:

- Analysis team costs
- Production support
- Purchased services

EXPENSE ITEM	# OF PERSON DAYS EXPENDED		EXPENSE ESTIMATES		
	TRNG STAFF	OTHERS	TRNG DPT BUDGET	OTHER BUDGETS	TOTAL
• STRATEGIC TRAINING PLANS					
- EMPLOYEE TIME					
- PURCHASED SERVICES					
- TRAVEL & LIVING					
- OTHER MISCELLANEOUS					
SUBTOTAL					
• ANNUAL TRAINING PLANS					
AND BUDGET					
- EMPLOYEE TIME					
- PURCHASED SERVICES					
- TRAVEL & LIVING					
- OTHER MISCELLANEOUS					
SUBTOTAL					
• ORGANIZATIONAL UNIT					
TRAINING PLANS					
- EMPLOYEE TIME					
- PURCHASED SERVICES					
- TRAVEL & LIVING					
- OTHER MISCELLANEOUS					
SUBTOTAL					
• INDIVIDUAL TRAINING PLANS					
- EMPLOYEE TIME					
- PURCHASED SERVICES					
- TRAVEL & LIVING					
- OTHER MISCELLANEOUS					
SUBTOTAL					
• PROJECT PLANS					
- EMPLOYEE TIME					
- PURCHASED SERVICES					
- TRAVEL & LIVING					
- OTHER MISCELLANEOUS					
SUBTOTAL					
• DELIVERY PLANS & SCHEDULES					
- EMPLOYEE TIME					
- PURCHASED SERVICES					
- TRAVEL & LIVING					
- OTHER MISCELLANEOUS					
SUBTOTAL					
• TOTAL COST OF PLANNING					
- EMPLOYEE TIME					
- PURCHASED SERVICES					
- TRAVEL & LIVING					
- OTHER MISCELLANEOUS					
TOTAL					

Figure 7-3 Planning System Costs Spreadsheet

- Travel and living expenses
- Other miscellaneous costs.

For each of these items you should estimate

- Number of person days expended by training staff
- Number of person days expended by other staff
- Estimated training department budget
- Other budgets.

Use the spreadsheet in Figure 7-4 to estimate these costs.

Instructional Design, Development, and Maintenance

Expense line items for instructional design and development and for course maintenance are the same. However, expense line items for these processes can vary depending on the delivery strategy of the course being developed or maintained. Figure

| EXPENSE ITEM | # OF PERSON DAYS EXPENDED | | EXPENSE ESTIMATES | | TOTAL |
	TRNG STAFF	OTHERS	TRNG DPT BUDGET	OTHER BUDGETS	
• NEEDS ANALYSIS					
- ANALYSIS TEAM COSTS					
- PRODUCTION SUPPORT					
- PURCHASED SERVICES					
- TRAVEL & LIVING EXPENSES					
- OTHER MISCELLANEOUS					
SUBTOTAL					
• CURRICULUM ARCHITECTURE					
- ANALYSIS TEAM COSTS					
- PRODUCTION SUPPORT					
- PURCHASED SERVICES					
- TRAVEL & LIVING EXPENSES					
- OTHER MISCELLANEOUS					
SUBTOTAL					
• TOTAL NEEDS ANALYSIS & CURRICULUM ARCHITECTURE					
- ANALYSIS TEAM COSTS					
- PRODUCTION SUPPORT					
- PURCHASED SERVICES					
- TRAVEL & LIVING EXPENSES					
- OTHER MISCELLANEOUS					
TOTAL					

Figure 7-4 Needs Analysis Curriculum Architecture Costs Spreadsheet

7-5 shows the expense line items for instructional design, development and maintenance as well as how they vary depending on which of the five major delivery strategies is chosen (conventional classroom instruction, self-paced classroom, self-paced on the job training, computer based training, and video teleconferencing).

Instructional Design/Development and Maintenance	Conventional Classroom Instruction	Self-paced Classroom	Self-paced OJT	CBT	Video Tele-conferencing
Expenses					
• Instructional designers, analysts, writers	X	X	X	X	X
• Content experts*	X	X	X	X	X
• Project managers	X	X	X	X	X
• Project committee*	X	X	X	X	X
• Production support staff*	X	X	X	X	X
• Administrative support staff*	X	X	X	X	X
• Audio/video studio staff*	X	X	X	X	X
• Purchased materials	X	X	X	X	X
• Purchased services	X	X	X	X	X
• Purchased rights to use licenses	X	X	X	X	X
• Equipment rentals	X	X	X	X	X
• Computer time*	X	X	X	X	X
• Computer programmer time*	X	X	X	X	X
• Purchased software	X	X	X	X	X
• Audio/video studio rental*	X	X	X	X	X
• Video teleconferencing changes*					X
• Travel and living expenses*	X	X	X	X	X
• Office rental*	X	X	X	X	X
Capital expenditures					
• Laboratory/simulator equipment and construction	X	X	X	X	
• Special classroom equipment, e.g., personal computers	X	X	X	X	X
• Training facility construction and furnishings	X	X	X	X	X
• Video teleconferencing network equipment					X

* Have potential hidden cost elements

Figure 7-5 Instructional Design, Development, and Maintenance Expense Line Items

EXPENSE ITEM	# OF PERSON DAYS EXPENDED		EXPENSE ESTIMATES		TOTAL
	TRNG STAFF	OTHERS	TRNG DPT BUDGET	OTHER BUDGETS	
• INSTRUCTIONAL DESIGNERS, ANALYSTS, WRITERS					
• CONTENT EXPERTS					
• PROJECT MANAGERS					
• PROJECT COMMITTEE					
• PRODUCTION SUPPORT STAFF					
• ADMINISTRATIVE SUPPORT STAFF					
• AUDIO/VIDEO STUDIO STAFF					
• PURCHASED MATERIALS					
• PURCHASED SERVICES					
• PURCHASED RIGHTS TO USE LICENSES					
• EQUIPMENT RENTALS					
• COMPUTER TIME					
• COMPUTER PROGRAMMER TIME					
• PURCHASED SOFTWARE					
• AUDIO/VIDEO STUDIO RENTAL					
• VIDEO TELECONFERENCING CHANGES					
• TRAVEL AND LIVING EXPENSES					
• OFFICE RENTAL					
TOTAL					

Figure 7-6 Instructional Design and Development and/or Maintenance Spreadsheet

The spreadsheet in Figure 7-6 can be used for estimating costs of instructional design, development, and/or maintenance.

Delivery

As was true for instructional design, development and/or maintenance, expense line items for delivery will vary depending on the delivery method. Figure 7-7 shows the expense line items for delivery as well as how these items vary by delivery method.

The spreadsheet in Figure 7-8 can be used for estimating delivery costs.

Delivery	Conventional Classroom Instruction	Self-paced Classroom	Self-paced OJT	CBT	Video Tele-conferencing
Expenses					
• Instructors/facilitators*	X	X	X	X	X
• Trainee time*	X	X	X	X	X
• Production support staff*	X	X	X	X	X
• Registration and scheduling staff	X	X		X	X
• Administrative support staff	X	X	X	X	X
• Audio/video studio staff*					X
• Purchased materials*	X	X	X	X	X
• Purchased services*	X	X			X
• Rights to use fees	X	X	X	X	X
• Equipment rentals	X	X	X	X	X
• Computer time*	X	X	X	X	
• Computer programmer time*	X	X	X	X	
• Purchased software	X	X	X	X	
• Video teleconferencing charges*					X
• Instructor/facilitator travel and living	X	X			X
• Trainee travel and living*	X	X		X	X
• Classroom/facility rentals*	X	X		X	X
• Equipment and lab maintenance	X	X		X	
• Shipping charges*	X	X	X	X	X
• Trainee overtime pay*	X	X	X	X	X
• Tuition paid to outside schools*	X				X
• Supervisor time*			X		
• Office rental*					

* Have potential hidden cost elements

Figure 7-7 Delivery Costs Expense Line Items

RESULTS SYSTEM COSTS

Results system costs include

- Developing results measurement tools
- Administering and processing trainee opinion surveys
- Processing mastery test data
- Administering and processing follow-up surveys to determine applications of training skills on the job

EXPENSE ITEM	# OF PERSON DAYS EXPENDED		EXPENSE ESTIMATES		TOTAL
	TRNG STAFF	OTHERS	TRNG DPT BUDGET	OTHER BUDGETS	
• INSTRUCTORS/FACILITATORS					
• TRAINEE TIME					
• PRODUCTION SUPPORT STAFF					
• REGISTRATION AND SCHEDULING STAFF					
• ADMINISTRATIVE SUPPORT STAFF					
• AUDIO/VIDEO STUDIO STAFF					
• PURCHASED MATERIALS					
• PURCHASED SERVICES					
• RIGHTS TO USE FEES					
• EQUIPMENT RENTALS					
• COMPUTER TIME					
• COMPUTER PROGRAMMER TIME					
• PURCHASED SOFTWARE					
• VIDEO TELECONFERENCING CHARGES					
• INSTRUCTOR/FACILITATOR TRAVEL AND LIVING					
• TRAINEE TRAVEL AND LIVING					
• CLASSROOM/FACILITY RENTALS					
• EQUIPMENT AND LAB MAINTENANCE					
• SHIPPING CHARGES					
• TRAINEE OVERTIME PAY					
• TUITION PAID TO OUTSIDE SCHOOLS					
• SUPERVISOR TIME					
• OFFICE RENTAL					
TOTAL					

Figure 7-8   Delivery Costs Spreadsheet

- Studies to determine value of training or cost of nonconformance to training standards
- Training department audits
- Cost of administering overall results function.

These costs can be estimated using the spreadsheet in Figure 7-9.

EXPENSE ITEM	# OF PERSON DAYS EXPENDED		EXPENSE ESTIMATES		TOTAL
	TRNG STAFF	OTHERS	TRNG DPT BUDGET	OTHER BUDGETS	
• DEVELOP TOOLS					
• ADMINISTER SURVEYS					
• PROCESS TEST DATA					
• CONDUCT STUDIES					
• AUDIT TRAINING					
DEPARTMENT					
• OVERALL					
ADMINISTRATION					
• OTHER MISCELLANEOUS					
TOTAL					

Figure 7-9   Results System Costs Spreadsheet

SUPPORT SYSTEM COSTS

Support system costs for which we need to account include:

- Information system cost
  - Hardware
  - Software
  - Operation/administration
  - Purchased services
- Communication
  - Writers
  - Printing and materials
  - Distribution
  - Video production
- Specialists
  - Salaries
  - Purchased services
  - Office space and equipment
- Administrative manuals
  - Printing
  - Distribution
  - Maintenance
- Financial administration
  - Personnel

          – Computer time
          – Office expense
- Facilities administration
  - Operation
  - Maintenance
  - Leasing.

The spreadsheet in Figure 7-10 can be used to estimate these costs.

ESTIMATED COST ROLL-UP

When you have completed your spreadsheet for the major training systems and processes, you should roll up the costs into a single spreadsheet like the one shown in Figure 7-11. When you add up all the costs of training, you may be shocked at how much training costs. This will be particularly true if you estimate individual managers sending people to seminars and workshops outside the training budget. When you add in these hidden costs plus the cost of the trainees' time while in training, it is not uncommon for the total cost of training to exceed three times the formally acknowledged training budget.

SUMMARY

Estimating the overall cost of training is important because your real objective is to get the total training job done at the least overall cost. Without a picture of what these costs are, you cannot begin to assess your progress against this objective. Estimating these costs consists of the following steps:

☐ Design a cost breakdown structure based on overall training system categories:

- Governance

- Planning

- Operations

- Results

- Support

☐ Develop spreadsheets for each of the following categories:

- Governance

- Planning

- Operations

  - Needs analysis and curriculum architecture

EXPENSE ITEM	# OF PERSON DAYS EXPENDED		EXPENSE ESTIMATES		TOTAL
	TRNG STAFF	OTHERS	TRNG DPT BUDGET	OTHER BUDGETS	
• INFORMATION SYSTEM					
COSTS					
- HARDWARE					
- SOFTWARE					
- OPERATION/					
ADMINISTRATION					
- PURCHASED SERVICES					
SUBTOTAL					
• COMMUNICATION					
- WRITERS					
- PRINTING AND					
MATERIALS					
- DISTRIBUTION					
- VIDEO PRODUCTION					
SUBTOTAL					
• SPECIALISTS					
- SALARIES					
- PURCHASED SERVICES					
- OFFICE SPACE &					
EQUIPMENT					
SUBTOTAL					
• ADMINISTRATIVE					
MANUALS					
- PRINTING					
- DISTRIBUTION					
- MAINTENANCE					
SUBTOTAL					
• FINANCIAL					
ADMINISTRATION					
- PERSONNEL					
- COMPUTER TIME					
- OFFICE EXPENSE					
SUBTOTAL					
• FACILITIES					
ADMINISTRATION					
- OPERATION					
- MAINTENANCE					
- LEASING					
SUBTOTAL					

Figure 7-10 Support System Costs Spreadsheet

EXPENSE ITEM	# OF PERSON DAYS EXPENDED		EXPENSE ESTIMATES		TOTAL
	TRNG STAFF	OTHERS	TRNG DPT BUDGET	OTHER BUDGETS	
• GOVERNANCE					
- EXECUTIVE BOARD OF					
EDUCATION					
- FUNCTIONAL					
CURRICULUM COUNCIL					
- TRAINING ADMIN.					
COUNCIL					
- ORGANIZATIONAL UNIT					
COMMITTEE					
- PROJECT COMMITTEE					
SUBTOTAL					
• PLANNING					
- STRATEGIC TRAINING					
PLANS					
- ANNUAL TRAINING					
PLANS					
- ORGANIZATIONAL UNIT					
PLANS					
- INDIVIDUAL TRAINING					
PLANS					
- PROJECT PLAN					
- DELIVERY PLANS AND					
SCHEDULES					
SUBTOTAL					
• OPERATIONS					
- NEEDS ANALYSIS					
- CURRICULUM					
ARCHITECTURE					
- INSTRUCTIONAL DESIGN					
AND DEVELOPMENT					
- DELIVERY					
- COURSEWARE					
MAINTENANCE					
SUBTOTAL					
• RESULTS					
SUBTOTAL					
• SUPPORT					
- INFORMATION SYSTEMS					
- COMMUNICATIONS					
- SPECIALISTS					
- MANUALS					
- FINANCE					
- FACILITIES					
SUBTOTAL					
• TOTAL COSTS					
- GOVERNANCE					
- PLANNING					
- OPERATIONS					
- RESULTS					
- SUPPORT					
TOTAL					

Figure 7-11 Training Costs Roll-Up Spreadsheet

- Instructional design, development, and/or maintenance
- Delivery

• Results

• Support

• Costs roll-up

☐ Use your spreadsheets to calculate present costs for each category of your cost breakdown structure.

☐ Based on current costs, future trends, rate of inflation, etc., estimate future costs for each category of your cost breakdown structure.

☐ Update the worksheets on a regular schedule as required by your steering committee.

8

MISSION
AND PHILOSOPHY

Until this point, everything that we have discussed is analysis. We have been looking back to establish a foundation for the strategies. Now it is finally time to look forward and begin creating

- A philosophy of training for the entire organization
- Mission statements and roles for each training department in the organization
- Roles for line and staff organizations.

The philosophy sets down your beliefs and principles about training and its place in the organization. We deal with it first because everything else should be based on it. It is your basis for decision making every step of the way through the strategic planning process.

The mission states in a few words the reason for the existence of each training unit. It gives you and everyone who reads it a picture of what the organizational unit is about.

The roles list says in more detail what a specific training unit will be expected to do (i.e., its key responsibilities). Similarly, the roles statement for line and staff management sets forth what they will be expected to do as part of the overall training system of the organization.

In this chapter, we explain philosophy, mission, and roles in more detail and provide you with some examples and methods for creating your own. These are important tools to use in explaining what your organization is all about.

PHILOSOPHY

The philosophy statement is like a creed or the Ten Commandments. You can hang it on the wall and use it to remind yourself of your principles when it comes time to make tough decisions. Without a set of principles, decision making becomes expedient, political, inconsistent, and often ineffective. Most of us have the principles in our minds, but many organizations have found that it is useful to get them out on the table and wrestle with them until they are shared by both the training community and the executive decision makers in the organization.

The working committee should address the following questions when establishing principles:

1. Why is the organization interested in training?
2. What do we expect training to accomplish?
3. What are the training's limitations?
4. What responsibility is expected of the individual employee?
5. What responsibility does the company assume?
6. What is generally expected of supervisors and managers?
7. What is expected of the training departments?
8. Is training an investment or an expense?
9. Do we eagerly embrace the value of continual learning and improvement or learn only when we can prove it is necessary?

The following paragraphs provide a menu of possible answers to these questions you can use to build your philosophy statement. This list is by no means exhaustive, and be sure to find or develop answers that are suited to the culture of your organization as well as the mission and goals. Note that each question may have more than one answer in your final philosophy statement.

1. Why is the organization interested in training?

- In a rapidly changing business environment, training is the only viable way to develop quickly the skills of new employees and keep the existing workforce skills current with technology, products, competition and regulation.

- Training has an important role to play in ensuring business performance in
  - Profitability
  - Quality
  - Market share growth
  - Compliance with law and regulations.

- Safety, occupational health, and protection of the environment require up-to-date skills and knowledge.

- Competence is the only asset that can provide a sustainable competitive advantage.
- The cost of not training far exceeds the cost of training.

2. What do we expect training to accomplish?

- Develop skills and knowledge required for improved job performance.
- Support organizational cultural change.
- Support the introduction of new systems, new technology, and new products.
- Support the company's quality goals.
- Bring new employees quickly to a basic level of competency.
- Provide a systematic means for employees, managers, and the corporation to manage competence.

3. What are the limitations of training?

- Training cannot solve problems due to deficiencies other than skills and knowledge, such as poor job design or lack of appropriate tools.
- If training is not reinforced by providing on-the-job application opportunity and coaching, the newly acquired skills and knowledge will not be used, may be forgotten, and will not have the expected payoff to the organization or the employee.
- Training is a very expensive and inappropriate way to make up for ineffective employee selection systems.
- Training is not a quick fix; it takes time to analyze training requirements, develop or acquire training materials, and deliver the training.

4. What responsibility is expected of the individual employee?

- Individual employees are responsible for maintaining their own competence.
- Employees are expected to take advantage of learning opportunities, particularly when these provide necessary skills and knowledge for performance of their assigned jobs.
- Employees are customers of the training system and are responsible for providing help in defining training requirements, designing training programs, and providing feedback on training effectiveness.
- The company expects employees to make an investment by devoting some of their own time to education and training.

5. What responsibility does the company assume?

- The company assumes the responsibility for providing the means (the training system) so employees can maintain their own competence.

- The company assumes the responsibility for providing the necessary time off the job to receive available training.

6. What is generally expected of supervisors and managers?

   - Supervisors and managers are responsible and accountable for the performance of their organizational units.

   - Supervisors and managers are expected to know what skills and knowledge are required for high-level performance in their work groups and to develop training plans for each employee and each work group or organization to maintain the skills inventory at the required level.

   - Supervisors and managers are expected to implement the training plans and to provide job assignment and coaching that reinforce formal training.

   - Supervisors and managers must cooperate with the training departments in staffing the training department with part-time and full-time content experts for developing training materials and delivering instruction.

7. What is expected of the training departments?

   - The training departments are responsible for articulating the training system and its subsystems and processes in partnership with their organizational customers.

   - The training departments are responsible for core education and training roles such as needs analysis, curriculum design, and delivery of instruction.

   - The training departments are responsible for applying the most effective and efficient training methods and techniques.

   - The training departments are expected to provide leadership coordination and specialized expertise to the corporation in meeting its education and training needs.

8. Is training an investment or an expense?

   - The competence of our executive, managerial, salaried, and hourly workforce is one of the most important assets of the business.

   - Training and education as a means of developing and maintaining competence is inherently an investment and should be managed as systematically and carefully as we manage other investments.

   - Failure to invest in training will result in a loss of competitive advantage.

9. Do we eagerly embrace the value of continual learning and improvement or learn only when we can prove it is necessary?

   - The need for continual learning is a core value in our corporate culture.

   - Executives and managers demonstrate their commitment to the value of continual learning by regularly spending time developing their own competence and by providing time, encouragement, and resources to permit continual learning throughout the organization, and by holding themselves and their subordinates accountable for maintaining and continually improving the competence of the workforce.

We have selected four examples to illustrate different forms a philosophy statement can take. The first (Figure 8-1) is General Motors' statement which was signed by the chairman, sent out to all organizational units, and hangs on the walls in GM's various training departments. The second (Figure 8-2) is found in the policy manual for GPU Nuclear's Nuclear Operations Training. The third (Figure 8-3) was created by Alcoa Laboratories when it established a formal internal education department. The fourth (Figure 8-4) was developed by Illinois Bell in a postdivestiture strategic training plan.

MISSION

A mission statement sets forth in a few words the reason for existence of an organizational unit. It should include ends, means, and scope. You should be able to read

---

Philosophy of Training

The worldwide performance of General Motors is the result of the dedicated performance of everyone in the business. The purpose of training is to increase the effectiveness of individuals so they can contribute to the organization's competitive posture. Thus the goal of training is to benefit individuals and the business. This is accomplished by enhancing the knowledge, skills, and attitudes of employees which have a positive impact on job performance.

Opportunities for improved performance exist at all levels of the organization. Managers in each unit are responsible for providing training based on an annual assessment of the needs of individuals and the organization. The establishment of training priorities must be integrated with business planning. The corporation has the responsibility for allocating financial and human resources for training.

Training is a continuing process. At a minimum, training must be provided

- When a person enters the organization
- When a person assumes new responsibilities
- When a person's job performance requires improvement
- When new conditions require changes in products, technology, policy, practices, or procedures.

The effectiveness of training will be measured by its contribution to the improvement of individual and organizational performance.

Figure 8-1 General Motors' Philosophy of Training

GPU Nuclear is an Electric Utility that owns and operates nuclear generating stations, including the Three Mile Island facility.

POLICIES

- **GPU Nuclear Commitment**

  GPU Nuclear is committed to the safe, economical, and efficient operation of its generating stations and the protection of the public health and safety. This commitment is accomplished, in part, by developing the knowledge, skills,and attitudes associated with the job performance of its personnel through effective training.

- **Basis for Training**

  GPU Nuclear considers training to be an important means of effectively developing personnel and solving or avoiding performance problems. Therefore, GPU Nuclear will provide efficient and effective training which develops the trainee's skills and knowledge as necessary to perform the job responsibilities.

  The decision on whether to train should be made after a needs assessment (which may include a formal needs analysis) has been performed, a need for personnel development has been verified, and training is found to be a solution.

- **Commitment to Training**

  GPU Nuclear has made an extensive commitment to training. This commitment includes
  - Dedicated training organizations.
  - Dedicated training facilities.
  - Management allocation of personnel in support of training.

- **Focus on Job Performance**

  Training programs utilize a systematic approach which focuses on job performance. This requires
  - The systematic analysis of job requirements.
  - Emphasis on measurable training objectives ties to job requirements.
  - Training evaluation systems that measure results in the training environment as well as performance improvements back on the job or under simulated job conditions.

- **Addressing Nonroutine Operations**

  The safe operation of a generating station requires that nuclear station personnel possess performance capabilities beyond those required for routine operations. To address both routine and nonroutine, generating station concepts coupled with practice in applying the theory and concepts over a wide variety of events should be provided. Simulation, regular Refresher Training, and on-the-job practice are important factors in being prepared to respond to nonroutine events.

- **Focus on the Trainee**

  Effective training is learner oriented. The attainment of this goal is the joint responsibility of the trainee and trainers.

- **Standardization**

  Training will be standardized between locations and divisions whenever training efficiency and/or effectiveness can be gained.

- **Assuring Training Effectiveness**

  To assure the effectiveness of training, a system of ongoing training evaluation will be utilized. This system will draw on the experience of the Training and Education Department, the trainee's management, the trainee, and other cognizant parties.

- **Examinations**

  GPU Nuclear considers the integrity of the examination process to be an important matter. All reasonable and appropriate steps are to be taken to ensure the security and integrity of the examination process.

- **Training Advisory Council**

  A GPUN Training Advisory Council shall be established to supplement interactions between the site training organizations and the user divisions to ensure that projected training priorities and programs meet long-range Divisional/Corporate Training needs. The Council shall also provide advice, guidance, and recommendations to the Director of Training and Education.

- **INPO Accreditation**

  GPU Nuclear will actively pursue and maintain INPO Accreditation in those programs which INPO accredits.

Figure 8-2   GPU Nuclear Philosophy of Training

Alcoa Laboratories is the Research and Development Unit of Aluminum Company of America.

Values

- Quality
  - Maintain and improve quality of Education and Training's products and services
  - Demand good return on educational investment

- Satisfaction of customer needs
  - View customers as partners
  - Anticipate customers' needs
  - Assist customers in identifying needs rather than merely respond to requests

- Personnel development
  - Fully utilize varied skills of Education and Training staff
  - Develop additional skills for all personnel

- Flexibility
  - View change as a challenge rather than a road block

- Safety
  - Practice and support company safety policies

- Entrepreneurial spirit
  - Lead organization in applying state-of-the-art technologies
  - Generate additional revenue

Figure 8-3   Alcoa Laboratories' Philosophy of Training

a mission statement and quickly tell what this organizational unit is all about, what it is expected to do, and generally what is not included in its role.

The mission statement provides an important focus for planning. It defines broadly what the organizational unit will do and what it will not do. It also helps inform management and client organizations what they can expect and what not to expect from the organization. In a large organization, an important function for developing the mission statement is to reveal role conflicts or gaps between the various training units. You should be able to lay all the mission statements for the training units side by side on a table and identify important areas of overlap or gaps. These overlaps and gaps then should become issues to be addressed in your strategic training plan. The sample mission statement for a corporate technical education unit shown in Figure 8-5 illustrates the main points that need to be covered in the mission. In this mission statement, the end is to keep the company at the leading edge of technology. The means is by providing technical

Illinois Bell is a telecommunications company with about 20,000 employees.

Philosophy

- Our clients are the reason we exist, their needs are our first priority.

- Active partnerships between training and our client organization produce the most effective solutions
  - To develop employees to their fullest potential
  - To integrate training into broader solutions where required.

- We provide the skills and knowledge needed for present or future job performance.

- To be effective, training must be reinforced in the job environment.

- In the last analysis, every employee is responsible for his or her own competency and development, however, Corporate Education exists to assist each employee in that endeavor.

- Training should contribute to the overall profitability of the company.

Figure 8-4   Illinois Bell's Philosophy of Training

The mission of Corporate Technical Education and Training is to keep the company at the leading edge of technology by providing technical education and training to technical professionals and managers in the Headquarters, the Business Units, and the R&D Lab.

Figure 8-5   Sample Mission Statement

education and training. The scope is limited to training technical professionals and managers in the headquarters, the business units, and the R&D lab.

If you were the head of this organization and someone asked you for negotiation skills training, what would this mission tell you? Probably that it is not your job. There is undoubtedly another training department whose mission does include management and personal skills training. If there is not, you either need to revise your mission or develop a training organization that has these responsibilities.

Figure 8-6 provides some example mission statements from real training organizations. These may be useful when developing your own.

Let's look at a fictitious manufacturing company, UTX Corporation. UTX has a corporate education department, training departments in each of three business units, and

Organization	Mission Statement
Contel	The mission of Contel training is to support the business goals of the corporation by managing the total training process to bring about changes in people and processes that improve employee job performance and so contribute to the company's business objectives, including financial performance, quality, customer satisfaction, and employee motivation.
Alcoa Laboratories	It is the mission of the Education and Training Department to lead the company into creating a culture where life-long learning is expected and supported. We will support corporate business goals by providing high-quality, timely, and cost effective educational programs and consulting services.
Commonwealth Edison	The mission of the Personnel Development Department is to provide company-wide programs and services that support and encourage the development of skills, knowledge, and attitudes of our management team. We also provide programs and services that compliment those noted above to our employee group.

Figure 8-6   Example of Mission Statement

training departments in each plant. Mission statements should be developed for each of these groups, as shown in Figure 8-7.

The mission of education and training in UTX (Figure 8-8) is a global mission for the entire company. The mission statements for each of the education and training units (Figure 8-9 through 8-11) should show how they contribute to this global mission. As you can see, this mission is all encompassing. The scope of business unit training departments is more limited. The scope of plant training is even more narrowly defined.

In a large corporation, there may be literally dozens of training departments. In this case, you will not be able to glance through the mission statements to see whether there are significant overlaps or gaps. A useful method for comparing a large number of training units within a corporation is to map their missions onto a matrix. The resulting mission map or role/responsibility matrix will give you a clearer picture of what is covered and where there are gaps. The simplified example in Figure 8-12 will give you an idea of how this works.

A complete matrix would have more columns to the right, including engineering functional skills, manufacturing functional skills, quality concepts and tools, etc. It also may have more training departments listed on the left-hand side. Reading down each column, there is a potential overlap if the same role or responsibility occurs for more than one training department. These overlaps may be appropriate but at the least require careful coordination. In some cases, significant savings can be made by eliminating the overlaps.

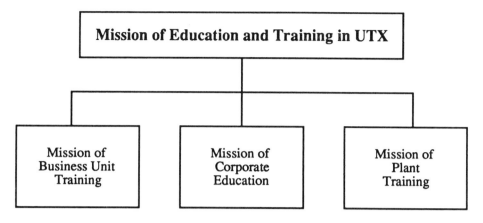

Figure 8-7 UTX Family of Mission Statements

<u>Ends</u>

Education and training at UTX develops needed skills and knowledge for attainment of business performance goals as set forth in the Corporate and Business Unit Business Plans.

<u>Means</u>

The means for achieving these ends include

- Company-sponsored schools
- Structured on-the-job learning
- Partnerships with educational institutions
- Use of other outside learning resources.

<u>Scope</u>

The scope of education and training in UTX includes all skills and knowledge required to meet expected business performance:

- Educational fundamentals
- Technical
- Supervisory, managerial, and executive
- Personal, interpersonal, and team skills
- Functional job skills.

Trainees include all employees, executive through hourly, including contract and part-time employees. Trainees also include employees of suppliers, distributors, and customers.

Figure 8-8 Mission of UTX Education and Training

Ends

Support the mission of UTX Education and Training.

Means

Provide leadership, coordination, specialized expertise for all UTX education and training in the areas of

- Strategic Training Plans
- Needs analysis and curriculum architectures
- Methods, procedures, and standards for courseware development, delivery
- Common training administrative systems
- Partnerships with educational institutions.

Scope

Develop and deliver those training programs that are needed across the business or that can be most economically or effectively provided by a centralized organization.

Figure 8-9   Mission of UTX Corporate Education

Ends

UTX Business Unit Training develops needed skills and knowledge for attainment of business performance goals as set forth in the Business Unit Business Plans.

Means

Provide leadership, coordination, specialized expertise, and resources to accomplish Business Unit training by

- Sending trainees to corporate schools
- Providing local delivery of corporate education programs
- Developing and delivering training programs unique to the Business Unit
- Analyzing Business Unit Training needs
- Developing and maintaining Business Unit Strategic training plans and curriculum architecture.

Scope

The scope of Business Unit Training includes employees of the Business Unit and its suppliers, distributors, and customers, including other business units who are suppliers or customers.

Figure 8-10   Mission of UTX Business Unit Training Departments

---

Ends

Plant training develops skills and knowledge needed to meet plant business performance goals.

Means

Provide leadership, coordination, specialized expertise, and resources to meet plant training needs through

- Sending trainees to corporate and Business Unit Schools
- In-plant delivery of corporate and Business Unit training
- Developing and delivering training programs unique to the plant
- Analyzing plant training needs
- Developing and maintaining plant training plans and curriculum architecture
- Supporting structured on-the-job training.

Scope

The scope of Plant Training includes employees of the plant and its suppliers and distributors and customers, including other UTX plants and organizations.

Figure 8-11   Mission of Training Department in UTX Plants

TRAINING DEPARTMENT ROLES

Roles and responsibilities lists define explicitly what a training unit is expected to do and, by omission, those things it is expected not to do.

Core Roles

The following are core training department roles. These are roles that most training departments are expected to play

- Performance and needs analysis

- Curriculum architecture design

- Training materials development or acquisition

- Training delivery

- Evaluation of training effectiveness

- Administrative management of trainees

Training Department	Type of Training								
	Generic Skills			Business Unit Business and Products			Marketing Function Skills		
	Training Population								
	Exec	Mgmt	Con-trib-utor	Exec	Mgmt	Con-trib-utor	Exec	Mgmt	Con-trib-utor
Corporate Education	1-7	1-7	1-4, 6,7	1-7	12-7	1-4, 6,7	1-7	-	-
Business Unit Training	-	1-3, 5-7	1-3, 5-7	1-7	1-7	1-7	-	1-7	1-7
Plant Training	-	5-7	5-7	-	-	5-7	-	-	-
Marketing Institute							-	1-7	1-7

Roles/Responsibilities

1. Strategic Planning
2. Needs Analysis
3. Curriculum Architecture
4. Development
5. Delivery
6. Administrative systems
7. Evaluation

Figure 8-12   Training Department Role and Responsibility Matrix

You do not have to do all of these to be a top drawer training unit. We know of several major corporate training units that have been established for the purposes of performance and needs analysis, curriculum architecture design, and developing courseware that is needed across a number of divisions or business units. The divisional and/or business unit training departments are left with the responsibility of delivering the actual training.

Secondary Roles

Training departments often take on additional roles, including the following:

- Provide information and advertising on course content, schedules, etc.
- Provide and operate a student or a trainee registration system.
- Provide materials for training to be conducted on the job or by other organizations within the corporation (or its subsidiaries or dealerships).
- Keep training records.
- Provide and manage training facilities and equipment.
- Develop strategic and current plans for carrying out the aforementioned roles.
- Represent the corporation in professional training circles.
- Provide performance consulting.
- Provide specialized consulting to other training departments in the areas of
  - Testing and measurement
  - CAI (computer aided instruction)
  - Instructional design
  - Artificial intelligence
  - Etc.
- Sell training materials to other organizations to help defray the cost of training.
- Manage the academic tuition reimbursement plan.
- Provide follow-up coaching to trainees after they have returned to the job.
- Develop job performance aids.
- Facilitate worksite task teams.
- Provide an information center and registration center for outside workshops and seminars.
- Operate assessment centers.

When selecting a set of roles for your training department, ask yourself these questions:

- What roles will contribute most to overall business success?
- What roles is our customer most comfortable having us play?
- What roles do we have the expertise to play now?
- What roles could we develop expertise for in three to five years?

- How can we avoid getting our resources spread too thin by concentrating on the roles we can master and perform with excellence?

In our experience, it is much better to focus on the core roles first and add others as you grow in experience, resources and reputation.

LINE AND STAFF MANAGEMENT ROLES

It is important to spell out not only the roles of the training department, but the roles of line and staff managers in the training system. The training department can do its job perfectly, yet the whole system will fail if line and staff management is not carrying its own weight.

Supervisors and managers have the primary responsibility for the job performance of their subordinates. They must determine the training needs of individual employees. If training is available, they are responsible for seeing that the employee receives the right training at the right time, and also for providing job experiences and feedback which reinforce the skills and knowledge acquired in training once the employee returns to the job. In many cases, training is actually conducted on the job either by the supervisor or the supervisor's delegated trainer. The effective performance of these roles by supervisors and managers requires that the training department provide them with course descriptions, training road maps, and other necessary aids.

Line Management Roles

The following are typical line management roles:

- Develop with each employee an individual training plan at least once a year.

- Facilitate employee registration in training events.

- Review progress on individual training plans quarterly.

- Develop a training plan for each organizational unit at least once a year.

- Establish clear objectives and accountability for on-the-job training (OJT).

- Maintain a library of OJT materials.

- Personally provide on-the-job training or make clear assignments of responsibility for OJT.

- Provide a mentor or personal coach for new employees to help them learn the ropes.

- Brief employees to establish expectations before they attend formal training, and debrief after training.

- Provide work assignments that give employees the opportunity to apply newly acquired skills and knowledge, monitor performance, and provide coaching if needed.

- Teach or lecture in training department courses.

- Serve on project committees or other training advisory groups.

- Maintain up-to-date information on available training.

- Provide expert resources to help with needs analysis, instructional development, and instruction.

- Give feedback on training effectiveness.

- Maintain a skills and knowledge inventory.

Corporate Functional Staff Roles

If you are in an organization that has functional staffs such as marketing and engineering, they can play some additional important support roles for the training function, including the following:

- Chair advisory groups.

- Select line participants for advisory groups.

- Help recruit content experts.

- Serve as the content authority for training content.

- Provide early warning on changes such as new technology and new policies that will have a training impact.

- Provide source material for training content.

- Take responsibility for addressing nontraining issues that emerge from needs analysis, such as methods and procedures problems.

In modern complex organizations that are constantly undergoing change, these roles can be crucial to the performance of the training function. We have found that in most cases it is necessary to approach each staff unit and have the unit members appoint an individual as the training liaison. This way it is clear who has the responsibility for these roles, and the training department will not have to beg for support each time some help is needed. We have seen many cases where these responsibilities have turned into important full time jobs.

SUMMARY

Mission, philosophy, and role statements lay the foundation for your entire strategic training plan. You should develop them and obtain consensus for them as early in the planning process as possible. Specifically, you should

☐ Develop a written list of philosophy statements for the overall training organization in response to the following questions:

1. Why is the organization interested in training?
2. What do we expect training to accomplish?
3. What are the limitations of training?
4. What responsibility is expected of the individual employees?
5. What responsibility does the company assume?
6. What is generally expected of supervisors and managers?
7. What is expected of the training departments?
8. Is training an investment or an expense?
9. Do we eagerly embrace the value of continual learning and improvement or learn only when we prove it is necessary?

☐ Develop a written mission statement covering

- Ends
- Means
- Scope

for each individual training unit.

☐ Develop a matrix for all the missions that identifies

- Types of training
- Types of skills
- Training populations
- Roles and responsibilities

for each training department.

☐ Develop a written list of roles for

- Each training unit
  - Core roles
  - Secondary roles
- Line management
- Corporate functional staffs.

☐ Print and post your mission and philosophy statements to remind yourselves and your customers of your purpose and values as you carry out your training plan.

9

STRATEGIC VISION AND GOALS

After developing and reviewing your analysis of the business goals and training implications, your assessment of the strengths and weaknesses of the existing training system, and the training philosophy and mission that you have developed, you can now begin to invent the future.

Let's say you have chosen a three- to five-year planning horizon—what do you expect things to be like three to five years from now? How do you propose to get there? These are the questions that should be answered in preparing your vision and strategic training goals.

Alvin Toffler said, "You've got to think about the 'big things' while you're doing the small things, so that all the small things go in the right direction." Developing your strategic vision and goals is thinking about the big things. The vision is a story that you make up to describe the future (the "big things"), and the goals are a short list of things that must be done if today's vision is to become tomorrow's reality (the "small things"). Both are important if you want to get there.

THE VALUE OF VISION

Making up the vision can be fun and exciting. If the vision is shared by the right people, it will become a self-fulfilling prophecy. A shared vision becomes the rallying point for leadership to mobilize energy and resources.

Within the time horizon you have chosen, what is the best situation you can realistically conceive? It has to be achievable, perhaps requiring great effort, changes in attitude, more resources, but really achievable. Recognize that making major changes takes time, but given a shared vision and long-term commitment, your vision can become a reality.

A few stories will help you see how this can work.

Bell System Center for Technical Education

In 1965 Chuck Sener, who was an engineering manager for Illinois Bell at the time, conceived the idea to create a technical education center to serve the engineering departments of the twenty-two Bell System Operating Companies. His concept was to develop and deliver those courses which were either so specialized or required such expensive equipment that the individual operating telephone companies could not afford to provide for their own training. In addition, the center would create course materials that were needed in common by the telephone companies to avoid duplication of expensive course development effort. These materials would be provided for local delivery in the telephone company engineering training groups. Another part of Chuck's vision was that this center should be self-funding and not become a part of the AT&T headquarters overhead budget. The activities of the center and the resources would be controlled by a board of advisors made up of engineering executives from the telephone companies and from the AT&T general departments. The telephone companies would voluntarily contribute to a course development fund, and delivery would be supported through tuition.

Chuck traveled around and gained support from several other telephone companies. He then approached top management at AT&T for permission to develop an implementation plan. Chuck was placed on special assignment to develop the plan. The center, known then as the Bell System Center for Technical Education (BSCTE), opened for business in 1968. The original building was constructed using the architecture of a motel because there was disbelief among top management that the telephone companies would voluntarily financially support such an institution, so if it did not work, the building could be converted into a motel.

Ten years later, by 1978, Chuck's entire vision had been accomplished and expanded on. The BSCTE had a live-in capacity for approximately 425 students, with plans on the drawing board to add another 400-student unit. Every technical executive and manager in the Bell System thought of the institution as a strategic resource for implementing new technology throughout the business. The governing structure had grown from the original board of advisors made up of operating company engineering vice presidents and AT&T assistant vice presidents to include three subordinate boards representing major subfunctions and fifteen curriculum planning councils, each governing its own specialty curriculum. At divestiture in 1984, the center was physically split, with half going to AT&T and half to Bellcore.

Motorola Training and Education Center

In 1980, Motorola had no corporate education function. It had recently abandoned its management institute at Carefree, Arizona. Top management at that time was creating a new vision for the future of the company which included a high quality education system as a major component. Management hired a consulting firm to develop a five-year plan for Motorola education out of which emerged the vision for the Motorola Training and Education Center (MTEC). Bill Wiggenhorn was hired from Xerox and charged by top management with executing the five-year plan.

The original vision was that MTEC would be limited in its roles to providing educational leadership for the corporation and developing curricula in engineering, marketing, manufacturing, and generic management skills. It would develop the training materials but not actually deliver training. The delivery of training was to be performed by the business sectors. Within five years, this vision had been successfully achieved. In fact, the members of MTEC were so successful that they outstripped the ability of the business sectors to deliver the training and subsequently added training delivery to their mission. Bill Wiggenhorn continues today as Vice President of Education for Motorola and President of Motorola University. He has written about the vision and evolution of education and training at Motorola in "Motorola U: When Training Becomes an Education", *Harvard Business Review* (July-August, 1990).

Exxon USA Exploration

In 1982, the Exploration Department of Exxon USA recognized that it had a serious internal education issue. Many of the experienced geologists and geophysicists were leaving either through retirement or for other reasons, and the company was faced with hiring a large number of new professionals. There was no formal internal training program in place that could help these new geoscientists to fully master the exploration art in the quickest possible time frame. Given the demographics, this was an unacceptable situation. A task force of eight of the company's most senior geologists and geophysicists was appointed to create a training system that could bring a professional up to mastery performance in as short a period as possible.

This task force created a performance model to describe all the tasks and the related skills and knowledge associated with the exploration function. A modular curriculum was then designed around the concept that most of the training would be done on the job by senior professionals acting as mentors using modular training materials created by a centralized training group. Only a small amount of training would actually be delivered centrally. The system was designed so a new professional could flexibly learn whatever was required for the immediate job tasks that were assigned under the direction of his or her mentor. A vision for this system was sold by the task force to the company's exploration management group. Jack Barnes, the task force chairman, was appointed to head the small centralized development staff charged with creating the learning modules and the administrative systems to support the mentors, trainees and supervisors in the field.

In every successful case we know, there was a champion, usually the training director, who was able to communicate and sell the vision to upper management and to the user community, often through several rounds of meetings with people and through "playing around with ideas" until the vision gelled.

DEVELOPING YOUR VISION

What should be included in your vision? Here's a partial list of ingredients.

- A brief overview of today's training system
- Training support for important business goals
- Training as an instrument of change
- The kinds and quantities of training to be provided
- Important training systems to be employed
- Strengthening parts of the training system
- Organization and administration of training
- Governance of training
- Present and future comparison charts
- The costs and benefits of training.

Figure 9-1 provides an excerpt from a vision statement for training in a large plant that is just completing a $500 million program to modernize its production equipment. It is couched in terms of a report the company would like to be able to deliver in five years.

Your vision may be several pages of story that helps the reader visualize what could be if you put your proposed system in place.

STRATEGIC GOALS

The purpose of strategic goals is to focus on a few things that must be done if today's vision is to become tomorrow's reality. Try to keep the goals list to ten or fifteen at most. Few of us can keep even that many clearly in mind without referring to notes. A good way to develop these goals is to review your vision and determine the things that must be done to actualize the vision and group integral statements. These goals become the bridge (see Figure 9-2) between today's reality and your vision of the future.

We like to start goals with action verbs, while others prefer to state an end condition as completed. Take your pick. You should follow the pattern set by your organization's overall business goals. Here are some examples of possible strategic goals:

Training:

One of the major factors in the present success story has been a rather massive training effort. The plant adopted a policy five years ago that all employees should be trained to perform to their maximum capacity at their assigned tasks. Over the last five years, $50 million has been invested in training. The payoff in asset utilization alone has been estimated at $300 million. The hourly operations and maintenance workforce backed by an expert team of technical specialists has achieved a high level of proficiency in operating and maintaining the high-tech plant in a statistically controlled environment.

The Engineering and Technology Group has developed in-depth expertise in all our critical technologies and processes. We realized that our modernized high-tech plant could not reach its performance potential unless our people also reached their performance potential. Therefore, we adopted a policy that we would put a high priority on learning, invest significant resources to achieve the necessary competence, and devote serious management attention to achieving our learning goals.

Today there are active training committees in Operations, Maintenance, Engineering and Technology, Customer Technology, and Comptrollers. These committees identify learning requirements, devise strategies for meeting these requirements, and establish priorities for training.

An expanded Training Department in Human Resources develops and delivers performance-based training supported by content experts from the other departments. Five years ago, technical or job-specific skills training were a small percentage of the total training. Today they represent 85 percent of all training. All major new systems require a comprehensive training plan to be executed, which has resulted in dramatic improvement in learning curves after commissioning.

Human Resources keeps a detailed list of required skills, and employees are certified once they have demonstrated a skill. This database allows us at any time to assess the skills inventory of the workforce.

Figure 9-1   A Training Report from the Future

- Develop performance-based curricula for each of the company's eleven major functions.

- Establish a governance structure for training which includes an executive board of education and curriculum councils at director level for each of the eleven functional curricula.

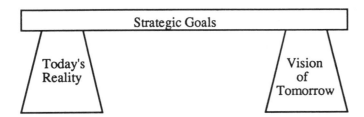

Figure 9-2 Strategic Goals Bridge

- Create an executive development program to keep executives at the cutting edge and to prepare people for future leadership roles.

- Revise the supervisory and management skills curriculum to support the new participative, quality-driven organizational culture.

- Implement a new computer-based training system to train the sales and repair force on all new products and product changes.

- Establish a corporate education department, headed by a vice president, with responsibility for developing any training program or material needed by three or more business units, delivering specialized high-cost, low-volume training, and coordinating all training across the corporation.

- Create a customer training system to train engineers, operators, maintenance technicians and managers in our customer companies to properly design, use and maintain our products and systems

- Develop a curriculum to support the company's drive to implement a Total Quality Management system.

- Create a manufacturing technology institute to support the company's drive to implement modern manufacturing technologies.

- Establish a system to hold managers at all levels accountable for keeping their workforce trained to be capable of peak performance and to measure both the cost of conformance and the cost of nonconformance to this standard.

- Develop an online training information and administration system to enable all employees to access their own training records, develop individual training plans, register for training events, order materials, and provide feedback on training received.

- Establish a technology seminar series to keep middle managers abreast of rapidly changing product, process and information technologies.

Many of these goals will have evolved from the analysis work you did. You can see from this list that accomplishing ten or twelve major goals like this will be a challenge for any organization. You may want to prioritize the goals and put them on a time line like the one shown in Figure 9-3.

While the goal statement itself should be one sentence, each goal is worthy of a page or more of explanation. You should develop a full explanation for each goal on your strategic goals list. Figures 9-4a, 9-4b, and 9-4c provide sample explanations for three of the example goals listed earlier in this section of Strategic Goals.

You can check your goals list by rereading your vision to see what parts of the vision will be actualized if the goals are met, and what will be lacking. You may need to add one or two goals to cover important areas missed. Or you may need to revise your vision if the number and size of required goals proves to be unmanageable.

A good example of a vision statement can be found in the Executive Summary from IRS *Training 2000*. It identifies the major challenges facing the IRS, training implications of these challenges, and a vision and goals for what must be done. The complete report is called *Training 2000*, and it is available from the Department of the Treasury, Internal Revenue Service, Publication 1480 (11-98).

SUMMARY

Taking a cue from the idea that "If you don't know where you are going, you might end up someplace else," we suggest that you create a vision and strategic goals for the future to define where it is that you want to go and what you will need to get there. To do this, you should take the following steps:

☐ Review the analysis work you did in chapters 4 through 7:

- Training implications of business challenges and goals

- Internally identified strengths and weaknesses

- Strengths and weaknesses compared to competitors

- Strength and weaknesses compared to best-in-class

- Estimated cost of training.

☐ Review the groundwork you laid in chapter 8:

- Mission of training organization(s)

- Philosophy

- Roles
    - Training
    - Line.

☐ Develop a written vision of training in your organization in five years.

☐ Develop a list of ten to twelve major strategic goals for achieving that vision.

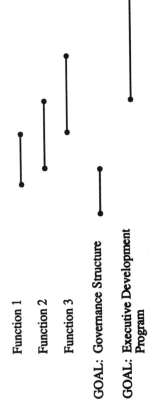

Year 1

Year 2

Year 3

J F M A M J J A S O N D | J F M A M J J A S O N D | J F M A M J J A S O N D

GOAL: Performance Curriculum

Function 1

Function 2

Function 3

GOAL: Governance Structure

GOAL: Executive Development Program

Figure 9-3 Strategic Goals Bridge

Goal: Develop performance-based curricula for each of the company's eleven major functions.

Functional training today is hit or miss except for the Sales function. We lack organized training paths for employees entering new jobs.

Our goal is to define curricula in each of the following functions in priority order:

- Engineering
- Manufacturing
- Marketing
- Customer Service
- Product Line Management
- Distribution
- Procurement
- Information Systems
- Accounting/Financial
- Human Resources.

These curricula will be designed based on analysis of responsibilities, tasks, and the required skills and knowledge to perform them from hourly through executive ranks. The curricula will include the needs of all Business Units and be flexible to accommodate specialized modules for individual Business Units.

Middle management Curriculum Councils will be formed to oversee the design, development, and implementation of these curricula. These councils will be chaired by functional directors on the corporate staff, with high-level functional representation from key business units.

The Corporate Education Department will provide a standard process and format for these curricula and will facilitate their design, development, and implementation.

Within five years we expect to have an organized learning path available to every employee who takes on a new job whether newly hired, transferred inside the company, or promoted to a higher-level position.

Figure 9-4a Example Goal

☐ Plot those goals on a time line.
☐ Write a full explanation for each goal.

Having done all this, you should now have

- A detailed project plan for your strategic planning process

---

Goal: Develop a curriculum to support the company's drive to implement Total Quality Management.

The company officers have recently adopted a strategic goal to implement TQM across the company and to be in position to win the National Baldrige Quality Award in five years. An essential prerequisite to achieving this goal is to develop and implement a quality curriculum for all employees, hourly through executive. The quality curriculum will include

- TQM concepts and vocabulary
- Our company's vision, values, and strategic plans for implementing TQM
- The chain of quality from supplier through our internal processes to our final customers
- The role of each department in the chain of quality
- Corrective action team skills
- Beginning, intermediate, and advanced skills on an array of quality tools and skills.

Training will be provided in a phased schedule that is driven by the company strategic TQM plan.

The Corporate Quality Council will oversee the design, development, and implementation of this curriculum.

The functional Curriculum Advisory Councils will integrate the quality curriculum into their functional curricula and recommended training paths.

The Corporate Education Department will facilitate the curriculum design and develop the training materials. They will deliver all executive and middle-management training and will train facilitators in the Business Units to deliver the remainder of the training. They will evaluate the effectiveness of the quality training programs.

Business Unit General Managers will account to the Corporate Quality Council for their implementation of quality training as part of their accountability for TQM implementation.

Figure 9-4b Example Goal

- An assessment of your strengths and weaknesses
  - Based on internal standards
  - Compared to your competitors
  - Compared to best-in-class
- An estimate of training costs for your total training system

Goal: Create a customer training system to train engineers, operators, maintenance technicians, and managers in our customer companies to properly design, use, and maintain our products and systems.

Customer training today is hit or miss and depends on the individual decisions of product managers, who are often driven by short-term expedience. An independent survey of our customers reveals that we are behind our competition and losing ground fast. In spite of our superior technology, our most sophisticated customers are already switching to competitors, who provide comprehensive performance-based training (recognizing that this training significantly reduces their overall cost of ownership).

Our goal is that, beginning immediately, all new product plans will incorporate a comprehensive customer training curriculum, which will be developed as a part of our investment in the product development. This training may be provided as a bundled part of the product price or sold separately at the discretion of Product Management. Existing products will be reviewed on a case-by-case basis to determine which products would provide sufficient return on our investment in a customer curriculum. Some entry product lines are too short and some are adequately supported today by customer-developed and provided training.

Corporate Education will support this goal by facilitating curriculum design in partnership with Product Management, developing the training materials, and training trainers in the product organizations. For large systems, Corporate Education will provide centralized laboratories for hands-on installation, operation, and maintenance training.

Figure 9-4c Example Goal

- A clear sense of your purpose as a training organization, including ends, scope, and means
- A list of your training philosophies and values
- A list of training roles for your organization and line organizations
- A vision for the future

- A list of strategic goals to get there.

That is, you now know who you are, where you have been, where you want to go, and how you think you are going to get there.

At this point you should put all this information into a written document and make a presentation for executive review. Phase 1 has been completed and you need full approval and buy-in for continuing with phase 2. Chapters 10 through 18 provide detailed information for carrying out phase 2.

10

DEVELOPING THE QUANTITATIVE PLAN

Chapters 10 through 18 discuss a systematic process for calculating the forecasted need and developing the quantitative three- or five-year plan that is the output of phase 2 of the strategic training plan process. The methods discussed have been developed over the last seventeen years and used successfully in a wide variety of situations with many different clients. This chapter is an overview of the process for developing the quantitative plan. Chapters 11 through 18 provide details, worksheets, and examples.

Developing a quantitative plan is the hard part. Doing the work leading up to the strategic vision and goals is relatively easy. But once you have the vision and goals, several quantitative questions must be answered:

- How much training do we need?
- How much would it cost?
- How much can we afford to do?
- How fast could we gear up if we had a blank check?

Your quantitative plan should be a series of charts, as shown in Figure 10-1. These charts tell you three important things:

1. The total amount of forecasted training needed
2. The amount of training you have been providing
3. The amount of training you plan to provide to begin to reach the forecasted need.

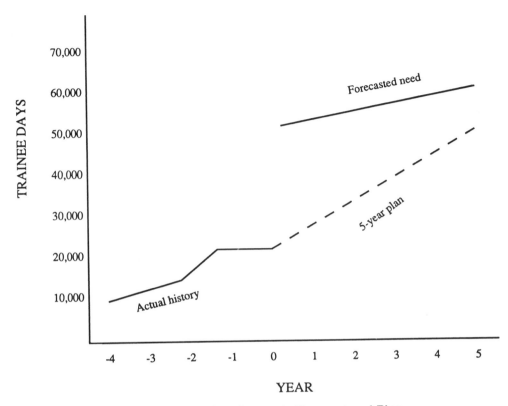

Figure 10-1 Training Requirements Forecast and Plan

Trainee days as the measure of delivery is the number of trainees times the number of days of training they received. Ten trainees in a five-day class produces fifty trainee days of delivery volume. For most organizations, estimating training in terms of trainee days makes sense, but some organizations may prefer to estimate need in trainee hours or trainee weeks.

The forecasted need is the amount of training you would have to do to meet the needs of the business as set forth in your vision and goals. The actual history is the amount you have been doing, and the five year plan is what you intend to do.

You can produce a whole series of these charts illustrating the plan for each important area of training (e.g., marketing training or management skills training).

You may be asking, why not plan to meet the total forecasted need? The answer is that you are only meeting a fraction of the real need today; many changes will be needed that cannot occur overnight. You may have to design and develop massive amounts of new training material, acquire and train a larger training staff, build facilities, and develop new administrative systems. Your user community will have to become educated to plan for and use the training they need as it becomes available. Just because you forecasted the need and make it available to them does not automatically mean they will use it. You want to project toward meeting the need at a reasonable rate that is actually feasible.

Of course there will also be financial limitations. One of the purposes of quantitative planning is to see how much it will cost to meet various percentages of the forecasted need, estimate the penalties associated with the remaining gap between supply and need, and let top management decide what level of resources to provide. We have found that management is generally very receptive to this approach to decision making.

When we first started doing strategic training plans, we did not have the "forecasted need" line on the graph. This made a rapid growth pattern much harder to sell even if we could show specific objectives that were to be accomplished. Putting the need line on the graph provides a bounded space for decision making that is easy to comprehend and deal with. Without it, the sky is the limit. The need line also helps people to visualize the size of the all important gap between what training is needed and how much is currently being delivered.

You need to realize that even if top management were to give you a blank check and expect you to meet the forecasted need, you may not be able to gear up that fast, particularly if you are in a large organization. One of our clients had a training organization of 200 people supporting a corporation of 20,000 employees. A conservative estimate of the need suggested that the training organization would have to double to about 400 to meet the need. There was no way the client could accomplish that much growth in the three years of the plan. The officers decided to authorize a 30 percent growth over three years, or sixty more people. This was a manageable amount of growth. The decision to authorize this growth came in a period when the rest of the company was downsizing 5 percent per year.

PROCESS OVERVIEW

Figure 10-2 presents a simplified schematic of the overall process for developing the quantitative plan. We briefly explain each block of the flow chart in this chapter, and then in chapters 11 through 18 we provide expanded flow charts, guidelines on how to do the data collection and calculations, and advice based on our experience in packaging and presenting such a plan to top management.

Carrying out this process is not a trivially simple exercise. In the preceding example of the 200-person training organization, it involved a planning team of two people and about two months of full-time effort working with a database and spreadsheet program, with about five days of coaching from us. The report documenting the work was about 150 pages long, and the presentation to management consisted of fifty slides.

We can give some general advice based on our experience with the process. As we have previously stated, do not attempt this without a spreadsheet and database program. There is a great deal of computation involved, and you will want to change assumptions, ask what-if questions, and generate several planning scenarios. You can do the calculation by hand, but it gets very tedious, it is easy to make mistakes, and doing so tends to inhibit the development of alternative scenarios.

If yours is a large organization, you will need to dedicate one or more people to

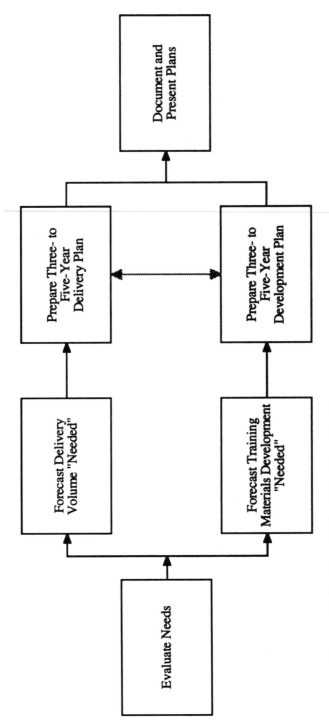

Figure 10-2 Quantitative Plan Flow Chart

this process for a solid block of time. Failure to have someone dedicated to this task usually means failure to accomplish it. In subsequent years, as you update your plan, it will take only a fraction of the time since your spreadsheet model and databases will be built and you will simply extend them a year and run them with new data and new assumptions.

Evaluate Needs

The first step in the quantitative planning process is to estimate the training needs in some detail for all segments of your target audience including employees, customers, and suppliers, if appropriate. Chapter 11 explains the needs analysis process, and chapter 12 explains how to develop the curriculum architecture in detail.

Inputs to this step are the training implications of business plans, training vision, and strategic objectives developed in the first phase of your planning process. Other important inputs are data from any formal needs analysis, existing course descriptions, and existing curriculum architecture designs.

The questions to be answered here are how much and what kinds of training are required for each individual in each segment of your target audience. The answers must include both training required for the new person entering that segment to become fully competent and estimated annual training for experienced people to keep up to date with changes, enhance their skills, and provide career development.

For example, a new account executive selling complex computer systems might require 130 days of initial training spread over the first two years of employment and then a minimum of ten days per year to keep up with new product releases and changes in the industry. Figure 10-3 shows how these numbers were derived.

If only part of the needed entry program exists today, and there has been no formal needs analysis or curriculum architecture designed for the account executive position, you will have to estimate the length of training based on what you have found other leading companies to be doing, what you believe is required to learn the job, and conversations with people who are familiar with the job. If the user community helps you with the estimates, your data will be more believable. If there are formal needs analysis data, or better still a curriculum architecture, the estimate is much easier. If you are not familiar with curriculum architecture as a concept, chapter 12 provides an overview.

Figure 10-4 presents another example for customer training.

The complete needs statement will include tables like the ones in Figures 10-3 and 10-4 for every segment of your target audience. For a large, complex organization, this could run to 100 or more tables by the time you include employees, customers, and suppliers.

Forecast Delivery Volume Needed

The concept of forecasting the needed delivery volume is relatively simple. Basically, you multiply the needs tables generated in the previous section by the number of trainees forecast for each year of the plan, usually three to five years.

Training Requirements	Days
<u>Entry Training</u> • Orientation to company, industry, job • Data processing systems architecture • Telecommunications networking • Product-specific knowledge (hands-on job training) • Basic selling skills • Managing the territory • Analyzing customer needs • Developing the systems plan • Developing and presenting the proposal • Supporting implementation and account maintenance • Competitive products	 10 15 5 50 5 5 10 10 5 5 10
TOTAL	130
<u>Annual Training</u> • New product releases • Industry trends • Advanced skills and career development	 5 5
TOTAL	10

Figure 10-3 Account Executive Training Requirements

Using the account executive example, let's assume there are currently 250 account executives and there are 10 percent new account executives every year to replace losses due to promotion, retirement, and resignation. No growth is planned over the five-year planning period. The calculation to forecast the annual delivery volumes needed looks like this:

Account executives		Training required		Annual delivery volumes needed
225 experienced	×	10 days/year	=	<u>2,250</u> Trainee days for experienced
25 new	×	130 days	=	<u>3,250</u> Trainee days for new
				<u>5,500</u> Total trainee days needed

System 3867 Customers	Length of Training (days)
• Management overview • Basic system operation • Software maintenance • Hardware maintenance • Advanced system troubleshooting	2 5 10 10 15
• Annual operations updates • Annual hardware maintenance updates • Annual software maintenance updates	1 2 2

Figure 10-4   Customer Training Requirements

If you have historical data on account executive training, you can now plot two parts of the planning graph, as shown in Figure 10-5. The graph shows a gap of 4,000 trainee days between the 1,500 days per year provided in the last year and the 5,500 days needed for the no-growth assumption. Another way of putting this is that we are providing only 27 percent of the calculated need.

The delivery volume need forecast is complete when you have performed this exercise for all segments of the target audience and summed up subtotals and totals.

One difficult part may be getting the forecast of the numbers of potential trainees for each segment of the target audience. Unfortunately, most organizations do not have an accurate personnel forecast broken down in sufficient detail. Most organizations do have a personnel database that will at least give you a head count of today's workforce. The most difficult number to project is the number of new people entering a given segment. If you are lucky, the personnel database will give you historical data on the number of new entries, and you can project on that.

Doing the need forecast this way is always an eye opener, sometimes a real shocker. We recommend using conservative assumptions throughout so when you present the results everyone will agree that the real need is probably much higher. Even with conservative assumptions, you will likely be surprised by the total need.

One final point: If you suspect the need is much higher than the present level of delivery, you do not need great accuracy in your need estimate since your three- to five-year plan probably will not bring you close to the need line anyway.

Prepare a Three- to Five-Year Delivery Plan

This is the point at which you plan what will be delivered and how and figure out how much it will cost. As you saw in Figure 10-2, there is a strong interaction with the

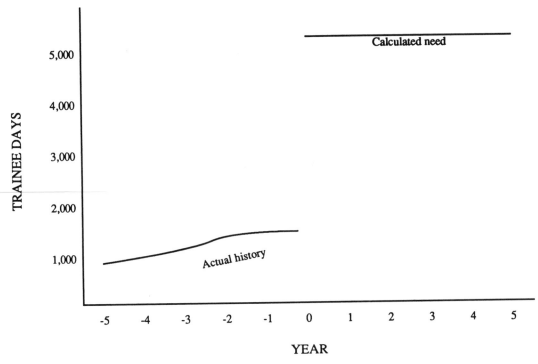

Figure 10-5 Account Executive Training Need Graph

development and acquisition plan, since you cannot deliver training that has not been developed or acquired. Therefore, you need to keep in mind as you go through phase 2 that this is an interactive process rather than a linear one. Over time, you will gain experience and become aware of how all the pieces of the process affect each other.

The major steps in developing your delivery plans are as follows:

1. Select target delivery volumes for each year in the planning period.
2. Plan the mix of delivery strategies
3. Estimate resource requirements; people, facilities, equipment, and money.

You may do this three-step process a number of times to generate different planning scenarios involving different target delivery volumes and different mixtures of delivery strategies and requiring different levels of resources.

By delivery strategies we mean any differences in methods of delivering training that require different types or levels of resources per unit of training delivered. Examples include

- Conventional classroom instruction, centralized
- Conventional classroom instruction, traveling instructors
- Laboratory or simulator training
- Structured on-the-job training
- Computer-based training at worksite
- Video teleconferencing

We discuss delivery strategies in more detail in chapter 13.

The planning charts that result may look like Figure 10-6. Figure 10-7 illustrates the assumed delivery strategies mix that was used to project the plan for scenario 2 in Figure 10-6. This scenario uses a starting point of 100 percent classroom delivery in the present year with 75 percent centralized and 25 percent delivered by traveling instructors. The scenario accomplishes double the delivery volume with a minimum increase in the number of instructors by shifting delivery strategies, since computer-based training at the job site and structured conventional OJT require no instructors. Adding computer-based

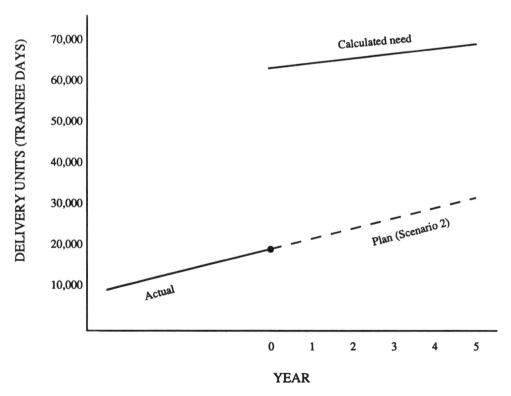

Figure 10-6   Delivery Plan Scenario

Delivery Method	Percent Distribution by Year					
	Present	1	2	3	4	5
Classroom, centralized	75	70	65	50	40	30
Classroom, traveling instructors	25	25	25	25	25	25
Lab/simulator	0	0	5	10	12	15
Computer-based at job site	0	0	0	5	10	15
Structured conventional OJT	0	5	5	10	13	15

Figure 10-7   Scenario 2 Delivery Strategies Mix (%)

training and structured OJT will run the development costs up because these forms of instruction cost more to develop, but reduced delivery cost and trainee travel time as well as improved effectiveness may make this a good trade-off.

Forecast Training Materials Development Needed

An important part of the quantitative plan is to figure out how much training must be developed to meet the estimated training need. There are four basic areas to estimate:

- New core curriculum
- Replacement of existing materials or courses
- Change-driven training
- Maintenance rates.

Core Curriculum   The core curriculum refers to all needed courses required for a new person in every segment of the target audience to become fully competent. You could define this curriculum by doing comprehensive needs analyses and curriculum architecture designs for each segment. If you worked at developing this curriculum for a number of years, eventually most of the needed materials, courses, etc. would be in place. The goal is to estimate how much training there is in the core curriculum, how much already exists, how much remains to be developed, and how much needs replacement.

In our previous example, the core curriculum for new account executives includes twenty-six weeks of training. The results of our analysis might look like Figure 10-8.

Total curriculum	26 weeks
Available today	-10 weeks
Existing, to be replaced	<u>- 3 weeks</u>
To be developed	13 weeks

Figure 10-8   Needed Core Curriculum Development for Account Executives

Change-Driven Curriculum   Change-driven training is the training material you will have to develop each year to keep up with change. This is training for new technology, new products, new systems, new methods, new laws, etc. In today's rapidly changing world, this represents an enormous instructional development load that never goes away. We have not found any organization that is able to forecast these changes, accurately and in detail more than one year ahead. The best approach we have found is to take the present year and maybe the next year, identify the changes and estimate the amount of training to be developed to support them. Then estimate the *rate* of change in the three- to five-year planning period compared to these base years and use that as a factor for projecting amount to be developed.

Let's assume that our analysis of account executive training showed an average of four weeks per year of new account executive training material needed this year to keep up with changes in the product line and in the industry. Let's say we also found out that product development is being accelerated as a matter of business strategy so the rate of change will increase. The forecast might look like the one in Figure 10-9. At this point, we are in a position to plot our need forecast. We take the backlog of core curriculum development and spread it over the five years (or spread it in some other way) and add the change-driven training.

For the account executive example, the thirteen weeks of needed new core curriculum, if spread evenly over five years, is 2.6 weeks per year. The need forecast looks like Figure 10-10. You can plot this on a graph showing the historical development output for comparison, as shown in Figure 10-11. This graph shows visually that the development output has historically been only half what will be required if all the needs are to be met. Preparing this chart, as with the similar chart for delivery, is usually an eye opener.

Prepare a Three- to Five-Year Development Plan

At this point, you can plan how much development you will actually do and estimate how much it will cost. The basic steps are as follows:

1. Develop a unit cost table.
2. Select target development amounts for each year of the plan.

Year	Amount of Change-Driven Development
1	4 weeks
2	5 weeks
3	6 weeks
4	6 weeks
5	6 weeks

Figure 10-9   Example Change-Driven Development Forecast

Year	New Core Curriculum	Change-Driven	Total to be Developed
1	2.6	4	6.6
2	2.6	5	7.6
3	2.6	6	8.6
4	2.6	6	8.6
5	2.6	6	8.6

Figure 10-10   Core and Change-Driven Forecast

3. Estimate or plan the mix of delivery strategies.
4. Plan the mix of development strategies.
5. Calculate the resource cost.

You will repeat steps 2 through 4 several times to generate different planning scenarios.

A unit cost table states your estimates of the resources required to develop one unit of instruction for each of the delivery strategies you intend to use as well as the development strategies. Figure 10-12 shows a unit cost table for four delivery strategies (group-paced, self-paced with conventional media, computer-based, and video network) and three development strategies (in-house development, contract development, and procurement of off-the-shelf materials). In this example it takes thirty days of developer time to develop one day of group-paced (conventional classroom) instruction.

This cost table is usually a shocker to management. They want to know why everything costs so much. We usually explain it as analogous to product development or systems development. Good instruction takes time to develop. You have to go through specification, analysis, design, development, testing, revision, and implementation

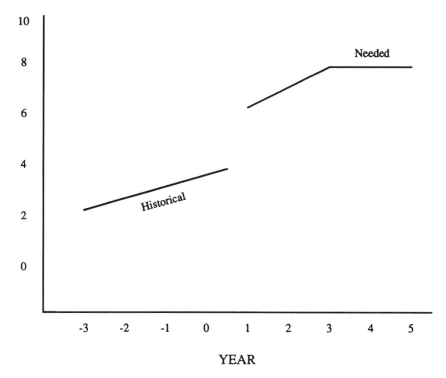

Figure 10-11   Development Needs Forecast

phases just as you do with any new development. This analogy usually makes the point and gives management a new appreciation for the process of instructional development.

The numbers you select for this chart directly establish the quality level of the training you expect to produce. The best data is your own experience data (i.e., what it has previously cost to do these kinds of developments).

The mix of delivery strategies you should use is the one for material you are going to develop in contrast to the mix for needed delivery volumes. The two are not the same. For example, if you are delivering 95 percent classroom, group-paced instruction now, your development program may require 100 percent computer-based development to achieve the 50 percent computer-based training in your delivery mix in five years.

The development strategy mix depends on your staffing situation. If you want to make a fast increase in development output capacity, contract some of the development out while you build up your staff. If you have a peak development period for a few years to work off the backlog, contract out the peak load so you do not have to build up and then reduce your development staff.

The percentage of off-the-shelf procured material depends on the type of courseware to be developed. There is good off-the-shelf material available in generic management skills, selling skills, computer languages, etc. You should also work with your procurement organization to specify training to be supplied by your vendor for major

Cost per day of material developed/acquired

Type of Course	In-house Development	Contract Development			Procured Off the Shelf		
	Developer Days	Project Manager Days	Contract Developer Days	Out-of-Pocket Dollars	Project Manager Days	Out-of-Pocket Dollars
Group-Paced	30	10	20	14,000	15	6,000
Self-Paced Conventional Media	60	15	45	36,000	30	10,000
Computer-Based	200	20	180	153,000	60	15,000
Video Network	100	15	85	72,250	50	10,000

Figure 10-12 Course Development Unit Cost Estimating Table

systems, software and equipment. There are two problems with off-the-shelf material. It usually does not exactly fit your need and will require some customization, and it is not as big a bargain as it looks because you still have to specify what is needed, do the in-depth analysis, shop the market, try out candidate products, customize if needed, and then implement. One big advantage of some of the commercially available products is that they have been thoroughly tested over time and represent very high quality instruction.

Maintenance Planning   Another issue you have to face in development planning is maintenance of the instructional material in your curriculum. Changes are occurring all the time that make your course material obsolete. We have found that courses are not maintained well unless the maintenance workload is forecasted, planned, and budgeted for. For mature curricula, a high percentage of the course development resources should go into maintenance.

The best way we have found to estimate maintenance is as a percent of the replacement cost of the material. For a curriculum with average content volatility, we usually expect to see 10 to 15 percent of the total replacement cost budgeted for maintenance *each year*. Our best advice is to track your own maintenance requirements over a period of years and trend them to use for estimating. Your ratio could vary from 8 to 30 percent for various parts of your curriculum depending on the content volatility.

Figure 10-13 shows an example profile of development resources over time for the various components of the development resource budget. The two segments of this chart that we have not explained yet are replacements and opportunity conversions.

Replacements   As you examine your curriculum you will discover that some programs just are not worth maintaining and should be replaced with new ones. This could occur because the original program was poorly designed, the target population for the course has changed dramatically, or years of maintenance have rendered the course a patchwork that really does not work well anymore.

Opportunity Conversions   Let's say your plan has uncovered an opportunity to save delivery expense and improve timeliness by converting part of your classroom-style curriculum to computer-based jobsite training. This adds no new curriculum but does require substantial development resources for the conversion. You must look at the trade-off between delivery savings and reduced training time and the development cost of the conversion to determine whether the conversion is worthwhile.

More information about completing your delivery and development plans is included in Chapters 13 through 17.

Document and Present Plans

You have now completed the elements of your quantitative plan. What remains to be done is to document it and present it for decision making.

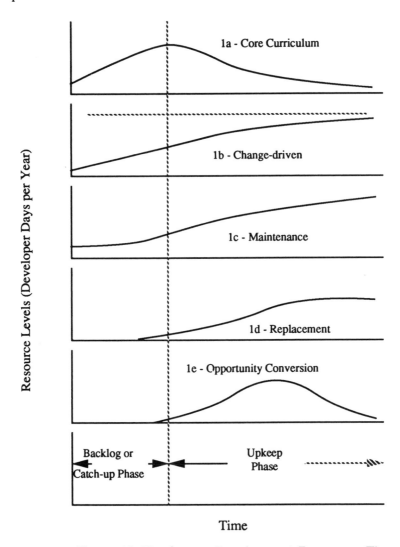

Figure 10-13 Course Development Resources Time Profile

The documentation does not have to be elaborate, but it should be complete enough so someone can follow what was done to update the plan a year or two later. The minimum that should be documented includes

- Training needs estimates, sources of the data, and who participated
- Forecast of delivery volume needed and sources of data

- Forecast of training materials development needed, assumptions on which the forecast is based, and sources of data

- Three- to five-year delivery plan scenarios, and resource requirements for the scenarios, resource estimating assumptions (unit cost tables)

- Three- to five-year development plan scenarios, resource requirements for the scenarios, and resource estimating assumptions (unit cost tables)

- Summary resource requirements and management decision choices

- Enough information on spreadsheets and computations so they can be updated in a year.

We have found that, even if we personally did all the work, we can not remember the details sufficiently to update it a year later unless we do a fairly complete job of documentation. If someone else has to do the updates, it is impossible for them. Another reason for documenting the plan is that it will be used as a basis for all parts of operational planning and decision making. If the documented plan is not available as a roadmap, you may have wasted your effort.

The rubber meets the road when you take your plan to the executive decision makers and ask them to choose the planning scenario and resourcing level they feel best meets the needs of the business. You should work out a presentation strategy that fits your organization and the individual executives in the decision making group. The trick is to reduce all the data you have produced to a relatively simple set of alternatives and clearly communicate what is at stake in terms of business results and resource costs. We usually prefer a formal set of presentation charts in the form of transparencies or slides, with lots of backup charts to answer questions and to let executives know that this is a thoroughly researched plan.

If the plan is to be presented for decision making to a group of officers, whether your executive board of education, the president's cabinet, or a special committee convened for the purpose, you may want to carry the plan around and present it to individual members of the group to give them time to ask individual questions, consult others, and form some opinions before being asked to participate in group decision making. Even if you do not do this, it is a good idea to go through a formal dry run with one member of the group, such as the Human Resources Vice President. This person can critique your plan and your presentation and give you some information about how the group is likely to respond.

Our experience in presenting to members of these groups and watching our clients present to them is that the executives will ask enough probing questions to assure themselves that the work you have done is sound, and then there will be testing of the alternatives and the business consequences for the alternatives. They may ask you to go back and run some additional scenarios. They may thank you and excuse you while they privately deliberate over their decision. If you have done all the homework we have suggested, you will probably be congratulated for your thoroughness and for clearly presenting the choices. Now it is up to them. Do not try to push them too hard for your favorite outcome. Choosing a scenario is their job.

Chapters 11 through 18 give you detailed procedures, worksheets, and examples to help you build the quantitative plan.

TRAINING NEEDS ASSESSMENT

The first step in identifying the amount of training that needs to be developed and delivered is to do a formal training needs assessment for the target audience(s) that fall within the scope of your strategic planning project. If you are doing a strategic training plan for an entire corporation, then you will undertake a needs analysis for the entire corporation. If your plan is for R&D, then your needs analysis will be limited to R&D, and so forth.

The purpose of this formal assessment is

- To develop performance models for each job function in the target audience that identify
    - The mission and rationale of the job
    - The major responsibilities of the job
    - Outputs for each responsibility area
    - Performance measures for each output
    - Tasks required to produce the outputs
    - Typical deficiencies in performance
    - Causes of the deficiencies
    - Priority for training
- To develop knowledge and skill matrices for all knowledge and skill items required to do the job, including
    - The major categories of knowledge and skill items for the job
    - An indication of the importance of the knowledge and skill items required to do the job

- An indication of the degree or depth of knowledge for items required to do the job
- Estimated training time required to teach someone the knowledge or skill to the depth required
- Priority for training
- Whether or not training already exists for the item
- To identify other training issues and concerns of the analysis groups.

Carrying out this assessment is extremely important and is fundamental to completing the rest of the quantitative plan. In phase 1 you determined what the foundation of the structure you are building looks like. To put up your framework and girders, you have to know how high the structure needs to be, how much weight it needs to hold, etc. Doing the needs assessment gives you this information. It tells you

- What people have to do on their jobs

- What they have to know to do it

- What training you do and do not have in place to support that knowledge.

Ultimately, the performance models and knowledge and skill matrices developed in this step will lead to the development of a curriculum architecture (covered in Chapter 12), which will form the girders and framework of your training system.

NEEDS ASSESSMENT PROCESS

Figure 11-1 is a schematic view of the process that is used to conduct a formal training needs assessment. The remainder of this chapter provides more information on how to do steps 1 through 6 of the training needs assessment process.

Step 1. Develop a Project Plan for the Training Needs Assessment Project

As we stated earlier, you do a separate project plan for several parts of the strategic planning process. Needs assessment is a project in itself and deserves its own project plan. As with any project plan, the plan for your needs assessment project should spell out

- Purpose of the project

- Scope of the project

- Target audience

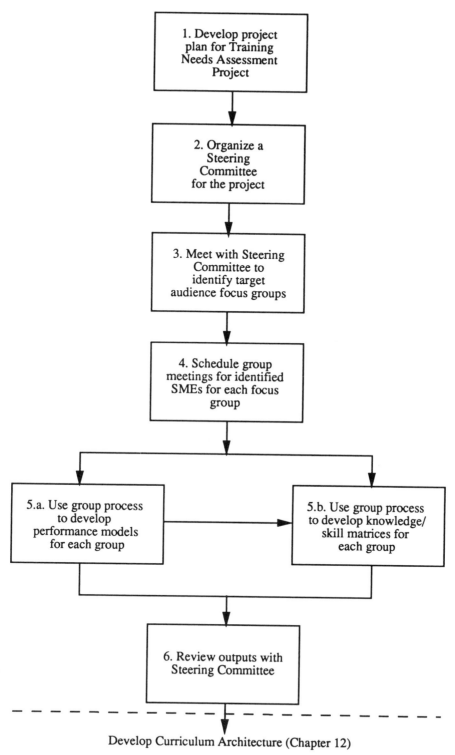

1. Develop project plan for Training Needs Assessment Project

2. Organize a Steering Committee for the project

3. Meet with Steering Committee to identify target audience focus groups

4. Schedule group meetings for identified SMEs for each focus group

5.a. Use group process to develop performance models for each group

5.b. Use group process to develop knowledge/ skill matrices for each group

6. Review outputs with Steering Committee

Develop Curriculum Architecture (Chapter 12)

Figure 11-1   Training Needs Assessment Process

- Outputs and expected results
- Roles
- Project tasks
- Resources
- Schedule.

Preparing this plan is important because it forces you to consider all the issues needed for the project to succeed. It also serves as a communications medium to let all the participants know what is going on, why, and what their expected role is. Figure 11-2 is a sample task, resource, and schedule list for a training needs assessment project.

Step 2. Organize a Steering Committee for the Project

The ultimate purpose of the Steering Committee is to ensure that the curriculum developed as a result of the needs assessment process truly addresses the important training needs of the identified target audience. The role of the committee within the needs assessment process is to

- Determine how the target audience should be divided
- Select master performers and experts to participate in analysis groups
- Review analysis group outputs.

The steering committee is usually selected by a top level person within the target audience to be addressed by the needs assessment. For example, if the target audience is the R&D function, the steering committee may be selected by the Vice President of Engineering or someone reporting directly to the Vice President. This person will usually chair the steering committee as well. The remaining members should be upper middle managers drawn from the organization, functions, or subfunctions that make up the target audience. The choice of members on this committee is extremely important. The committee will have a major influence on the content of the curriculum by their own actions and by their selection of people for the analysis groups. They will also have a major influence on the level of political support for implementation and funding. The size of the steering committee is not as important as having all stakeholders represented in the group. If an important group is left out, it will have less buy-in to the outcome and could later cause difficulty by its lack of acceptance of the curriculum. A good steering committee will give you valuable guidance, provide top caliber resources, and provide strong political support for implementation and funding.

XTELCO ENGINEERING
PROJECT PLAN

	Estimated Resources (Days)							Schedule	
	Svenson & Wallace			XTelco				Start Date	End Date
Project Tasks	CS	WP	GA	PM	PT	SC	MP		
PHASE I. ANALYSIS									
1. Steering Committee Review of Project Plan									
a. Coordinate Steering Committee meeting	-	-	-	.5	-	-	-	1/5	1/9
b. Prepare presentation material	.5	1.0	.25	-	-	-	-	1/1	1/9
c. Conduct meeting	1.0	-	-	.5	.5	.5	-	1/10	1/10
- Review Project Plan									
- Identify group analysis meeting participants									
2. Analysis Meetings (three, 3-day meetings)									
a. Coordinate selection and attendance	-	-	-	2.0	-	-	-	1/11	1/31
b. Prepare for analysis meetings	.5	1.0	-	-	-	-	-	1/11	1/31
c. Conduct analysis meetings	9.0	-	-	9.0	9.0	-	3.0	2/1	2/15
d. Document performance models and skills/knowledge matrices	2.0	7.0	3.0	-	1.0	-	-	2/16	2/26
e. Edit results	1.0	2.0	-	-	-	-	-	2/27	2/28
3. Steering Committee validation meeting to review Performance Models									
a. Prepare for meeting	.5	2.0	.5	.5	-	-	-	3/1	3/5
b. Conduct Validation Meeting	1.0	-	-	1.0	1.0	1.0	-	3/6	3/6
c. Document meeting outputs	1.0	1.0	.5	-	-	-	-	3/7	3/10
SUBTOTAL (in days) - Phase 1	16.5	14.0	4.25	13.5	11.5	1.5	3.0		

KEY   **Svenson & Wallace, Inc.**   **XTelco**
              CS = Consultant   PM = Project Manager
              WP = Word Processing   PT = Process Trainee
              GA = Graphic Arts   SC = Steering Committee
                                         MP = Master Performers/Subject Matter Experts

Figure 11-2   Sample Project Plan Schedule for Needs Assessment

Step 3. Meet with the Steering Committee to Identify Target Audience Focus Groups

Your first meeting with the steering committee is an important one because it sets the tone for all future meetings. It is important for you to be

- Prepared
- Organized
- Professional
- Knowledgeable.

The following tips will help you present this image:

- Schedule the date for the first meeting well in advance and confirm it with a written memo.
- Be sure the room is reserved, is comfortable, and has adequate seating and table space.
- Send agendas out ahead of the meeting.
- Be prepared with charts and graphs for your presentation.
- Keep the meeting on track and within the allotted time.

Figure 11-3 presents a typical agenda for the first meeting of the steering committee.

The first critical decision the steering committee makes is which functions or subfunctions are to be analyzed. People performing the same function, such as sales, will typically have similar tasks and require similar skills and knowledge no matter what division or geographical region they are in. There may also be some division-specific or region-specific needs. We have found that doing the needs analysis (and curriculum design) by function (vs. by topic) is the best way to link training to expected job performance and will provide the most complete curriculum maps. The functional curricula can be compared to identify common needs and avoid duplication. Examples of this type of potential duplication include generic management skills, personal skills, some product knowledge, and use of personal computers.

A list of functional curricula to be developed might look like this:

Corporate Functional Curricula

- R&D
- Marketing
- Manufacturing

1. Introductions
2. Orientation to performance analysis and curriculum architecture design
3. Overview of project plan including Steering Committee roles
4. Selection of analysis focus groups
5. Selection of participants for analysis groups
6. Tentative schedule expectations and date for Steering Committee Meeting to review analysis data

Figure 11-3   Typical Agenda for First Steering Committee Meeting

- Distribution
- Sales
- Customer services
- Procurement
- Product management
- Human resources
- Information systems
- Accounting
- Legal

Other Curricula

- Executive development
- Customers
    - Users/operators
    - Maintenance
- Suppliers.

Executive development for general manager levels and up is cross-functional. These people are learning the art and science of leading and governing the organization across all functions.

One drawback to the functional approach to needs assessment and curriculum development is that the opportunity to do cross-functional training could be missed if you are not careful, and the training itself can by default preserve old communication barriers between functions. We deal with this more in chapter 12.

In the R&D project illustrated in Figure 11-2, the steering committee selected three subfunctions for analysis:

- Hardware developers
- Software developers
- Product development managers.

There was debate about whether project leaders represented a significantly different subfunction since they are not classified as managers but are performing managerial tasks. The committee decided to include them with managers, which in retrospect worked out well.

There were other subfunctions not included, such as laboratory technicians, model shop, etc. These were left out of the initial project for economy and because the largest populations with the most important training needs were judged to be in the three groups selected.

The second decision the steering committee makes is who should participate in the analysis groups. The analysis groups must be able to represent their subfunctions not only as they are being performed today but as they will ideally be performed in the future. Most jobs are in transition in the real world. Most steering committees do not want a curriculum that represents yesterday's way of doing things. Therefore, the groups must be able to look ahead.

The best mix in an analysis group usually contains master performers from the line organization, experts from the staff, and supervisors of the line performers. Master performers are people who everyone recognizes as consistently producing superior work and who can represent the job at its best today. The staff experts and line supervisors will often have a clearer view of the future. The analysis group brings all these elements into dialog in a structured, facilitated group process.

We always tell the steering committee that the names of the analysis group members will appear on the analysis reports and curriculum documents. They should select participants whose names will automatically generate respect for the products produced.

Step 4. Schedule Group Meetings for Identified Subject Matter Experts (SMEs) for Each Focus Group

This step is primarily a logistical one. It is important that all participants are notified well in advance of the meeting and that they have some information in writing as to what the meeting is about and what their role is going to be. We have facilitated meetings like this when the participants had no idea what it was going to be about or why they were there. Some of them thought they were coming to be trained, some to provide training, etc. This creates a great deal of unnecessary confusion and turmoil. In addition, be sure you have a big enough room, with seats and tables, refreshments that meet your cultural guidelines, an overhead projector and screen, flip chart easels, paper, and markers. We like to use double-wide easels (45") for this process if they are available. It makes it much easier to document the outputs.

Step 5. Meet with Analysis Groups to Develop Performance Models and Knowledge and Skill Matrices

The analysis groups will each meet for a two- to three-day intensive process to describe and analyze the work of the functions and subfunctions and then analyze the knowledge and skill requirements for that work. These groups, containing a representative mix of master performers, staff experts, and supervisors will perform the analysis tasks under the direction of a facilitator, trained in the process, who is usually not an expert in the jobs being analyzed.

We have found that the best group size is between six and twelve. Fewer than six leaves the coverage a little thin and may reduce the amount of dialog. More than twelve can get unwieldy, take longer, and result in some people not participating much.

The same data can be collected through a series of individual interviews, but each person and organizational unit sees the work differently and represents it differently. In a group process, these differences can be discussed and a consensus view developed. There is no way to develop a consensus view through individual interviews. The interviewer must integrate the data and present it back to the steering committee. We have found that this can be a hard sell since the integrated view is different from what any individual contributed. We have had outstanding success gaining organizational support for analysis data generated through the group process.

The major drawback to the group process is that it requires a highly skilled facilitator to bring the group through the process, collect all the important data, and finish in the allotted time. The stakes are high. If the group bogs down, will not agree, or does not see how to proceed, a great deal of talent is being tied up in a highly visible way, so a failure can have big repercussions.

Performance Modeling   The first task of the group is to develop performance models for the jobs in their function or subfunction. This usually takes the entire first day and sometimes more if there are several jobs or the jobs are done differently in different places.

We usually use 45"-wide easel paper to document the work and post each page so the group can see the job definition and performance analysis emerging on the walls and can go back and forth to edit various parts. Electronic whiteboards are an alternative, but you cannot post the results on public display for constant referral.

For example, the first question to the group is, "What is the Mission of the subfunction or job? Why, in a few words, does the company need hardware developers? Why do you exist?" It may take up to a half hour to arrive at a consensus mission statement. For example, the mission of a hardware developer might read something like this:

> The mission of a hardware developer at Luxor Computing Corporation is to conceive, plan, design, develop, and support solutions to customer problems or needs in the form of

processes, device drivers, terminals, and peripherals in conjunction with software development and/or product management.

The second question is, "What are the major responsibilities of the job?" For some jobs, these responsibilities may fall in a major process flow.

Here is a typical set of responsibilities for product developers in an engineering or R&D department:

- Product conceptual planning (with marketing and others)
- System design and subsystem specification
- Detailed design
- Development and testing of prototype
- Preparation of manufacturing and maintenance specifications
- Support for manufacturing
- Support for field service
- Technology surveillance, assessment, and transfer.

Here is a typical set of responsibilities for mid-level managers in a utility installation and maintenance function.

- Managing work
  - Create annual plan
  - Create workforce plans
  - Monitor/control work performance
  - Manage internal/external projects
  - Manage customer/community relationships
- Managing people
  - Personnel planning and staffing
  - Personnel orientation and training
  - Support individual/group performance
  - Administer compensation
  - Career planning
  - Labor relations
  - Support personnel-related programs
- Managing the environment
  - Organization design
  - Job design
  - Workflow design
  - Develop or implement methods and procedures

    –   Implement new management systems.

We have always found it convenient and workable to break management responsibilities into the three areas of managing work, managing people, and managing the working environment. The subresponsibilities will vary somewhat, particularly in the area of managing work, but all managers are able to relate to this general framework.

It is important to work with this responsibilities list until it gives a compact representation of the job without leaving anything out, without duplication, and without one really being a subtask of another.

Now we take each responsibility and break it down. The analysis format is created on the easel like the one shown in Figure 11-4. This example is for the utility company middle management group. The first responsibility is "managing work: annual planning and budgeting." The principal information on this chart includes outputs from the responsibility, performance measures, tasks, typical deficiencies in performance, causes of the deficiencies, priority for development of training material, and placement of the task training in the eventual curriculum.

The outputs are a statement of the principal outcomes from the responsibility, in this case the annual plan, budget, and periodic budget revisions. The measures relate to each output or to all of the outputs, and may include such things as quality, quantity, timeliness, etc. All the measures identified on this page are quality measures. Tasks represent the activities required to produce the outputs.

Deficiencies are typical deficiencies in performance using the measures in the second column as a reference. The causes of the deficiencies are identified and then evaluated in two categories: deficiencies of environment (DE), and deficiencies of knowledge (DK). In this case, you can see that almost all of the deficiencies were caused by deficiencies of the environment. Only two causes had knowledge components. This suggests that training alone is highly unlikely to resolve these deficiencies.

The priority column indicates that this analysis group rated the priority for training on this responsibility at eight on a twelve-point scale which would be a medium priority. The module placement information is not recorded until the curriculum is designed and module numbers or a module coding scheme is established. So this column is left blank during the analysis meetings.

The analysis process simply follows this format through each responsibility in the job until the room is covered with charts like this. When the analysis is complete, you can walk around the room and see the entire job or collection of jobs mapped out in considerable detail. A common reaction from the participants is that this is the first time they have ever seen their work laid out in this comprehensive fashion. Most of them request copies of the information to take home for their own use in more effectively managing their work.

The columns for information you collect could change for different groups. Figure 11-5 shows a similar chart from an R&D hardware developer group.

Knowledge and Skills Analysis   The next major series of activities involves completing the knowledge and skills analysis for the job. The first task is to establish

1. Managing Work Segment: A. Annual Planning and Budgeting

Outputs	Measures	Tasks	Deficiencies	Causes	dE	dK	Pr	Mod Plcmt

• Annual Plan
  - Objectives
  - Action Plans
 	
• Budget
 	
• Periodic Budget Revisions
	• According to policies and procedures if available
	
	• Plans should relate to strategic objectives
	
	• Reviewed and revised as required
	
	• Plans should reflect efficiency gains if possible
	
	• Adequate rationale to support budget requirements
		1. Review:
		  - Previous year's plan
		  - Historical data
		  - Forecasts from marketing
		  - Cutover schedules
		  - Obsolete equipment lists
		  - Demands of interexchange carrier for the year
		
		2. Obtain input from
		  - First-level managers
		  - Engineering
		  - Staff
		  - Marketing
		
		3. Prepare and submit for approval
		
		4. Revise as required
		
		5. Implement
		  - Communicate to subordinates
		  - Obtain outside support
		  - Create/modify tracking system as needed
		
		6. Update as required
			1. Plan/budget inaccurate
			
			2. Planning process not done
				• Unknowns
				
				• Top down budgets cause inappropriately allocated funds
				
				• Contingency plans not included
				
				• Inaccurate forecasting
				
				• Customer demands change
				
				• Technology changes may affect plan
				
				• Funds taken out of alternative account because appropriate account is underbudgeted
				
				• Lack of predictability
				
				• Low priority
				
				• Demands force reactive mode rather than planning mode
					X
					X
					
					X
					X
					X
					
					X
					
					X
					
					X
					X
					X
						
						X
						X
							8	600 Series

Figure 11-4   UTX Corporation Mid-Level Manager Performance Model

194

Responsibility: Product Development

Outputs/Tasks	Level*	Performance Measures	Typical Deficiencies	Causes	dE	dK	Module Placement
Design, Implementation, Integration Phases							12001
1. Develop block diagrams, circuit design, flow charts, timing analysis, rules checking	E-S	• Rate of changes after design freeze (Pareto analysis tool)	• Too many changes	• Changing requirements and/or definition	√		12002
				• Design errors	√		91401
2. Perform competitive analysis • Features • Function • Quality • Cost • Reliability (ongoing throughout development and implementation)	I/S	• Completeness • Selling propositions rearticulated		• Inadequate margin analysis	√	√	98002
				• Incomplete/inadequate vendor review	√		
				• Premature design freeze	√		
3. Perform simulation	E-S	• Actual versus planned schedule	• Not meeting schedules	• Lack of advanced product development	√		
4. Prepare BOM	I/S			• Accelerating complexity	√		
5. Analyze reliability	E-S						
6. Mechanical layout	I/S						
7. Tolerance study	E-S						
8. Thermal analysis	I/S						

* Entry-, Intermediate-, or Session-level person

Figure 11-5 Hardware Developer Performance Model

195

with the analysis group a list of knowledge and skill categories. The list of categories below came from the Utility middle management jobs analyzed in the performance modeling section.

Example Skills/Knowledge Categories
Utility Middle Managers

- Organizations
- Company policies and procedures
- Administrative systems and associated reports
- Records, reports, and forms
- Management/interpersonal skills
- Computer tools
- External regulations
- Service/product offerings
- Miscellaneous

These categories are useful in classifying skills and knowledge that relate back to the job responsibilities and tasks. You should be able to look at the list of external regulations that these managers must be familiar with and make an assessment as to whether all the important regulations have been identified. Without these categories, this becomes an impossibility, since you would have policies, products, services, and regulations all intermixed, making it impossible to judge whether there is a complete list.

Again, the 45"-wide easel paper is used to document important information in each of these categories. Figure 11-6 shows an example, "Category D, Records, Reports, and Forms," from the aforementioned mid-level manager project. The first three columns indicate which aspect of the work each record, report and form applies to; managing work, managing personnel, and managing the environment. The next column asks the question, "Is training appropriate for mid-level managers?" As you can see, only three items on this list were judged to require high-level training. The next column indicates that all the remaining items are appropriately trained at first or supervisor level. The depth column is an estimate of the required depth of coverage for the training, conceptual overview, in-depth knowledge, or skill building. The volatility column estimates whether the content volatility of the training will be high, medium, or low. The estimated length gives a rough estimate of the amount of training, which is also a further check on the depth of training expected. We do not expect at this point to get an accurate estimate of the length of training, but we will find out whether we are dealing with something small, medium, or large. The groups will generally be able to discriminate between two hours of training, two days, two weeks, or two months. This is very important later on when it comes time to estimate the resource requirements for course development.

Category D. Records, Reports, and Forms

Item	Mg Work Grp 1	Grp 2	Mg P	Mg E	Mid Level Trmg?	If no, What?	If yes, Depth	Vol	Est Lgth	Pr	Module Placement
• Workbook of Various Records/Reports/Forms											
- Attendance	X	*	X		No	First Level					
- Payroll	X	*	X		No	First Level					
- Accident and Injury	X	*	X	X	No	Supervisor					
- Management by Objectives	X		X	X	No	First Level					
- Personnel Records	X	*	X	X	No	First Level					
- Vacation Schedule	X		X		No	First Level					
- Workload Schedule	X				No	First Level					
- Held Orders	X				No	First Level					
- Morning Report	X	*	X	X	No	First Level					
- Overtime Report	X		X		No	First Level					
- Tool Report	X				No	Supervisor					
- Expense Vouchers	X	*	X		No	Supervisor					
- Official Services Request	X	*			No	First Level					
- Corporate Telephone Service Application	X	*			No	First Level					
- Grievance Form/Disciplinary Record	X	*	X		No	First Level					
- UTX Accident Prevention Plan	X	*	X		No	First Level					
- Budget Report	X	*	X	X	Yes	First Level	3	M	1 day	5	100 Series
- Upgrade & Transfer Report	X	*	X		No	First Level					
- Top Customers/Customer Advocate/Service Pro	X				No	First Level					
- Training Forms	X		X		No	First Level					
- Building Operations Center Order	X			X	No	First Level					
- Plant Work Recommendations	X				No	First Level					
- Appraisal Forms	X		X		Yes		3	L	.5 day	3	100 Series
- Major Failure Report	X	*	X		Yes		3	H	1 day	9	200 Series
- Time and Materials	X				No						
- Damage to Company and Others	X				No						
--Facility						First Level					
--Property						First Level					

Figure 11-6 UTX Corporation Mid-Level Manager Knowledge and Skill Matrix

The priority column is the group's assessment of the relative priority of each of the training needs against all of the other training needs. We do not do the priority exercise until the entire job analysis is done and all the skill and knowledge areas are identified. Then we go back through all the responsibility sheets and all of the skill and knowledge sheets and vote priorities.

The priority voting process is simple and is useful in a variety of situations. Everyone gets one vote. A high priority counts two points; a medium, one point; and a low, zero points. If there were eight people voting, then the maximum score for any item would be sixteen. If everyone voted "medium," the score would be eight, and so on. Voting is by a show of hands, it is remarkably fast, and the groups usually accept the outcome. If there is a dispute, we usually let those who are dissatisfied make a little speech to persuade their peers and then revote. Sometimes the vote changes and sometimes it does not but everyone has been heard.

The module placement column again is left blank until the curriculum is designed and the numbering plan established.

Other Training Issues and Concerns   Generally, at the conclusion of these analysis meetings, we try to get some closure by having the group talk to us about any other issues and concerns they might have about the training system. We document the statements they make on the flip chart. We find that they give us a lot of useful information that comes in handy when designing the curriculum architecture. For instance, in the mid-level manager example, the analysis groups provided us with the following comments and suggestions:

- Maximum of four one-week sessions per year

- Average course length should be five days.

- Two to four weeks of training in the first six months on the job of the core curriculum for
  - Managing work
  - Managing people

- Group-paced learning
  - Mandatory self-study precourse work
    - Readings
    - Interviews
    - Assignments
  - Case study format using "In Basket" concept (items placed in trainees "in basket" that he/she has to respond to based on case study information)

- Mentored instruction
  - Self-selected mentor
  - Peer or higher-level manager other than immediate manager

- Maximize use of self-paced materials

- Consideration should be made to include time during training to access office automation tools and handle business matters.
- A mix of divisions is helpful—interaction among the divisions leads to shared experiences
- The curriculum should be modularized to allow mid-levels from one function to attend another function's training and to allow for expansion to other groups and functions at a later date.

Training Delivery Issues

- No more than five days per month off the job for training
- Need to be away from jobsite to reduce potential for interruption
- Initial training should be concentrated within the first six months of being on the job.
- Use current and/or previous mid-levels to conduct training. Perhaps team teachers could be used to avoid biases and disbelief directed at the instructor from participants who work in the same division as the instructor.
- It may be good for each of the Divisions to host the course delivery.

Training Administration Issues

- Do not charge at the district level for training, keep it at the general manager level.
- An evaluation of training can be conducted by sending information to the supervisor regarding objectives, content, etc., and then follow up six months later to determine how quickly the skills are assimilated into the job performance.
- Make certain that this training does not affect the performance appraisal.
- Advertise curriculum through local training areas—make certain it is visible up to the third level.
- Initial session should be mandatory for all newly promoted mid-level managers.
- Keep the course useful and interesting—must be updated.
- Have a one- to two-year term for the course facilitator or use existing mid-levels to facilitate the course. Be certain to recognize the assistance formally.
- Assign the task of keeping the course updated.
- Obtain support from each division's management
- Offer an overview or pilot course to third and fourth levels in the divisions.
  When you have obtained all the analysis data, have it typed on 8½" × 11" sheets

so copies can be distributed to group participants and to the steering committee for review. A few caveats about the process:

- The process should be facilitated by someone who is well versed in group facilitation methods and needs analysis processes.

- The group is likely to feel confused at first and wonder where all this work is leading, but in the end participants almost always feel it was well worth it.

- The formats we have presented are typical and are meant to serve as guides, but they are not the only possible formats to use. We usually end up with a different format for each client because we have to modify the data needed depending on each client's situation.

Step 6. Review Outputs with Steering Committee

Once you have documented the outputs from all of your analysis meetings, it is time for your second meeting with the steering committee. The purpose of this meeting is for the steering committee to review the analysis data and make any changes it feels are needed. It is not at all uncommon for steering committees to make changes that better represent a future view of the jobs. The give and take between the ground-level view of the analysis groups and the high-level view of the steering committee produces a superior overall result. We advocate having one representative from each of the analysis groups attend the steering committee meeting to represent the work of the group, since the facilitator is not an expert and often cannot adequately answer questions of substance or adequately represent the analysis groups' viewpoint.

At this second meeting, the steering committee can help establish some curriculum design criteria or guidelines. Examples include issues like, "How long is it permissible to take someone off the job for training; can job site workstations be used for on-the-job computer-based training?" etc. We deal with this in more detail in chapter 12.

Figure 11-7 presents a typical agenda for the second steering committee meeting.

SUMMARY

In this chapter, we dealt with the the following steps of the needs assessment process:

- [ ] Develop a project plan for the needs assessment project.
- [ ] Organize a steering committee for the project.
- [ ] Meet with the steering committee to
  - Review project plan and set schedule
  - Identify analysis groups.

1. Review functional performance model
2. Review skill/knowledge analysis data
3. Establish curriculum design criteria

Figure 11-7 Second Steering Committee Meeting Agenda

- Select participants for analysis groups
☐ Schedule analysis group meetings.
☐ Facilitate analysis group meetings to
    - Develop performance models
    - Develop knowledge/skill matrices
    - Identify other training issues.
☐ Document the analysis results.
☐ Review results with the steering committee

You will use the data obtained in this chapter to develop curriculum architecture(s), as explained in chapter 12.

12

CURRICULUM ARCHITECTURE DESIGN

In this chapter, we present a curriculum architecture concept and design process developed by us and our colleagues at Svenson and Wallace over the last twelve years and used successfully with many larger corporate clients.

A curriculum architecture is essentially a multidimensional map or logic diagram that relates modules of training to segments of the target audience and to other modules of training. For example, the curriculum architecture could tell you what training modules are appropriate for a new account representative selling computer systems in the Western Region. It could tell you if there is a required or preferred sequence to take the training modules in. It should tell you how the training is linked to job performance. You should also be able to look at the curriculum architecture and notice that some training programs are appropriate for people in more than one type of job.

Developing a comprehensive curriculum architecture for a large organization is a major challenge, but we know of no better way to provide an organized, systematic framework to use in managing training. The curriculum architecture will avoid gaps and unnecessary overlaps in content. It will identify common needs across several job functions and help avoid unnecessary duplication of training development. It provides a menu of modules to be prioritized for training materials acquisition or development. It provides the information needed to construct learning paths for typical jobs. It can also be used to develop reference manuals for supervisors to use in planning training with their subordinates.

There are several different types of needs assessment and curriculum architecture classified by the type of need that is driving it.

Type of Need	Results In
Functional or job specific	Core curriculum for function or job
Cross-functional needs	Cross-functional curricula such as • Generic management skills • Personal skills • Quality skills
System or product related	Cross-functional curricula to support a system or product

The results of all of these are interdependent—in other words, the complete functional curriculum for product managers contains modules from all the appropriate cross-functional, system, and product curricula.

You should consider developing performance-based curriculum architectures for all major job functions in your organization. For a large corporation, accomplishing this in two to three years would be an excellent and achievable goal.

We also strongly recommend using this process for mapping the training required to support the introduction of all new systems, products, and corporate initiatives. Examples of this kind of application include

- CAD/CAM system
- Mechanized materials management
- Total Quality Management
- Performance appraisal system.

CURRICULUM ARCHITECTURE DESIGN PROCESS

In this section, we introduce you to the process of developing a curriculum architecture. Curriculum architecture design consists of mapping all the training requirements identified by the analysis groups into a curriculum structure. The basic tasks include

1. Establish design criteria.
2. Create the curriculum structure.
3. Map the training requirements into the structure.
4. Evaluate existing available training.
5. Define modules and link back to job models and knowledge/skill matrices.
6. Define typical learning paths.
7. Review with the steering committee.

Step 1. Establish Curriculum Design Criteria

When establishing curriculum design criteria, four elements should be considered:

- Target audience background
- Training development issues
- Training delivery issues
- Training administration issues.

As we said in chapter 11, in general, curriculum design criteria in these areas are established by the steering committee as part of its review meeting for the analysis data. The committee should address the issues raised by the analysis group (see Chapter 11 for examples) and use them as a basis for developing a set of design criteria. Some of the types of questions the design criteria should answer are as follows:

- What is the maximum length of time we are willing to have employees away from the job for training at one stretch?
- Are we willing to send people away for training?
- Do we have or are we able to get facilities for high tech training such as Computer-based Training (CBT), interactive videodisc, etc.?
- Will our curriculum be used by other groups outside our function?
- Will our training be developed and delivered by subject-matter experts or instructional designers?
- What is the population of the target audience we are addressing?
- What is the total amount of time we are willing to have employees trained per year?
- What is our preferred delivery method?
- Should training be on site or off site?

In addition, the steering committee should address the question of target audience background. The background of the participants in the target population should be one of the prime elements considered. Trainees may potentially come from various functional or staff backgrounds and possess a wide variety of experience levels in former positions. The curriculum can then be structured in a way to accommodate the wide variety of experience levels and backgrounds of the target participants. When reviewing target audience background, any changes in promotional patterns must also be considered.

Step 2. Create the Curriculum Structure and Architecture

The curriculum structure organizes all the content into important or significant groupings. The example of the utility mid-level curriculum used in chapter 11 is continued in this chapter. Note that this is an example of a functional curriculum architecture. In this case, a curriculum structure was developed with five learning experiences, each customized to accommodate managers in five subfunctions (called disciplines) across five divisions. The subfunction and division flexibility is handled by the internal modularity of each of the five learning experiences.

The chart in Figure 12-1 provides a visual representation of the overall curriculum architecture with an overview of five main training experiences or courses. This structure is based on the information obtained in the job analysis phase of this project. Each of the five shaded boxes in the curriculum structure represents one of the five training experiences for the mid-level manager. The five learning experiences include

- Three initial training experiences in which the new manager learns and develops the basic survival skills to cope with the day-to-day activities of his or her job. These should occur in the manager's first year on the job.

- Two advanced training experiences which address issues that concern a mid-level manager. These should occur in the manager's second year on the job.

Completing the five training experiences requires ten to twelve total training days in the manager's first year and six days in the second year. These five training experiences are summarized in Figure 12-2.

Each of these training events is composed of one or more discrete modules. This modularized approach allows for flexibility and specificity in designing a training program that will address the needs of five target audiences across five different divisions. New managers will be coming to the job from various backgrounds with varying levels of experience. In addition, this approach provides for further expansion of the curriculum to include other functional areas in the future.

Step 3. Map the Training Requirements into the Structure

To give you an idea of the five training events and the modules that they are comprised of, we describe them in further detail in the following sections. This will give you an idea of how the various training requirements defined in the analysis get mapped into a curriculum structure.

First Training Event (Basic)   This first training event is "Orientation to New Managers (Managing Work)." Its structure is depicted in Figure 12-3. The initial phase of the mid-level manager curriculum begins with self-paced modules developed specifically for each of the five subfunctions in each of the five divisions. The 100 series modules assist the new manager in orienting himself or herself to the position, the

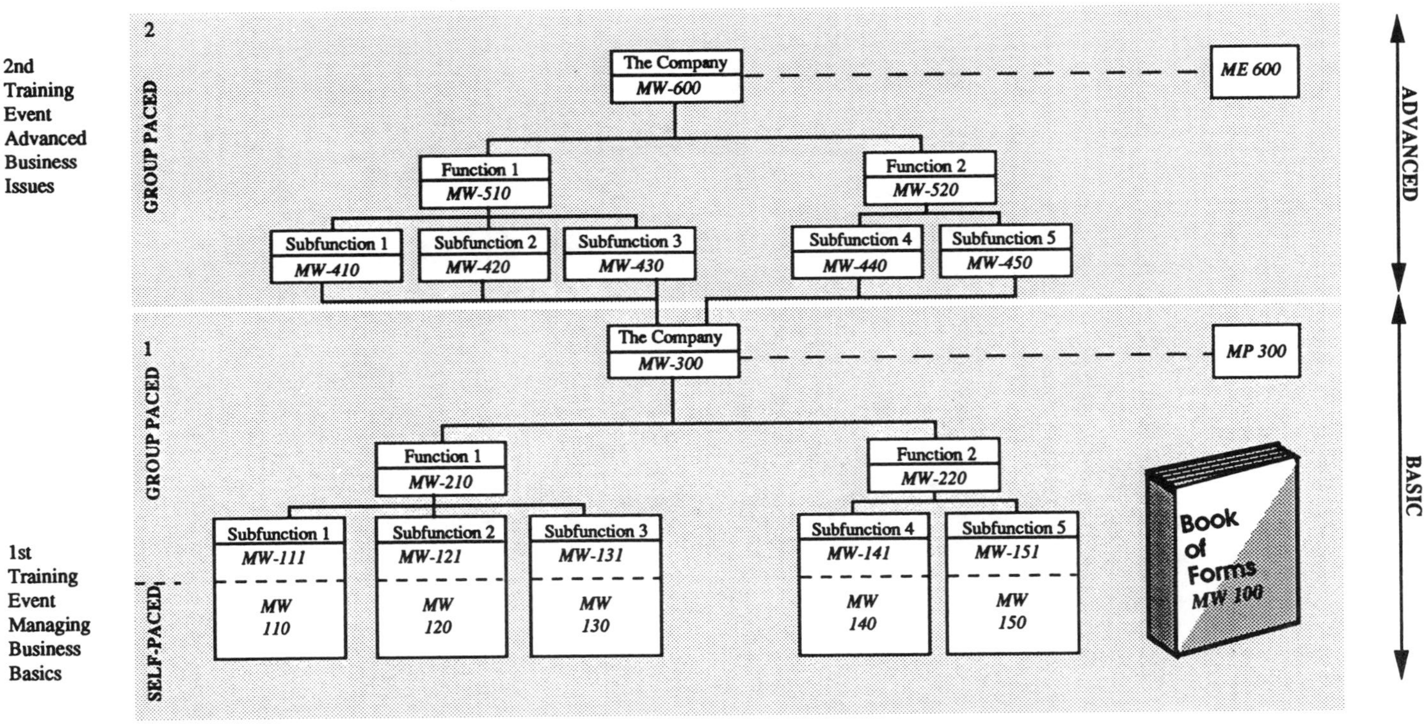

Figure 12-1 UTX Corporation Curriculum Architecture

ADVANCED

BASIC

ME 600

MP 300

Book of Forms *MW 300*

2nd
Training
Event
Advanced
Business
Issues

1st
Training
Event
Managing
Business
Basics

The Company
MW-600

The Company
MW-300

Function 1
MW-510

Function 2
MW-520

Function 1
MW-210

Function 2
MW-220

Subfunction 1
MW-410

Subfunction 2
MW-420

Subfunction 3
MW-430

Subfunction 4
MW-440

Subfunction 5
MW-450

Subfunction 1
MW-111

MW
110

Subfunction 2
MW-121

MW
120

Subfunction 3
MW-131

MW
130

Subfunction 4
MW-141

MW
140

Subfunction 5
MW-151

MW
150

GROUP PACED 2

GROUP PACED 1

SELF-PACED

Curriculum Architecture Design by Guy W. Wallace, Svenson & Wallace, Inc.

MW = Managing Work Modules
MP = Managing People Modules
ME = Managing the Environment Modules

206

Event	B/A*	Title	Series	SP/GP**	Length	Category	Purpose
1	B	Orientation	100	SP	110 pgs	MW	Orientation to organization, position and resources
2	B	Managing Business Issues	200-500	GP	5 days	MW	Skills need to manage day-to-day work
3	B	Managing Managers	500	GP	3 days	MP	People management skills, especially how to manage Manager
4	A	Advanced Business Issues	600-900	GP	3 days	MW	Advanced business skills for mid-level management
5	A	Managing Environment	900	GP	3 days	ME	Environmental issues that affect mid-level management

* = Basic or Advanced
** = Self-paced or Group-Paced

Figure 12-2   Overview of Training Events

organization, and the resources available. Each new manager will receive only the self-paced materials that pertain to his or her function and his or her division. The new mid-level manager should receive the training material for this module along with the Book of Forms within the first few weeks of assuming the position. The Book of Forms is a job aid developed to assist the manager in determining when a particular form should be filled out, how it should be completed, and where it should be sent once it is completed. The Book of Forms will also include an acronym guide to familiarize the new manager with many of the terms he or she will encounter daily. The materials are reviewed and studied at each manager's pace and serve as a reference guide for the manager.

Second Training Event (Basic)   The modular structure of the second training event, "Managing Business Basics," is depicted in Figure 12-4. The second training experience in the initial phase is group-paced, classroom instruction to be attended by all new mid-level managers within the first six weeks of being placed in the position. This portion of the training program instructs new managers on the basics that are necessary to manage their portion of the business effectively. The 100 through 300 Series of modules are combined to create the single, five-day training event. The information to be contained in this training event is modularized as follows:

- 100 Series contains training unique to each subfunction.

- 200 Series contains training that addresses issues specific to the functional group.

- 300 Series contains training that applies across all functions and divisions of the company.

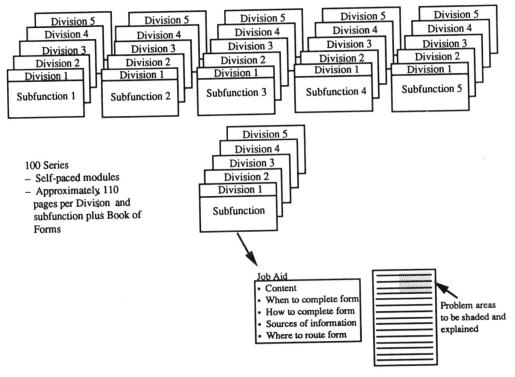

Figure 12-3 First Training Event Modular Structure

The format for this course is as follows:

- All participants will be brought together for an introduction to the course.

- Participants will then be separated by subfunctions and discuss issues such as workforce planning and monitoring and controlling work performance.

- Participants are then grouped by function to cover critical administrative systems and associated reports that apply to all subfunctions within the organization.

- At the end of the course, all participants are brought back together to discuss topics common to all divisions and functions. Topics include
  - Company policies and procedures
  - Customer and community relations
  - Customer service issues
  - Regulatory overview
  - Basic people management/interpersonal skills.

Third Training Event (Basic)   The modular structure of the third training

Training
that is
generic
across the
company

Company

300 series

Training
that addresses
issues specific
to the
functional
group

Function 1   2   Etc.

200 series

5 days
Group-Paced

Training
unique to each
subfunction

Subfunction 1   Subfunction 2   Subfunction 3

100 series

Subfunction 4   Subfunction 5

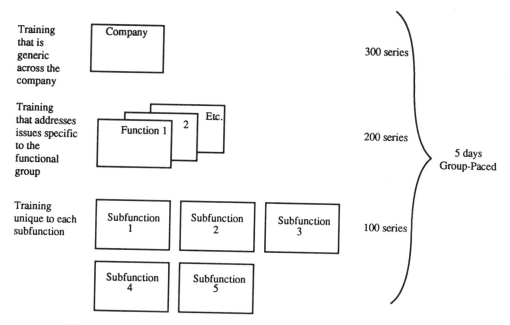

Figure 12-4   Second Training Event Module Structure

event, "Managing Managers," is depicted in Figure 12-5. Developing the skills required to supervise and direct other managers is important for the mid-level manager. He or she must be able to deal with issues concerning

- Personnel planning and staffing
- Compensation administration
- Reviewing employee performance and establishing goals
- Career planning
- Labor relations
- Etc.

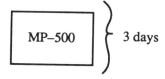

MP–500   3 days

Figure 12-5   Third Training Event Modular Structure

This event is a three-day course to be attended by all new managers, regardless of discipline or division.

Fourth Training Event (Advanced)   The modular structure of the fourth training event, "Advanced Business Issues," is depicted in Figure 12-6. The fourth training event occurs in the manager's second year on the job. Modules included in this training event are the 400 through 600 Series from the Managing Work portion of the curriculum architecture, which combine to create a three-day course. These modules focus on higher-level training topics such as annual planning and budgeting and advanced administrative procedures. The mid-level manager must be able to understand and apply this information, but it is not critical to functioning on a day-to-day basis. The information to be contained in this training event is modularized as follows

- 400 Series contains training unique to each subfunction.
- 500 Series contains training that addresses issues specific to the functional group.
- 600 Series contains training that applies across all functions and divisions of the company.

The format for this course is as follows:

- All participants will be brought together for an introduction to the course.

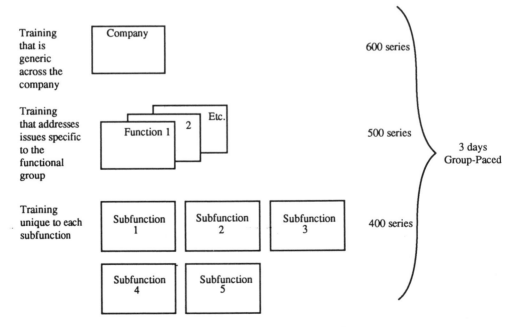

Figure 12-6   Fourth Training Event Modular Structure

- Participants will then be separated by disciplines and discuss issues such as annual planning and budgeting.

- Participants are then grouped by function to cover noncritical administrative systems and associated reports that apply to all subfunctions within the organization. Managers will understand how to manipulate systems to generate desired reports.

- At the end of the course, all participants are brought back together to discuss topics common to all divisions and functions. Sample topics include
  - Operations system common architecture
  - Operations system support planning
  - Network strategies.

Fifth Training Event (Advanced)   The modular structure of the fifth training event, "Environmental Issues as a Mid-Level Manager," is depicted in Figure 12-7. Managing the environment in which the work is performed is yet another concern for the mid-level manager. He or she must design the organization to run efficiently and effectively, design the jobs within the organization, and manage the workflow. The fifth training experience is a single, three-day class to be attended by second-year managers from all functions of each division.

Curriculum Architecture Scope

This curriculum architecture covers the tasks and knowledge/skill items necessary for a mid-level manager to be effective in his or her position within a reasonable amount of time. Training is not a substitute for years of experience; however, it does serve to shorten the learning curve considerably if implemented properly.

This curriculum does not address personal development courses nor does it address many of the skills needed for managing people. Personal development courses focus upon honing useful skills such as

- Computer skills

- Time management

- Stress management

- Presentation skills

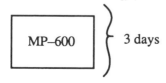

Figure 12-7   Fifth Training Event Modular Structure

- Etc.

Skills necessary for managing people include

- Leadership
- Delegation
- Interviewing
- Etc.

The participants felt that training on these topics and others should be a part of the first-level curriculum rather than a part of the mid-level management curriculum. Mid-level managers could, of course, take these courses as needed.

Note that in this second-level example, the typical learning sequence is implicit in the design of the curriculum. In other curricula there may be a number of typical paths depending on the subfunction, division, previous experience, etc. Figure 12-8 provides an example of a curriculum for which there are several possible learning paths.

Step 4. Evaluate Existing Available Training

Once you have developed the overall curriculum structure and identified all the modules that comprise it, you need to evaluate your existing training to determine which modules you already have available for the curriculum. Go through the list of modules and determine the following:

- Do you have training that is usable as is for this module?
- Do you have training that can be modified or adapted to meet the need of this module?
- If training needs to be adapted, approximately what percentage of the existing training needs to be changed?

This information will be refined and detailed further when you develop your curriculum development and organization plan (chapter 14). For now it gives you a broad picture of the amount of development work to be done to meet the need defined in the curriculum.

Step 5. Define Modules

Each module in a curriculum structure is specified in further detail on a module specification sheet, as shown in Figure 12-9. Each module definition sheet includes

- Curriculum segment of the module

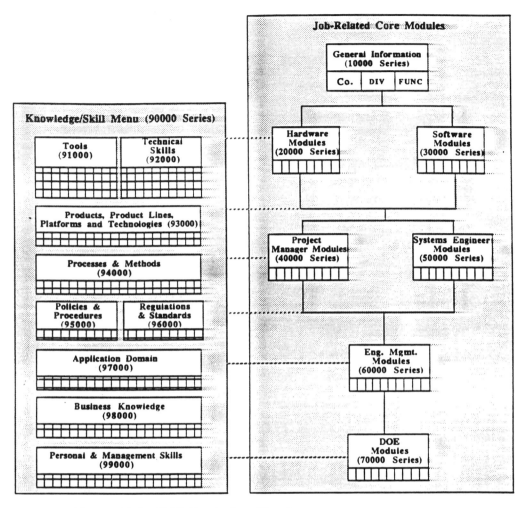

Figure 12-8 R&D Curriculum Structure

- Module title
- Intended target audience for the module
- Temporary module number
- Module intended for basic or advanced phase of training
- Depth of content coverage needed in module
- Learning difficulty of content
- Volatility of content
- Course availability and source

- Suggested method for course development
- Preliminary delivery strategy
- Estimated length of course
- Preliminary content listing.

The example in Figure 12-9 is for one module in the utility company mid-level manager curriculum.

You now know how much training material must be developed and approximately how much and what kinds of training each person will need. To verify that you have covered all the needs defined in the analysis process, you can now link the module definition sheets back to the job models and knowledge and skill matrices discussed in chapter 11. This is a simple matter of completing the last column of each of these documents with the number of the module in which that task or knowledge/skill item will be covered.

Figure 12-10 reviews how the entire process works, from job analysis through curriculum, structure, module definition and link of modules back to job analysis.

Step 6. Define Typical Learning Paths

As we said earlier, in many curriculum structures, particularly those that cover a large division or function or an entire company, there will be many possible learning paths an employee could follow depending on his or her

- Job responsibilities
- Level of education
- Experience on the job
- Prior experience.

It is valuable to develop a set of typical learning paths for the curriculum that supervisors and managers can use as guidelines in developing individual learning plans with employees. Typical learning paths should be developed for

- New-entry employees in each job function
- One- to two-year employees in each job function
- Experienced (three plus years) employees in each job function.

Figure 12-11 shows some example typical learning paths for some of the job functions represented by the curriculum structure presented previously in Figure 12-8.

Sample
Module Definition
Mid-Level Management Curriculum

Curriculum Segment	Module Title	Target Audience	Module No.
Managing Work	Orientation for New Managers	_X_ Func. 1 ___ Func. 4 ___ Func. 2 ___ Func. 5 ___ Func. 3	MW-111

Training Phase	Depth of Coverage	Learning Difficulty	Content Volatility
_X_ Basic ___ Advanced	_X_ Overview ___ Detail ___ Build Skill	___ High ___ Medium _X_ Low	___ High _X_ Medium ___ Low

Courses Available   [X] No   [ ] Yes   [ ] Use As Is   [ ] Modify   %

Title _____   No. _____

Development Method	Preliminary Delivery Strategy	Estimated Length
___ Training Development Standards _X_ Modified Development Process	Self-paced	110 pages

Preliminary Content Listing (not all-inclusive)

- **Overview of the Job Model**
  - Objectives
  - Priorities
  - Key issues
  - Key tools
  - Systems
  - Work progress
  - Internal/External projects

- **Organization Overview (By Division)**

- **Interface Organizations (By Division)**
  - Marketing
  - Human Resources
  - Support Staff
  - Etc.

- **Installation and Maintenance Function Overview**

- **Interview Guide**
  - Superior
  - Peers
  - Subordinates

- **Job Assignments**

- **Checklists**

- **Resource Guide (By Division)**

- Curriculum Overview

- Administrative Systems Overview

- Guide to Records, Reports, and Forms used by a Mid-level Manager.

Design by Svenson & Wallace, Inc. • Naperville, Illinois • (312) 416-3323

Figure 12-9 Module Definition Sheet

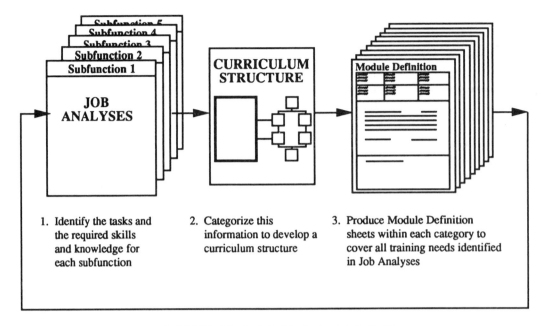

1. Identify the tasks and the required skills and knowledge for each subfunction

2. Categorize this information to develop a curriculum structure

3. Produce Module Definition sheets within each category to cover all training needs identified in Job Analyses

4. Link Modules back to Job Analyses to indicate which modules relate to which training/skill and knowledge requirements

Figure 12-10   Curriculum Structure Process

Step 7. Steering Committee Review

The steering committee or curriculum council now has enough data needed to review the draft curriculum architecture and module definitions and establish priorities for developing or acquiring the modules. It may also, at this same meeting, review and help with implementation issues. At this meeting, the steering committee should become a permanent curriculum council to oversee the implementation and evolution of the curriculum and to provide a point of accountability for the effectiveness of the training. Figure 12-12 presents a sample agenda for the third steering committee meeting.

In the future, the job analysis data and knowledge and skills analysis data should be reviewed once a year for changes, and the curriculum architecture and module definitions should be brought up to date. Doing so is easier if all the data is stored in a database.

SUMMARY

We have presented a method for systematically designing curriculum architectures to accommodate the training requirements identified in chapter 11. The steps in this process are as follows:

	Required	Days	Recommended	Days	Electives	Days
New Appointee **1st Year** Average Amount of Training = 16-20 days	• Project Management (40001)	5	• Conducting Meetings (99015)	1	• Other Personal and Management Skills	(3)
	• Project Management Tools (91401)	1	• Influence Management (99019)	2		
	• Cost Estimation/BOM (HW) (91403)	0.5				
	• Software Change Control Tools (SW) (91404)	1	• Principles of Contemporary Management			
	• Project Estimation Tools (SW) (91405)	1	• New Manager Orientation			
	• Product Dev. Process Overview (12002)	0.25				
	• TPM	1				
	• Process Management	2.5				
2nd Year Average Amount of Training = 13 days	Targeted Selection	2-3	• Negotiation (99012)	1-2	• Technical and Personal and Management Skills as required	(3)
			• Group Dynamics (99020)	2		
			• Team Building (99035)	2		
			• Leadership and Leadership Styles (99027)	2		
Experienced Average Amount of Training = 10 days/year					• Technical and Personal and Management Skills as required	(10)/ year

Figure 12-11 Typical Learning Path

---

1. Review Curriculum Architecture Design
2. Review Module definitions
3. Establish priorities for courseware development
4. Discuss continuing role as a standing Curriculum Advisory Council

---

Figure 12-12   Steering Committee Review Agenda

☐   Establish design criteria in conjunction with the steering committee.

☐   Create the curriculum structure, accounting for

- Orientation
  - To the company
  - To the division
  - To the job
- Job related skills
- Generic skills
  - Communication
  - Management
  - Office tools, etc.

☐   Map the training requirements into the structure.

☐   Evaluate the existing available training.

- What is available as is?
- What can be modified or adapted?

☐   Define modules and link back to job models and knowledge/skill matrices.

☐   Define typical learning paths.

- New entry people in each job function
- One- to two-year people in each job function
- Three-plus-year people in each job function

☐   Review with the steering committee

- Curriculum architecture design
- Module definition
- Priorities for courseware development
- The steering committee's continuing role as the curriculum advisory council.

13

DELIVERY STRATEGIES

One of the most intriguing issues in designing a world-class training system is planning the delivery strategy mix. A delivery strategy is an alternative means of delivering instruction. Centralized classroom training led by an instructor is a totally different strategy than instruction on a personal computer at the worksite driven by the individual learner. In this chapter, we catalog the major delivery strategies, give a brief description of each, discuss the strategic implications of each, compare the pros and cons for various applications, and show you how to set up a decision guide for selecting delivery strategies appropriate to your situation.

The delivery strategies that people are most familiar with are unstructured, informal, on-the-job training and centralized, group-paced lecture and lab training. There are many others, listed in Figure 13-1. These strategies are often used in various combinations, so they do not necessarily represent a unique list of distinct strategies.

The delivery strategies have major implications for

- Cost of developing and maintaining the courseware

- Instructional effectiveness

- Scheduling flexibility

- Cost of delivery

- Trainee time away from the job

- Trainee exposure to corporate culture and contacts outside trainee's own work environment

By Location

- Centralized (e.g., Corporate Education Center)
- Regional (e.g., Southwest Region, Europe, etc.)
- Work location (e.g., in or near a plant or group of offices)
- Centralized instructors, distributed class (e.g., video teleconference)

By Instructional Modality

Group-paced, instructor driven:
- Lecture/discussion
- Case group
- Laboratory
- Video

Self-paced:
- Conventional paper-and-pencil media
- Computer based and interactive videodisc
- Simulator
- Laboratory
- Video
- Expert systems
- Embedded (as in help screens on a computerized order entry system)
- Tutorials
- Structured OJT
- Unstructured OJT and work assignments

Figure 13-1 Delivery Strategies List

- Control of results
- Administrative support systems required
- Skills required of courseware developers and instructors.

Factors to consider in determining the appropriate delivery strategy mix include

- Target audience size
- Content and objectives of the training program
- Geographical dispersion of the target audience
- Education level of the target audience
- Maturity of the corporate learning culture
- Stability of the content
- Consequences of taking trainees away from the job.

Computer-based interactive videodisc training can be a highly effective, efficient way to train large numbers of people on standard tasks (e.g., a computer company with thousands of sales representatives to train each year on new product releases). This type of training can save up to half the trainee time (more if you save travel time), all the instructor time, and it guarantees that all trainees completing the program have mastered each of the training objectives. These benefits are balanced by the high cost of developing the software and the cost of delivery stations distributed to the sales offices. Video teleconferencing is another effective way of providing information-based training, such as training all managers in a corporation to administer a new drug testing policy. Key managers at all sites having a downlink can attend a live session, which is videotaped and then repeated locally for all other managers and supervisors within a week or two.

In the following sections, we discuss each of the major training strategies as a prelude to the courseware development and delivery planning information in chapters 14 and 15.

STRATEGIES BY LOCATION

Centralized Training at the Corporate Education Center

The advantages of centralized training at a corporate education center include:

- Exposure of trainees to peers from other parts of the Corporation

- Communication of corporate culture and values

- Efficient use of corporate experts and notables in the training programs

- Efficiencies for low-volume training of distributed target audience

- Efficiencies for teaching where high cost labs or simulators are required

- Provisions for excellent control over instructional quality

- Efficient use of instructors

- Efficient use of the training facility.

The disadvantages and limitations of centralized training include

- High cost of trainee travel

- Trainee travel time

- Limited capacity to train large numbers quickly

- Content not adaptable to local needs

- Preclusion of direct involvement of local management.

Appropriate applications include

- Training with high cost lab equipment and simulators
- Low volume training
- Middle management and executive education and training
- Professional and specialist training
- Corporate orientation for new professional and managerial employees.

Corporate education centers were in vogue in the late 1960s through the 1970s. During the 1980s, there was a move to decentralize training, which followed the trends of decentralizing corporations, downsizing, and cutting corporate overhead staffs. Now we are seeing a reawakening of interest in the corporate education center as a vehicle for transmitting corporate culture, providing synergy among decentralized business units, providing a visible focal point for learning in the corporation, and providing high-cost, low volume training that can only be provided effectively at a central location. We believe that every large organization, certainly all of the top 500 industrial, and the top 500 service companies, can make a case for a corporate education center.

Training At or Near the Worksite

The advantages of worksite training include

- No trainee travel and living expenses
- Accommodations for large numbers of trainees
- Training on the trainees' actual equipment, files, tools, etc.
- Training for the trainees by their supervisor or others who carry their respect and whose word has authority in their location
- Work teams that can be trained as a unit
- Local content requirements that can be met precisely
- Less trainee time away from the job
- More transfer of new skills to actual job performance.

Disadvantages and limitations of worksite training include

- Some training is too expensive to provide locally because high-cost equipment is required or because there are not enough trainees.
- If there are not enough trainees, people who need training may have to wait too long for a class to be scheduled.

- Many worksites lack sufficient training expertise and support infrastructure to do a quality job.

Examples of appropriate uses of jobsite training include

- Jobsite orientation
- Structured OJT to learn basic job tasks and skills
- Team training
- Any training where there are large numbers of trainees at the site
- Embedded training in production systems
- Training on site-specific content
- Individualized learning through computer-based, self-paced, video, and other self-paced modalities
- Video teleconferencing.

The advances in computer and telecommunications technology are making it more feasible to deliver high quality instruction at the local site with centralized control over content and quality. Furthermore, the accelerating pace of change is forcing more locations to install a high quality local training infrastructure. The lion's share of all training in the twenty-first century will be provided at or near the worksite.

Regional Training Centers

Organizations that have large numbers of trainees dispersed over the globe or even domestically may find it an economic and practical necessity to open regional training centers. The major advantages over the centralized approach include

- Limiting travel time and cost
- Accommodating regional differences
- Keeping the corporate education center to a manageable size.

The principal disadvantages include

- Duplicate curriculum and faculty required at each center
- Difficulty of maintaining control of content integrity and quality
- Some training populations which will be too small to provide efficient and timely training (ten trainees per year is only enough to run one undersized class per year).

Third-Party Locations (Universities, Vendor Schools, Etc.)

Training by third party providers is growing and will continue to grow. For many training situations, this is the supplier of choice. Advantages of third party training locations include

- The provider assumes the cost of developing the courseware.
- The provider may have specialized expertise unavailable internally.
- Trainees gain exposure to peers from other organizations.
- It may be the only way to provide trainers for specialists where the trainee population is insufficient to justify mounting an internal training program.
- The provider may have made the investment in expensive lab equipment or simulators.
- The provider brings in knowledge, skills, and practices not available internally.

Disadvantages and limitations of third party training include

- Lack of control of content and instructional quality
- Exposure of employees to employment opportunities elsewhere
- Content not tailored to internal needs
- Travel and living expenses.

Examples of appropriate use of third party training include

- Executive education
- Specialist training and continuing education
- Any trainee group where the population is insufficient to justify an internal training program
- Training on vendor-provided hardware, software, systems and technology.

STRATEGIES BY INSTRUCTIONAL MODALITY

Group paced, Instructor driven; Lecture and Discussion

The major advantages of this mode include

- Low courseware development cost
- Easy to accommodate rapid changes in content.

The disadvantages include

- More difficult for trainees to develop mastery of skills
- Relatively low retention rate.

Examples of appropriate uses include

- Conceptual overviews
- Training which is largely information transfer
- In combination with other modes to prepare trainees for casework, simulation, or other practice exercises.

This is the most overused and abused training modality. Companies fall back on it because it is cheap and easy. It costs little to put a poorly prepared expert in front of a class to lecture. We believe that many people, including highly placed executives and managers, are negative about training because this is the only form of training they have ever experienced.

On the positive side, the lecture and discussion method can produce outstanding results for the class of situations it fits best and when the instruction has been well developed and is presented by a qualified instructor.

Group paced, Instructor driven: Casegroup and Simulation

In this strategy, a group of trainees is engaged in an exercise to analyze a case or simulate some actual performance. This can be one of the most powerful forms of training. Examples of appropriate application include

- Operating team training on a nuclear power plant simulator
- War games
- Business simulations
- Football scrimmage
- Case problems
- Team-building exercises
- A symphony rehearsal.

In this type of training, the instructor sets up the situation, possibly through a lecture; stands back and acts as a resource or facilitator as the learning team works through its problem; and then critiques their performance. The model, in this case, is the sports team in training with its coaching staff.

The advantages of this modality include

- Develops skills in handling realistic job situation
- A team can be trained to work together in a coordinated way.
- High probability of transfer of skills to job performance (if skills are relevant to the job)
- Team members help and reinforce each others' learning.
- Many trainees find this form of learning to be more fun and more stimulating than other forms.

The disadvantages include

- Courseware development can be expensive.
- It is difficult to measure the performance of individual trainees.

This form of training which has its origins in military and sports training thousands of years ago, is among the most effective means we have, yet it remains grossly underutilized by corporate education systems. It seems, we would prefer to subject the football team to an all-day lecture and discussion rather than have it out on the field running plays and practicing blocking and tackling.

Group paced, Instructor driven: Laboratory

The lab group is really just another variant of case group and simulation training. The lab is a simulator of some real world situation where trainees can practice without risk of damaging operating equipment or disrupting its operation. Appropriate examples of this type of training include

- Installation, servicing, and repair of equipment and software (from small radios to mainframe computers)
- Using analytical chemistry equipment
- Operating a printing press.

Group paced, Instructor driven: Video

This strategy has a couple of variants. In the simplest one, videotape is used with a class in lieu of a lecture to present information, demonstrate something, or dramatize something. The instructor then facilitates discussion, casework, and testing. One good example of this is training that was developed for people working in a chain of lumber and hardware stores. The training center developed a library of video-based training programs, trained local trainers to administer the training, and reproduced copies for each store. This permitted a consistent message, with effective role plays and demonstration available at every store. Local supervisors administer the training which predisposes them to reinforce the skills and principles in their daily supervision around the store.

The other main variation is the interactive video teleconference. This takes place in a video classroom where there is an instructor and sometimes a live class. Perhaps the best example of this is National Technological University (NTU), which broadcasts graduate-level and noncredit engineering courses from about twenty of the top universities and corporate transmitting sites to engineers located in the premier corporations and government labs around the United States. Trainees do homework and lab exercises, and they complete tests which are graded by centralized instructors.

Advantages of video instruction include

- Fast distribution to a large target audience

- Centralized control over content and quality

- No trainee travel and living cost

- No instructor travel and living cost

- Sessions can be taped for reuse

- Most people have become accustomed to watching TV as a means of acquiring information.

Disadvantages of video instruction include

- High production cost

- Video teleconferencing requires a network to be in place with video studio classrooms, uplinks, satellite transponders, downlinks, and video classrooms at receiving location

- Limited direct interaction between the expert instructors and trainee

- People's standard of quality for TV programs is commercial production which is very expensive.

Examples of appropriate application include

- Video demonstration of equipment or physical tasks

- Role plays of situation

- Messages from corporate officers or other notables
- An alternative to centralized training for management and professional continuing education.

With the widespread availability and low cost of VCRs, one of the main impediments to distributing videos to local sites has virtually vanished. Many professionals and managers are more than willing to take tapes home for viewing on their personal equipment.

Self-paced: Conventional Paper-and-Pencil Media

In this type of training, the trainee uses self-instructional textbooks or workbooks as the major structuring device for the training. The text may contain learning material, or it may direct the trainee to other sources. At a minimum, the text contains objectives, directions, exercises and tests.

Advantages of this form of instruction include

- Learning proceeds at one's own pace; large average time savings are possible
- Inexpensive to reproduce
- Scheduling flexibility
- Can be used in a learning center, at the jobsite, or for home study
- Can be used effectively with audio and video media and with lab and simulator training.

Disadvantages include

- Good material is expensive to develop.
- If self-administered
  - Low completion rates
  - Trainees get stuck and have nowhere to turn.
- If not well prepared, this type of instruction can be very boring, instilling an aversion to training.
- Difficult for trainees who are not accustomed to reading for long periods.

Appropriate application examples include

- Conceptual, informational content
- Training in nonphysical skills such as math, reading blueprints, flow charting

- Training for physical tasks such as automotive repair when used together with other media, especially video and lab or simulator training.

During the 1970s, the Bell System Plant Training Advisory Board discovered self-paced instruction. Some of their early experiments with it produced dramatic results. Encouraged by these successes, they developed hundreds of self-paced courses over a fifteen-year period. Some of these programs were outstanding examples of effective instruction. Some, on the other hand, put people who were used to working with their hands into self-paced learning stations where they had to read material all day that was not written to be interesting. Because of this experience, large numbers of people turned sour on self-paced instruction.

Self-paced, Computer-Based and Interactive Videodisc

In this strategy, the computer manages the instructional process and may also deliver the content. The power of the computer makes "branching" easier than it is with conventional self-paced training. In a branching system, the computer checks the knowledge and skill level of the trainee entering the program and branches the trainee around the lessons that are not needed. If a trainee is having trouble mastering a skill, the computer branches him or her into practice problems or more basic explanations, depending on the computer's diagnosis of the learning difficulty.

Coupling CBT (computer-based training) with videodisc technology provides an extremely powerful combination called interactive videodisc training. Here, the videodisc can contain up to 50,000 separately addressable video images, which can be individually accessed like slides or run sequentially like a videotape. A demonstration of a manual procedure can be slowed down, stopped, or rerun under trainee control.

At the low end of CBT, the computer is used like an electronic book: It simply presents pages of information. At the high end is extremely sophisticated real-job performance.

Advantages of this form of instruction include

- Learning proceeds at trainee's pace; large average time savings are available.

- The computer measures trainee learning by administering online mastery tests.

- Branching is more easily accomplished than with a paper-based self instructional program.

- The trainee is interacting with a system that has the feel of a live tutor.

- Trainees get immediate feedback on their performance, making corrections of errors quicker and learning faster.

- Many trainees today are computer literate and are used to learning from TV.

- High quality training materials can be quickly sent to geographically dispersed sites.

Disadvantages include

- High cost of developing the courseware
- High cost of maintaining the courseware when content changes
- Requires an investment in individual learning stations
- Requires specialized courseware development skills.

Appropriate application examples include

- Subjects with low content volatilities (e.g., basic prerequisites that do not change very fast)
- Subjects where drill and practice enhances learning and builds trainee confidence
- Conceptual knowledge
- Subjects where the number of trainees is large enough that delivery savings will override the high cost of development
- Subjects where large numbers of people need the same training at once (e.g., new product releases)
- Demonstrations of physical operation (e.g., auto maintenance)
- Training on procedures, especially where forms and information are used
- Simulation (e.g., pilot training to save time in expensive flight simulators).

As computers and videodisc technology continue to evolve and as authoring systems get easier to use, the array of application for this strategy will multiply. A growing percentage of workers have PCs or workstations that can alternately be used as learning stations. Pressures to keep employees at the jobsite and to train everyone quickly on new products and systems will further accelerate the deployment of CBT.

Self-paced: Laboratory

This is a variation on the use of labs for group-paced training. The lab, again, is essentially a simulation of some real world environment such as telephone poles to climb, a practice tower for fire fighers, or a radio repair station.

Advantages include

- The self-paced lab is a powerful method for training individuals when some physical skills must be acquired.

- Each skill can be practiced until mastered.

- High probability of successful skill transference to the job

- Can be used in combination with CBT or other conventional self-paced media

- Trainees like it because they can easily understand the relevance to their job.

Disadvantages include

- High cost of lab equipment and maintenance

- May require lower student/instructor ratio than other forms of training

- May require trainee travel to the lab site.

Examples of appropriate applications include

- Equipment installation

- Equipment operation

- Equipment maintenance

- Machine tool operation

- Programming of robots or programmable logic controllers

- Troubleshooting complex systems.

There are many fine examples of this strategy in operation. Telephone companies make extensive use of it in training their technical workforces. Equipment suppliers use it to train their own service people and also to train their customers. Military training makes extensive use of this strategy.

Self-Paced: Simulators

Simulators are a high-fidelity extension of the lab concept. The idea is to replicate as closely as possible some real environment like an airplane cockpit, the inside of a tank, an airport flight control room, or a nuclear power plant control room. The trainees are provided with visual, auditory and other sensory stimuli that may occur in a real job situation. They can be checked out on a complex array of operations, tasks, skills, and responses in a safe environment where neither people nor equipment will be hurt by errors.

Advantages include

- High-level simulation provides maximum assurance that skills will transfer to actual job performance.

- Can be used to practice skills seldom or never needed on the real job, such as flying a plane with two engines out, or responding to a nuclear reactor failure.

- Builds trainee confidence through realistic practice.

- Reduces risk of human error.

Disadvantages include

- High cost of simulators and maintenance

- Low trainee/instructor ratio

- Trainee travel to simulators.

Appropriate applications examples include

- Pilot training

- Nuclear power plant operation

- Operation of military, aircraft, tanks, etc.

- Maritime navigation and ship operation.

The airlines, the military and the nuclear power industry have all made impressive application of this delivery strategy. Though expensive, the stakes associated with human error far outweigh the cost of simulator training.

Self-Paced: Expert Systems

Expert systems have terrific educational potential. They can simulate the collected knowledge and experience of the best experts in any field. Once developed, an expert system can be replicated to serve as an expert tutor for large numbers of trainees who may be geographically dispersed.

Advantages include

- Economizes on the use of scarce instructor expertise

- Can be queried by trainees for suggested responses to an almost unlimited variety of conditions.

Disadvantages include

- Expensive to develop
- Requires specialized expertise to develop
- Limitations in the state of the technology
- Lack of awareness of the technology.

Appropriate application examples include

- Complex diagnostic situations
    - Oil exploration
    - Systems troubleshooting
    - Medical diagnosis
- Complex situational analysis
    - Systems selling
    - Military situations
    - Competitive business planning.

This relatively new technology is just coming into its own and will add a powerful new alternative to the educational tool kit in the next decade.

Self-Paced: Embedded Training

Embedded training comes as part of a product. The copying machine in your office has help screens, instruction diagrams, and diagnostics built in. A proficient PC user can learn a new piece of software by quickly scanning the manual and learning online using help screens and built-in diagnostics. As more information technology is built into production equipment and other products and systems, the opportunity to build in the capability for the machine to teach its operators and maintainers increases. This technology permits the integration of what used to be an operators' manual, a maintenance manual, job aids, and training into a single, menu-driven system. Systems with embedded training are user friendly.

Advantages of embedded training include

- Minimizes training time away from the job
- Learning takes place in the context of doing the work; hence, there is good transference to actual performance.
- Minimizes problems due to forgetting
- Saves instructor costs and expensive training facilities.

Disadvantages include

- May be expensive to develop
- Adds to the cost of the product or machine
- Requires cooperation between system designers and developers and training specialists throughout the design and development of the system
- Errors during on-line learning may disrupt production or be dangerous.

Appropriate application examples include

- Computer software systems
- Operation and maintenance of hardware systems
- Enhanced diagnostics
- Feedback to operators on incorrect procedures (e.g., failing to fasten a seat belt before operating a car).

During the last half of the 1980s, Apple Computer Corporation won significant market share for business applications of its Macintosh® line of personal computers because the computers and the software that run on them are easy to learn and use. This system is preferred by thousands of customers over others that may be more technically capable or lower priced. We can expect to see embedded training and user friendliness emerge as a major competitive strategy as information technology grows more powerful, less expensive, and more ubiquitous.

Self-Paced: Tutorials

Tutorials are a useful strategy for transferring specialized knowledge and skills to a small group of specialists in R&D labs or corporate staffs. The tutorial strategy works like this:

- A training specialist meets with the group that desires to acquire the new competencies.
- The group broadly identifies its learning objectives.
- It identifies the best sources of the knowledge (e.g., university researchers, consultants, etc.).
- A meeting is arranged with the expert sources where specific learning objectives are developed, a sequence of learning activities is planned, and roles are assigned to the players
- The learning program is carried out with support from training specialists.

Advantages include

- Avoids expensive courseware development
- Can be carried out very quickly
- Efficient use of expert sources
- Efficient and effective knowledge and skills transfer to small numbers of trainees.

Disadvantages include

- Not practical for large numbers of trainees
- Difficult to repeat
- Dependent on expert sources.

Appropriate applications include

- Transfer of knowledge to small groups
- Transfer of quality and process improvement.

In the 1980s Alcoa Laboratories included this strategy in its in-house education system as a means of transferring leading edge science and technology to small groups of R&D professionals. Many companies are using variations of this strategy for transferring process improvements from one plant or operation to another. (The medical community uses this strategy for moving new procedures from research into clinical practice.) This strategy works particularly well with groups of professionals such as scientists, engineers, and doctors who have highly developed learning skills.

Self-Paced: Structured OJT

On-the-job training has gotten an undeservedly poor reputation because so many people have been thrown into jobs, given a pile of manuals, and told not to worry, that they will soon figure out what to do. This unstructured OJT is responsible for much loss of productivity and poor performance and is responsible for worker frustration and many serious accidents. Structured OJT, in contrast, involves establishing individual learning, objectives, providing expert coaches or mentors to support learning and fully supporting the trainee in learning, practicing, and mastering skills while in the job situation.

Advantages include

- Can be much less expensive than other learning strategies
- High probability of transfer of new skills to actual job performance

- Recognition for people chosen as coaches or mentors
- Trainees have built-in support system
- Trainees know that what they are learning is exactly what their management and peers need them to learn.

Disadvantages include

- Requires strong management support and awareness of learning process
- Harder to control quality of instruction than offline training
- May be disruptive to production process
- May be too risky where human error carries high stakes
- Not very effective for conceptual learning (e.g., theory of hydraulics)
- Some procedures and skills are only required in unusual or emergency situations that are undesirable or impossible to create online
- Low instructor/trainee ratio (often one on one) interferes with production productivity.

Appropriate application examples include

- Training in production and maintenance tasks
- Training of professionals such as geologists and engineers to apply theoretical knowledge in real tasks
- Training of new workers by their work team.

Structured OJT requires strong cooperation between training specialists and line management to identify tasks and skills, and develop learning objectives, develop learning materials, develop and apply performance tests that measure the acquisition of new skills. In many operations, line management is so focused on production problems that proper attention to high quality OJT is difficult if not impossible. The growing popularity of Total Quality Management and self-managing work teams will make structured OJT a viable and preferred strategy for many situations.

DELIVERY STRATEGY DECISION GUIDE

The organizations that have done the best job of using a balanced mix of delivery strategies have decision guides that help select the delivery strategy to be used for individual instructional situations. Some of the best of these decision guides are mechanized to permit quick and easy cost trade-offs to be analyzed. These decision guides can be spreadsheet models, which provide

- Cost
- Delivery volume
- Timing information

for a variety of location and strategy scenarios to enable objective decisions about the trade-offs of various options.

Figure 13-2 provides a map of one spreadsheet model that we have developed for making these kinds of delivery decisions.

SUMMARY

There are many possible delivery strategies that can be used in providing training. This chapter provided an overview of some of the major strategies and their important features and benefits. The strategies include

☐ By location
- Centralized
- Regional
- Work location
- Centralized instructors, distributed class

☐ By instructional modality
- Group-paced instructor-led lecture and discussion
- Group-paced instructor-led case group
- Group-paced instructor-led laboratory
- Group-paced instructor-led video
- Self-paced conventional paper-and-pencil media
- Self-paced computer-based and interactive video disc
- Self-paced simulator
- Self-paced laboratory
- Self-paced video
- Self-paced expert systems

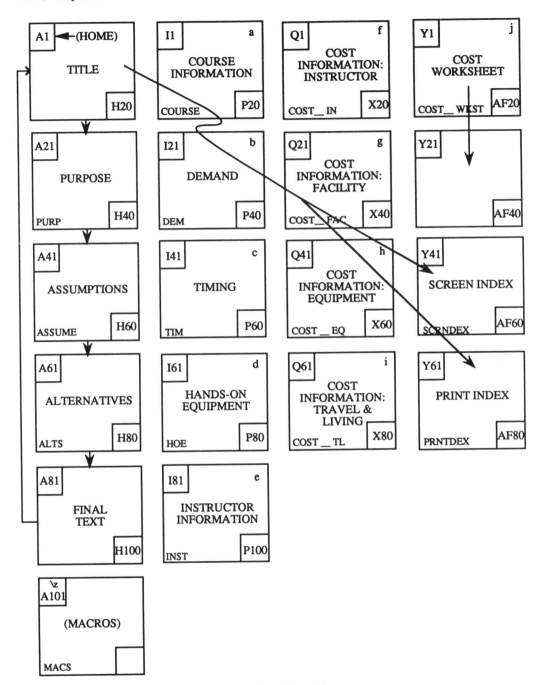

Figure 13-2 Training Delivery Decision Model

- • Self-paced embedded

- • Self-paced tutorials

- • Self-paced structured OJT

- • Self-paced unstructured OJT and work assignments

☐ A spreadsheet-based decision model that accounts for

- • Cost

- • Timing

- • Location

- • Strategy.

The variables of your specific situation will be factors in determining which strategy will work best for you.

Chapter 15 provides help on determining delivery volume, which is a factor in choosing appropriate delivery strategies.

14

STRATEGIES AND PLAN FOR CURRICULUM DEVELOPMENT AND ACQUISITION

In this chapter, we provide you with a methodology for developing strategies and plans for developing and/or acquiring the course materials required to meet the forecasted delivery need. The information in this chapter links tightly with chapter 13, "Delivery Strategies," and chapter 15, "Delivery Plan." You need to have some sense of the delivery strategies you intend to use, as they will have a direct bearing on your course development and acquisition decisions. You should also have some idea of the need for various types of training because it will affect these decisions.

Making these decisions about delivery and development strategies and plans is not a linear process. In writing it down, we are somewhat forced to make it appear linear, but in reality the process is iterative, with each piece influencing the other and sending you back to look at earlier pieces. It is like writing down the process for designing a building—you can make the process look somewhat linear, but an experienced architect already has some idea of what the building looks like and how much it will cost before he or she begins the design. As you gain experience with the process, you will have more knowledge about it and the process will be greatly simplified.

Figure 14-1 shows how the various pieces of the process link together and affect each other.

The final output you are trying to produce is the development plan, which spells out the number of person days or hours to be spent on development for

- Core (or base) curriculum
- Change-driven curriculum
- Courseware maintenance

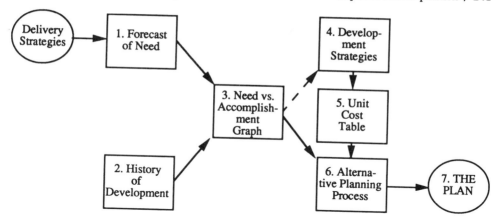

Figure 14-1 Course Development and Acquisition Planning Process

- Courseware replacements
- Opportunity conversions

for each functional curriculum for each year of the plan.
This chapter is organized as follows:

- Definition of curriculum categories
- Forecast of development need by category
- Unit cost assumptions
- Plan development.

DEFINITION OF CURRICULUM CATEGORIES

There are five kinds of course development activities to be considered in long-range planning:

- *Core curriculum:* Development of all the courses required for people entering the discipline to become completely competent at their assigned tasks
- *Change driven:* Development of courses required to keep people competent in the face of changing tasks, methods, technology, policy, etc.
- *Course maintenance:* Updating, repair, and improvement of existing courses
- *Replacement:* Complete redevelopment of courses which are not worth attempting to maintain

- *Opportunity conversion:* Alteration of a course or group of courses to capitalize on an opportunity, such as major delivery savings offered by computer-based instruction.

FORECAST OF DEVELOPMENT NEED BY CATEGORY

For each of these five categories, you forecast the amount of development needed. The following sections provide the steps for doing that.

Core curriculum

- Revisit the curriculum architecture (if you have one) and identify all the courses that are not developed or available.
- If you do not have a curriculum architecture, identify from the needs analysis data which courses are needed to teach people their basic jobs.
- Review priorities for development.
- Add up the total number of days of training to be developed (do these for each curriculum).
- Scan across all curriculums. Your forecast equals the total amount of core curriculum to be developed between now and eternity.

Change-driven curriculum

- Revisit the needs analysis and identify all courses needed to support future changes (new systems, new products, new technology, reorganization of work, regulatory change, corporate initiatives such as TQM, etc.).
- Do this for all identifiable changes across all curriculums. *Note:* Do this for next year only, because it is our experience that you can never foresee beyond one year all the changes that will hit, but you can come close for the next year. (After one or more years experience, you can begin to forecast using a corrective factor based on your experience with rates of change.)
- You can then forecast the rate of change for each curriculum over the forecast period.
  - Your simplest assumption is that the rate of change will stay about the same next year.
  - Change might go faster because of factors like an increasing R&D budget or major regulatory changes on the horizon or entering an era of major corporate change.
  - Change might go slower because you have just completed a major overhaul

of technology and therefore see static technological change over the next five years.

You want to end up with a number chart for the rate of change like the one shown in Figure 14-2. In this example, the rate of change for curriculum A is expected to increase by 40 percent four years from now and is greatly affected by an increase in R&D. Curriculum B is expected to remain the same (10 percent change per year). The rate of change for curriculum C is expected to slow down somewhat.

When you have the rate of change for each curriculum for each year, you can multiply year 1 volume by the rate of change for each curriculum for each year to get total expected volume of change-driven training for each curriculum for each year, as shown in Figure 14-3.

One way you can shortcut this process is to work with current volume and projected volume rather than rate of change, though this is not as precise. Either way, however, there is a certain amount of guessing and assuming, but your guesses and assumptions should be based on econometrics and leading indicators. The important thing is that the process forces you to think about relevant factors and impacts and issues on the horizon.

Maintenance

- One of the most overlooked areas in the course development budget is the cost of maintaining already existing courses. Only a minority of training departments that we are familiar with have a budget for maintenance, and even fewer have an adequate method for forecasting it. But in a mature curriculum, maintenance is going to eat the majority of your course development budget, so you had better learn how to forecast it if you are going to keep a viable curriculum. If you are just getting started developing a curriculum, maintenance will not be a big deal for the first two to three years, but after that it can eat you alive.

  Some of the things that drive course maintenance are
- Content changes—new products, technology, technical specifications, etc.
- Instructional design improvements
- Changing target audience(s)

CURRICULUM		YEAR 1	YEAR 2	YEAR 3	YEAR 4	YEAR 5
	A	1.00	1.10	1.20	1.30	1.40
	B	1.00	1.00	1.00	1.00	1.00
	C	1.00	0.90	0.80	0.80	0.80
	:					
	:					
	:					
	:					
	N	1.00				

Figure 14-2   Change-Driven Curriculum Rate of Change

YR 1 Volume
a
b
c
d · · · · · ·
n

X

	Rate of Change				
	1	2	3	4	5
A	1.00	1.10	1.20	1.30	1.40
B	1.00	1.00	1.00	1.00	1.00
C	1.00	0.90	0.80	0.80	0.80
D · · · · · ·	1.00				
N	1.00				

=

	Forecasted Volume				
	1	2	3	4	5
A	a	1.1a	1.2a	1.3a	1.4a
B	b	b	b	b	b
C	c	.9c	.8c	.8c	.8c
D	d				
· · · · · ·					
N	n				

Figure 14-3 Change-Driven Volume Forecast

- Different starting skills and knowledge
- Different levels of need for end competencies (e.g., cross-training)
- Cosmetic improvement of materials
  - Print media
  - Slides
  - Videos
  - Etc.

There are too many factors, and they are too varied to forecast with any real accuracy. You cannot look at all these details and forecast the amount of work you have to do based on that. Our experience is that you end up in a nightmare when you do so.

The method we use to forecast maintenance requirements is called the Investment Base Method. It was developed by one of this book's authors, Ray Svenson, when he was at Bell System Center for Technical Education (BSCTE) in the early 1970s. In 1972, the center had been running for four years. Complaints were piling up from the instructors that courses were out of date and student feedback confirmed it. There was a theory that the instructors were responsible for maintaining their own courses, but their delivery schedules were packed so tightly that there was less and less time for maintenance. In addition, the instructors were not measured on the amount of maintenance they did, but on the amount of delivery, so maintenance did not get done. Ray interviewed all the instructors and came up with an estimated maintenance need for 1973 of $250,000, and he sold this requirement to the board. In 1974, the estimated need was $500,000, and Ray realized he was going to need a better argument to convince the board. That was when he came up with the Investment Base idea.

Basically, the Investment Base equals the replacement cost of the existing curriculum. In 1974 Ray asked, "What is the investment value of this curriculum?" The answer was $5 million. Ray argued that it is not unreasonable to assume 10 percent change of curriculum every year just because of technology change. The board responded well to this argument because it was used to the idea of spending a percentage of money each year to protect capital investments. The board then decided to forecast maintenance over the next five-year period after the amount of courseware in the curriculum was forecasted, and it used a 10 percent factor as a starting place for developing a maintenance budget. At the same time, the board started a Controlled Quality Management Program for the courseware. That program forced the instructors in each curriculum to go through the courses and estimate maintenance for every year for all the drivers of maintenance, and price what it would take to do that. The board made it mandatory to put in these changes, or it would shut down the courses. The total requirements were then added up, and it was decided that the maintenance budget was short by about 50 percent. So the board went to 15 percent as an estimating factor and gradually built up to 17 percent by tracking the percentage of important and worthwhile maintenance being done given the current budget.

We have found that this 15 percent factor can be used as a starting point for maintenance in most curriculums. However, this is another example where you can estimate one year ahead, but then will need to develop correction factors for future years based on your experience. In addition, you do not want to make the mistake of using this number as a flat rate for each individual course. Some courses will need 40 percent maintenance in a given year, while others will not need any. You are trying to define the size of the overall pot. Then the various instructors and instructor teams will have to fight for their share of the maintenance pot once you have defined its size.

This system for incorporating maintenance costs is a major contribution to course development budgeting, particularly for mature organizations that have been around for five or more years. Most of these organizations have huge piles of courseware rotting on shelves but do not know how to fix it. Most of our clients are well aware of this problem, but do not know how to get started.

The steps you need to take for developing your maintenance budget are as follows:

- Add up the replacement cost of course material in the existing curriculum for each type of delivery strategy (e.g., number of days of group-paced, number of days of computer-based, etc.) because the replacement cost of each delivery strategy is different, and therefore so is the maintenance cost.

- Estimate the percentage of replacement cost that will be required if you are going to do a decent job of maintenance. The best way to do this is to have instructors do an inventory of existing courses and build your estimate based on that. However, for lack of better data or if you do not want to take the time, you can use 10 to 15 percent. Some of our clients have recognized that they have not done maintenance for the last five years and they know the existing courseware is poor, so they start at 20 to 25 percent, hoping to work this number down to 10 to 15 percent over the five-year period.

- Forecast the total amount of training in the curriculum over the five-year forecasting period. *Note:* You cannot actually carry this step out until you have figured out your development scenarios (which we cover later in this chapter), because for each scenario you will have a different amount of maintenance to do, depending on how much courseware is in place.

Replacement

- The idea behind replacement is that at some point you will realize that a particular course is now ten years old, over the years incremental changes have been made to it, but it now looks like an inner tube with twenty patches on it. Yes, it holds air, but it is time to replace it with a new tubeless tire. The trick in this situation is to figure out the rate at which these kinds of replacements will occur. You do this as follows:

- Go back and get a history of all courses that have been replaced and see what their age was at replacement. You may find that replacement is spread out over a range, such as two to ten years of age, but you determine the mean or average age is seven years.

- You can then develop a curriculum aging chart for the number of courses in the curriculum that are older than the aging factor determined in the previous step.

- Make the assumption that you are going to replace those, and then assume that resource requirements to replace the courses are approximately the same as those for developing new courses. (You might want to give yourself 10 to 20 percent for use of materials, but you will still need to go back and do a job analysis, etc., on the entire course.)

If you want to add a layer of sophistication to this, you can come up with different aging factors for each curriculum, because some curriculums are more volatile than others. For instance, basic math courses are normally fairly static, while the technology of digital communications is volatile. (This is true for maintenance as well.) As another example, basic personal and managerial skills do not change very quickly unless you follow the fads.

Opportunity conversions

The most common examples of opportunity conversions are converting existing classroom courses to computer-based instruction or the increasingly popular satellite delivery method. The steps in opportunity conversions are as follows:

- Revisit your delivery strategy mix (you should do this once a year). In chapter 13, we talked about ways to determine optimal delivery strategies for a particular program based on cost analysis.

- Go through the existing curriculum and determine which courses are in the wrong strategy, or where you have opportunities to improve instructional effectiveness or reduce cost or achieve some other advantage by converting.

- Make up a table like the one in Figure 14-4. This table shows you the amount of training that should be converted in terms of days if you are going to do it the most optimal way. For instance, in this example there are five days of group-paced training which should be converted to computer-based training.

- Figure out what it would cost in resource requirements to make this conversion, as shown in Figures 14-5 and 14-6. The calculation is person days (from Figure 14-4) times conversion cost (Figure 14-5) equals resources required (Figure 14-6).

- Finally, when you figure out your scenarios, you have to spread the resources required for the needed conversions over the next five years. For example, you could decide to do it all next year, or you could do 30 percent of it, or you could do none. This will depend on the other types of work that need to be done and the amount of resources you have available to do it.

EXISTING STRATEGY	Future Strategy			
	A. Grp-Paced Classroom	B. CBT	C. Video Net	D. Self-Paced
A. Group-Paced Class	-	5	2	1
B. CBT	3	-	6	2
C. Video-Net	0	0	-	0
D. Self-Paced	1	3	0	-

Figure 14-4 Opportunity Conversions in Person Days

	A	B	C	D
A	-	100	50	10
B				
C				
D				

Cost in Units (Development Days or Dollars)
to convert one day of existing strategy
to future strategy

Figure 14-5 Conversion Cost Table

	A	B	C	D
A	-	500	100	10
B				
C				
D				

Total number of developer days
required to make that conversion

Figure 14-6 Resources Required Table

We recommend that you do all this forecasting using spreadsheet models so you can tinker with your assumptions and try out a wide variety of scenarios.

UNIT COST ASSUMPTIONS

After you have completed your development for the five categories of curriculum development, you are ready to establish your unit cost assumptions which will be used later in developing your actual plan. This involves the following steps:

1. Review and select potential development and delivery strategies based on which ones look promising and feasible.

2. Identify types of development resources per development for all types you are likely to use, not just the ones you are currently using. Examples include

   - In-house development
     - Instructional designers
     - Subject-matter experts
     - Production staff
     - Project managers
   - Contract development
     - Project manager
     - Subject-matter experts
     - Contract dollars
   - Off-the-shelf
     - Project manager
     - Instructional designer
     - Subject-matter experts
     - Purchase cost.

3. For each delivery and development strategy, figure the unit cost:

   - Review your historical data on course development to determine the number of days you have been spending. You can do this by plotting the days on a scatter diagram like the one in Figure 14-7.

Using the scatter diagram, you could compute the overall average days per course day, but the problem is that shorter courses have a higher per unit cost than longer courses. We suggest that you compute average costs for one-day courses, two-day courses, three-day courses, etc. However, if you are willing to make the assumption that your statistical mix of course lengths is not going to change, then you can throw them all together and come up with the overall average cost per day of material developed. But if you are going to develop a strategy that calls for changing the average course length (e.g.,

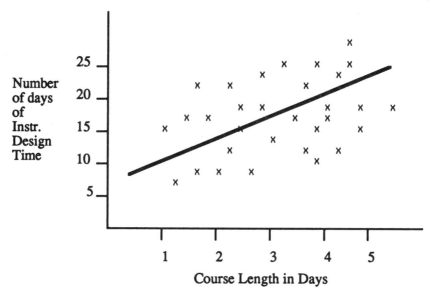

Figure 14-7 Instructor Days Spent by Course Length

toward shorter modules), it would be prudent to analyze what it is going to cost by course length. In our examples, we use a simple method for the sake of clarity.

If you have no historical data on which to base these calculations, you can do some research to determine what seems to be commonplace in the industry. There is data published by the American Society for Training and Development (ASTD), but we suggest that you talk to other training departments that are similar to yours. Also, we suggest that you do not use the ratios in our examples because these ratios are situationally dependent. Developing your own ratios will help in two other important ways:

1. It will allow you to account for differences in working cultures. We have seen situations where actual daily working time for instructional developers was less than three hours per day. The rest of the time was spent walking around, chatting, reading electronic news, making personal phone calls, arriving late, etc. In other situations instructional developers are putting in more than a full eight-hour day. Needless to say, these two companies will have widely varying development ratios.

2. It provides you the opportunity to discover that your ratios are way out of line with other organizations. For example, if you are at 100 to 1 and ASTD and/or your competitors are operating at 30 to 1, something is wrong. It may be that your instructional developers are wasting their time in idle activity. Now you can find out where your inefficiences are (e.g., lack of tight project control, etc.). Then you may want to forecast a 30 percent productivity improvement over the next five years so your ratio moves from 100 to 1 to 70 to 1.

In figuring out your ratio, you should also take into account the quality factor. Figure 14-8 shows a quality curve based on Pareto's law of diminished returns (You get 80 percent of the bang for 20 percent of the buck, after that it's all downhill). You should figure out where you have been operating historically. If you have been low on the quality curve, you may want to make an investment in quality until you get to the point of diminishing returns. You have to decide where you want to operate on this quality curve. Generally, it is preferable to have two courses produced at a cost of thirty units each than one course which is only 10 percent better produced at a cost of sixty units. One caution: in any development environment, designers are always yelling about needing more time to design. Meanwhile, the window of opportunity is going by. There are always trade-offs.

The bottom line is that you need to pick a set of numbers to come up with a completed unit cost table like the one in Figure 14-9. The numbers in this table are based on four main factors:

1. Historical data (including historical experience data from others)
2. Projected changes in mix of course length
3. Projected changes in course length
4. Projected changes in quality.

If you are projecting changes in these ratios, develop a table like the one in Figure 14-9 for each year of your projection.

It is important when doing all of this that you keep track of the decisions that are made and the rationale behind them so when you revisit the plan in the future you know

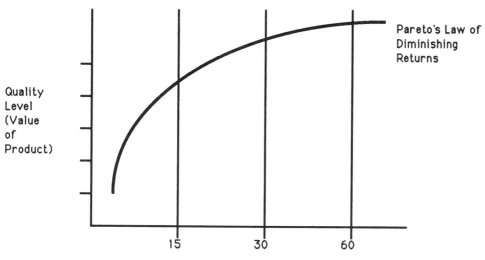

Figure 14-8 Quality Curve

RESOURCE TYPE	DELIVERY STRATEGY						
	GROUP	CBT	VIDEO	. . . .	. . . .	. . . .	. . N
IN-HOUSE - ID - SME - Production - Project Mgr TOTAL	30*						
CONTRACT - Project Mgr - SME - Contract $ TOTAL							
OFF-THE-SHELF - Project Mgr - ID - SME - Purchase $ TOTAL							

*Unit Cost = Total Resource Required to Develop One Training Day

Figure 14-9 Unit Cost Assumptions Table

where the numbers came from. Although it can be tough to document so the process is understandable and interpretable, it is critical.

DEVELOPING SCENARIOS

The objective of this section is to create a number of different scenarios and to analyze the resource cost compared to expected benefits for each, as well as compared to probable resource availability and ability to deploy the resources usefully.

The first step in this process is to research and graph historical resource deployment, as shown in Figure 14-10. You can further break this down by each development category:

- New courses
  - Core
  - Change-driven
  - Replacements
- Maintenance
- Opportunity conversions.

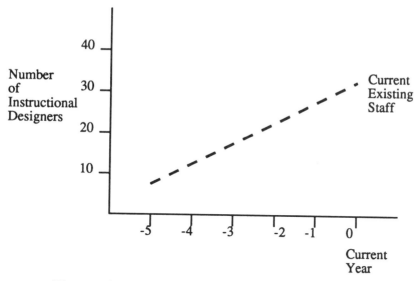

Figure 14-10   Historical Resource Deployment

In doing so, you do not kid yourself that you have thirty people available to develop new courses when you need 20 percent of them for maintenance and conversions.

Your next step is to develop a set of alternative five-year scenarios or plans. Your areas of choice in developing these scenarios are

- How to spread the core curriculum development over time
- Mix of development strategies
- Mix of delivery strategies
- Percentage of needs to be met
- Amount of opportunity conversion each year
- Relative priorities (i.e., core courses vs. change-driven courses, maintenance vs. conversions, etc.).

In assessing these choices, you must try to imagine the impact of each choice on the business. To use a change-driven example, it makes no sense to install a new corporate-wide computer information system without providing training on how to use it.

Figures 14-11 and 14-12 present alternative scenarios that could be developed. Scenario 1, "Hold Resources at Present Level," is one you always should do, because you may not be given any additional resources and you want to show what can be done with the present level of resources and what is going to be left out. In general, you want to work out at least three scenarios:

Scenario Description:	Hold Resources at present level					

Assumed Priorities:
1. Maintenance of existing courses
2. Top 3/4 of change-driven courses
3. Remainder spent on new core courses until there are no more resources, or all core courses have been developed

Other Aumuptions: All courses will be delivered as group-paced instrucor-led courses

Background Data:
- Present level of resources = 100
- Replacement cost of existing investment = 400 units
- Maintenance percent for the first year = 15%
- Change-driven new courses requires 40 units per year

Implications:

	Year 0	Year 1	Year 2	Year 3	Year 4	Year 5
No. of Resources	100	100	100	100	100	100
Maintenance	--	60	66	71	75	79
Change-Driven		30	30	29	25	21
(75 % of need)	--					
New Core	--	10	4	0	0	0
Total	--	100	100	100	100	100
Replacement Cost	400	440	474	503	528	549

Figure 14-11   Alternative Scenario 1

1. Present level of resources maintained
2. Maximum growth you can handle
3. Middle of the road.

You can also work out the various iterations of all these by changing your assumptions. You would only work out the fourth alternative, head count reduction, if you were mandated to do so by your executives. If you are asked to work out a reduced head count alternative, this method will show you the road to the least painful cuts.

You want to end up with a chart like the one in Figure 14-13 which shows the resource implications of all your scenarios.

If you want to get extra fancy, you can calculate the cost to the business of not doing the things left out . You are calculating the cost of lost opportunities. All of this gives you the information you need to stand in front of the company officers and explain

Scenario Description:	Maximum Service Scenario (also called "Modified Blank Check Scenario"). This is a combination of filling all the justifiable needs tempered by the maximum rate of growth you can manage.

Assumed Priorities:	1. Do all maintenance and replacements 2. Do all change-driven 3. Spread the new core courses over the shortest possible period

Other Auumptions:	The maximum digestible growth rate = 20%/year

Background Data:
- Present level of resources = 100
- Replacement cost of existing investment = 400 units
- Maintenance percent for the first year = 15%
- Change-driven new courses requires 40 units per year
- Aging table for replacement Courses =

Age	1	2	3	4	5	6	7	8	9	10
#of Units	40	30	20	10	5	--	--	--	--	--

	Year 0	Year 1	Year 2	Year 3	Year 4	Year 5
No. of Resources	100	120	144	173	207	249
Maintenance	--	60	69	80	92	106
Replacements	--	0	5	10	20	30
Change-Driven	--	40	40	40	40	40
Core	--	20	30	43	55	73
Opp. Conversion	--	0	0	0	0	0
Total	100	120	144	173	207	249
Replacement Cost	400	460	530	613	708	821

Figure 14-12 Alternative Scenario 2

what you need. It takes the training department completely out of a defensive position because you will have completely portrayed all the options, and now you can leave it up to management to make the choices. Knowing which particular scenario you wish to propose is a matter of reading the political and economical tea leaves at your company. You may wish to do some preliminary shopping around with the power players, who hopefully are members of the executive advisory board and they can help you make some judgments about what management might accept.

You do all this to decide that next year you will go from x to y. You have another

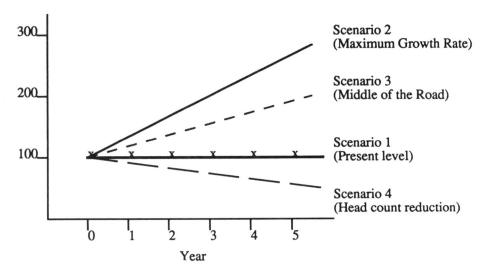

Figure 14-13   Resource Requirements for Alternative Scenarios

opportunity to decide where you will go in year 2 at the end of year 1. So management is not committing to year 5, it is only making a provisional commitment for year 1 and a planning intention for year 5. But you should still forecast for five years because

- Your forecast has implications for year 1
- It answers the question, "If we give you 20 percent per year when do you reach your capacity or limit of your ability to produce?"
- It tells you how long before you can reach the goal.

This falls in line with the TQM theme of managing quantitatively and getting your process under control, in this case with data.

SUMMARY

This chapter provided a methodology for developing strategies and planning the amount of resources required to develop or acquire courses to meet the delivery need. The steps are as follows:

☐ Forecast development need by category

- Core curriculum
- Change-driven curriculum

- Maintenance
- Replacements
- Opportunity conversions

☐ Calculate your unit cost assumptions

☐ Develop alternative scenarios

- Present level of resources
- Maximum growth
- Middle of the road
- Head count reduction.

15

DELIVERY PLAN

The purpose of this chapter is to provide you with a roadmap for developing the quantitative three- to five-year delivery plan. Chapter 10 provided an overview of the process. This chapter provides you with a more in-depth view of the mechanics.

The basis for this chapter is the spreadsheet system shown in Figure 15-1. We explain all the inputs, the spreadsheet setup and the outputs. You can use this as a model to design your own system. Unless you have an extremely simple situation, do not try to do this manually. PC-based spreadsheet programs are ideally suited for this type of quantitative planning and will save you many hours of tedious, error-prone computations. This is especially true as you experiment with different assumptions and different scenarios.

We illustrate the system with a relatively simple example. Your situation may require additional degrees of complexity, but the example will give you the basic framework to build on. Where appropriate, we list additional complexities to consider in designing your own system.

SPREADSHEET 1: FORECAST DELIVERY VOLUME NEEDED

The objective of this spreadsheet is to forecast the delivery volume needed

- By year
- By trainee population segment.

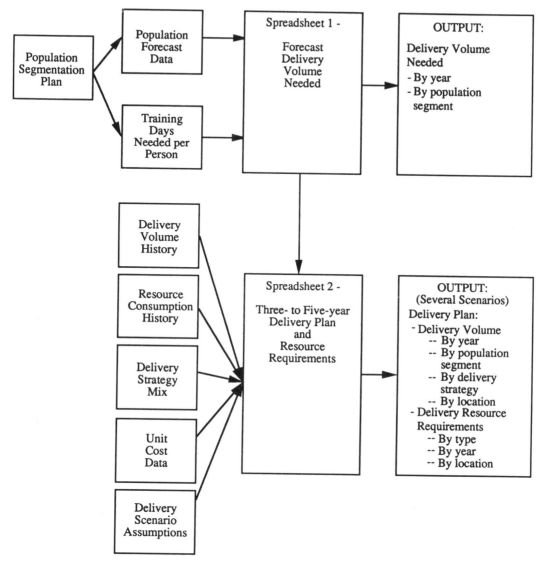

Figure 15-1 Spreadsheet System for Delivery Planning

We use *trainee days per year* as the unit of measure for delivery volume. You can just as easily use hours or weeks, whichever is the most convenient measure for your situation.

Step 1. Review the population segmentation plan

In chapter 3 we described segmentation of the training population. Figure 15-2 shows one of the examples from that discussion. For purposes of forecasting delivery requirements, you may want to subdivide the functional segments even further. Figure 15-3 provides an example partial breakout based on the structure in Figure 15-2 above.

You must carefully choose which breakouts are important for your forecast. The more complex your segmentation plan, the more complex your spreadsheet system will be. If you are developing this forecast for only one function (research and development) or one business unit (Airborne Electronics) or one plant (Smoke River Works), your task is greatly simplified.

Step 2. Obtain or develop population forecast data

You need two forecasts for each population segment.

1. The number of new people expected to enter the segment each year

2. The average number of experienced people in the segment for each year.

You need both of these because new people generally require much more training than experienced people.

Let's take a look at Figure 15-4, which shows a typical population forecast for just

Functional

- Research and Development
- Marketing
- Manufacturing
- Distribution
- Sales
- Customer Services
- Procurement
- Product Management
- Human Resources
- Management Information Systems
- Accounting
- Legal

Hierarchical

- Executives
- Middle Management
- Supervisors
- Professionals
- Exempt
- Nonexempt

Business Units

- Consumer Electronics Group
- Automotive Electronics Group
- Medical Electronics Group
- Airborne Electronics Group

Geographical

- U.S.
  - Eastern
  - Central
  - Western
- Europe
- Asia

Customers

- Engineers
- Operators
- Maintenance personnel
- Managers

Suppliers

- Engineers
- Production Management
- Quality Assurance

Figure 15-2 Electronics Manufacturing Segmentation

- Research and Development
  - Technology Research and Development
  - Hardware Development
  - Software Development
  - Manuafacturing Process Development

- Manufacturing
  - Production
  - Materials
  - Quality Assurance
  - Maintenance
  - Engineering

Figure 15-3   Functional Segments

the R&D function in one business unit (Consumer Electronics Group). If you are lucky, there will be a personnel forecast complete enough to give you this data. Generally, you will have to develop it by working with historical data, the business plan for the next few years, and informed judgment of executives and managers in the departments being served. You can see from Figure 15-4 that this can get very complex for a large organization with many functions, business units, and geographical locations.

Step 3. Obtain or estimate training days needed per person

For each segment of the training population, you need two numbers.

1. The number of training days required for the average new person entering the segment to become fully proficient (entry training).

2. The number of training days required per year for the average experienced person to stay current with change and develop enhanced skills (annual training)

The best plan to obtain these estimates is from the curriculum architecture and typical learning paths developed from it (see Chapter 12). If there is no such information available, then estimates must be built. One example is provided in Figure 15-5. The two numbers we need from this table for our forecasting purposes are

- 130 days entry training

- 10 days per year annual training

Remember that this is not the training level you plan to provide but the level you would provide if all important needs were to be met.

	Year 1		Year 2		Year 3	
	New	Exp	New	Exp	New	Exp
• Technology Research & Development						
U.S.						
Europe						
Asia						
TOTAL	50	250	55	275	60	300
• Hardward Development						
U.S.						
Europe						
Asia						
TOTAL	300	2000	300	2150	300	2300
• Software Development						
U.S.						
Europe						
Asia						
TOTAL	240	1200	240	1320	240	1440
• Mfg. Process Development						
U.S.						
Europe						
Asia						
TOTAL	150	750	150	825	150	900
• Total R & D						
U.S.						
Europe						
Asia						
TOTAL	740	4200	745	4570	750	4940

For all geographic areas, all subfunctions, assume:
  Executives = 0.5%
  Middle Managers = 3%
  Supervisors = 12%
  Engineers = 30%
  Technicians = 30%
  Others = 25%

Figure 15-4   R&D Forecast—Consumer Electronics Group

The chart in Figure 15-6 shows a table of average training needs for our R&D example. In this example, we have made the simplifying assumption that these numbers are the same regardless of business unit, geographical location, and year. This is generally not a bad assumption, but your situation may be different, requiring you to build a more complex table. For example, implementation of major new product technology may drive

Training Requirements	Days
Entry Training	
• Orientation to company, industry, job	10
• Data processing systems architecture	15
• Telecommunications networking	5
• Product-specific knowledge (hands-on job training)	50
• Basic selling skills	5
• Managing the territory	5
• Analyzing customer needs	10
• Developing the systems plan	10
• Developing and presenting the proposal	5
• Supporting implementation and account maintenance	5
• Competitive products	10
TOTAL	130
Annual Training	
• New product releases	5
• Industry trends	5
• Advanced skills and career development	
TOTAL	10

Figure 15-5   Account Executive Training Requirements

up the annual training requirements for a couple of years for hardware, software, and process development personnel.

Step 4. Calculate delivery volume needed using the data from steps 2 and 3 and spreadsheet 1

Spreadsheet 1 in Figure 15-7 shows how the population data from steps 2 and the training needs estimates from step 3 come together to make up the delivery requirements forecast. To simplify the illustration, we left out the extra complexity of geographical location (U.S., Asia, Europe).

	Trng Needed Per Person (Days)	
	Entry	Annual
• Technology Research and Development		
Middle Managers	40	10
Supervisors	40	10
Engineers	145	15
Technicians	96	10
Others	50	7
• Hardware Development		
Middle Managers	40	10
Supervisors	40	10
Engineers	120	15
Technicians	90	10
Others	50	7
• Software Development		
Middle Managers	40	10
Supervisors	40	10
Engineers	160	20
Technicians	100	15
Others	50	7
• Manufacturing Process Development		
Middle Managers	35	10
Supervisors	35	10
Engineers	110	15
Technicians	90	10
Others	50	7
• Executives	30	10

Figure 15-6   R&D Training Needed per Person

SPREADSHEET 2: THREE- TO FIVE-YEAR DELIVERY PLAN AND RESOURCE REQUIREMENTS

The objective of this spreadsheet is to develop alternative delivery plans (scenarios) and estimate the resources required for each alternative. The output for each alternative scenario should include

- Delivery volume
    - By population segment
    - By year
    - By location

POPULATION SEGMENT	Population Size						Trng Needed Days Per Year		Delivery Requirements Forecast (Trainee Days Per Year)								
	Year 1		Year 2		Year 3												
	New	Exp	New	Exp	New	Exp	New	Exp	New	Exp	TOTAL	New	Exp	TOTAL	New	Exp	TOTAL
	A	B	C	D	E	F	G	H	I	J	K	L	M	N	O	P	Q
CONSUMER PRODUCTS R&D																	
Technology R&D																	
• Middle Managers	2	8	2	9	3	10	40	10	80	80	160	80	90	170	120	100	220
• Supervisors	6	30	7	33	7	36	40	10	240	300	540	280	330	610	280	360	640
• Engineers	15	75	16	85	18	95	145	15	2175	1125	3300	2320	1275	3595	2610	1425	4035
• Technicians	15	75	17	82	18	89	96	10	1440	750	2190	1632	820	2452	1728	890	2618
• Others	12	62	13	66	14	70	50	7	600	434	1034	650	462	1112	700	490	1190
TOTAL	50	250	55	275	60	300			4535	2689	7224	4962	2977	7939	5438	3265	8703

NOTES:
A,B,C,D,E,F,G,H = Input Data
I=A x G, J=B x H, K=I+J
L=C x G, M=D x H, N=L+M
O=E x G, P=F x G, Q=O+P

Figure 15-7   Spreadsheet Number 1

265

- By delivery strategy
- Delivery resource requirements
  - By type
  - By year
  - By location
  - By delivery strategy.

The inputs required include:

- Needs forecast from spreadsheet 1
- Delivery volume history
  - By population segment
  - By year
  - By delivery strategy
  - By location
- Resource consumption history
  - By population segment
  - By year
  - By delivery strategy
  - By location
  - By type of resource
- Delivery strategy mix
- Unit cost assumptions
  - By delivery strategy
  - By location
  - By type of resource
- Delivery scenario assumptions.

The needs forecast from spreadsheet 1 has already been described. The remaining inputs are described in the next sections. In a mature training system, all this data is stored in a database and is easy to retrieve. In most cases, however, some of the data may be hard to access.

Delivery Volume History and Resource Consumption History

These data are the baselines for your three- to five-year plan. The forecast of delivery volume needed gives you your ultimate target. The baselines are your starting point. The breakdowns we typically look for include

- Delivery volume history
  - By population segment

- – By year
- – By delivery strategy
- – By location
- Resource consumption history
  - – By population segment
  - – By year
  - – By delivery strategy
  - – By type of resource.

For baselining purposes we generally do not recommend breaking these data into extremely fine grained segments.

Comparing Needs and History

The historical data can be juxtaposed with the needs data from Spreadsheet 1 (Figure 15-7) to yield some interesting comparisons. The three graphs in Figure 15-8 show how you can compare what has been provided to what is needed for the whole organization and for selected population segments. As this figure shows, simply looking at the numbers for all training can give a misleading picture of what is really going on.

Unit Cost History

Another set of useful comparisons comes from the delivery volume history and the resource consumption history. If the resources are all dollarized, you can trend cost per trainee day. You can also trend trainee days per instructor per year, trainee days per year per 10,000 square feet of training facility, and so forth, as shown in Figure 15-9.

Delivery Strategy Mix

The next step is to identify the delivery strategies to be supported during the three- to five-year planning period. (See chapter 13 for a review of available delivery strategies and their uses.) Later in developing your alternative delivery plan scenarios, you will select the distribution of delivery load among the delivery strategies.

For the sake of simplicity, to keep our examples easy to follow, we limit the delivery strategies to

1. Group-paced classroom
   a. Centralized
   b. Traveling instructors
2. Centralized self-paced classroom
3. Computer-based training (CBT) at the worksite
4. Structured on-the-job training.

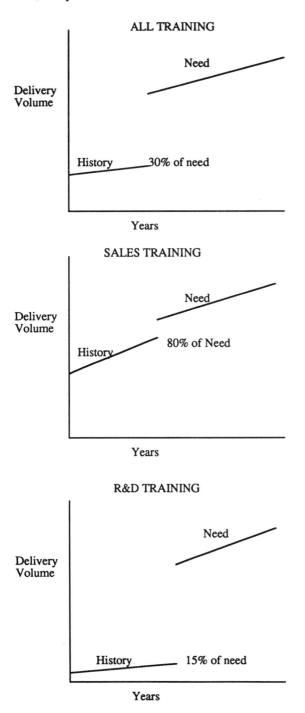

Figure 15-8 Needs/History Comparisons

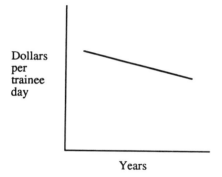

Dollars
per
trainee
day

Years

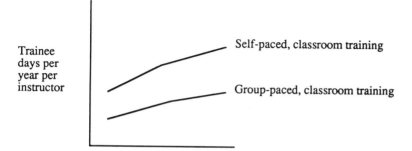

Trainee
days per
year per
instructor

Self-paced, classroom training

Group-paced, classroom training

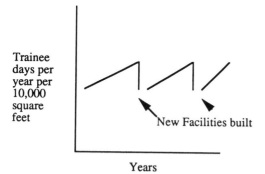

Trainee
days per
year per
10,000
square
feet

New Facilities built

Years

Figure 15-9   Unit Cost History

Unit Cost Assumptions

Now that we have identified the delivery strategies, the next step is to build a table of unit costs. The best source of this information is historical data, but if the data are not available you can build up the estimates. These unit costs will be used to develop

1. The total dollar cost of each planning scenario
2. The number of each type of resource needed for each scenario.

Assume that the cost elements to be considered include

- Instructors
- Administrative support
- Supervision and management of the delivery system
- Training materials and other similar costs, such as computing time
- Trainee travel
- Instructor travel
- Training facility cost.

These cost elements will be different for each delivery strategy so you need to develop a table or matrix of unit costs (See Figure 15-10).

Delivery Scenario Assumptions

In determining your delivery scenario assumptions, there are two major variables:

- Delivery strategy mix
- Percentage of need to be met.

Figure 15-11 provides three possible scenarios for delivery strategy mix. Scenario 1 assumes the strategy mix will stay the same as it is today. Scenario 2 assumes an increase of training which is composed of both CBT at the worksite and structured OJT. Scenario 3 assumes a conversion of most of the current group-paced training to self-paced training. Figure 15-12 provides three possible scenarios for percentage of need to be met.

The delivery strategies mix scenarios in Figure 15-11 and the percentage of need to be met scenarios in Figure 15-12 combine to form nine possible alternative scenarios:

- A1, A2, A3
- B1, B2, B3

INSTRUCTOR TIME	Group-Paced		Centralized Self-Paced	CBT at Worksite[1]	Structured OJT[2]
	Central	Trav. Instr.			
Total work days per year	261	261	261	261	261
• Vacation	12	12	12	12	12
• Holidays	11	11	11	11	11
• Sick/Personal	5	5	5	5	5
• Professional Development	10	10	10	10	10
• Course Maintenance	10	10	10	10	10
• Preparation to Teach	25	25	25	10	25
• Travel/Setup	10	38	10	0	30
• Administrative Duties	12	12	12	12	12
AVAILABLE DAYS TO INSTRUCT	166	138	166	191	146
Average Trainee to Instructor Ratio	15	10	30	100	10
Trainee Days per Year	2490	1380	4980	19100	1460
Staff Salary Cost per Instructor[3]	72266	72266	72266	72266	72266
Staff Salary Cost per Trainee Day	29	52	15	4	49

[1] Instructors at Corporate Education Center on a Help Hotline
[2] On-site Instructors
[3] Staff Cost Based on:
    Instructor Loaded Salary = $55,000
    One Supervisor per 6 Instructors at $70,000 Loaded Salary
    One Support Person per 5 Instructors at $28,000 Loaded Salary

Figure 15-10   Unit Cost Table for Instructor Time

	Now	Scenario 1 3 Years	Scenario 2 3 Years	Scenario 3 3 Years
Group-paced Centralized	65	65	30	10
Traveling lists	20	20	20	20
Centralized Self-Paced	--	--	--	20
CBT @ Worksite	5	5	25	25
Structured OJT	10	10	25	25
TOTAL	100%	100%	100%	100%

Figure 15-11 Delivery Strategic Mix Research and Development Example

NOW	A	B	C
15%	15%	85%	55%

Figure 15-12 Percent of Need to Be Met

- C1, C2, C3.

For example, suppose you choose scenario C2. In that case, you are planning for 55 percent of the need to be met in three years with the following delivery strategy mix.

- 30% centralized group-paced
- 20% traveling instructors
- 25% CBT at worksite
- 25% structured OJT.

Three- to Five-Year Delivery Plan and Resource Requirements

You now have all the data you need to complete your three- to five-year delivery plan and resource requirements, as shown in spreadsheet 2 in Figure 15-13. These figures require the total needed volume you calculated in Spreadsheet 1, your percentage of need to be met assumptions, and your delivery strategy mix assumptions. When you have completed this chart, you will know the total amount of delivery you plan to do for each delivery type over the next three years. You can now calculate the total dollar resources required to provide this.

The first thing you need to do this is a unit cost table like the one in Figure 15-14. (The numbers in this chart are for example purposes only and should not be used for your actual calculations. You will want to develop your own unit cost table based on actual history and experience data in your company.) By multiplying the delivery requirements in spreadsheet 2 by the costs in Figure 15-14 you can calculate the total cost of delivery over the next three years as shown in Figure 15-15.

| | Delivery Requirements | | |
	Year 1	Year 1	Year 1
Consumer Products R&D			
A. Total Needed Volume (from Spreadsheet 1)	6874	7939	8703
B. Percent of Needs to be Met (from Figure 15-12, column C) (Growth from 15%)	30%	45%	55%
C. Delivery Volume Forecast (A x B)	2062	3175	4787
Delivery Strategy Mix (From Figure 15-11—change over 3 years to Scenario 2)			
D. Centralized Group-Paced 1. Percent (Current = 65%) 2. Volume (D1 x C)	55% 1134	45% 1429	30% 1436
E. Traveling Intstuctor 1. Percent (Current = 20%) 2. Volume (E1 x C)	20% 412	20% 635	20% 957
F. CBT at Worksite 1. Percent (Current = 5%) 2. Volume (F1 x C)	10% 206	15% 476	25% 1197
G. Structured OJT 1. Percent (Current = 10%) 2. Volume (G1 x C)	15% 309	20% 635	25% 1197

Figure 15-13 Three- to Five-Year Delivery Plan and Resource Requirements

	Instr. Time	Facility	Student Trav	Instr. Trav	Mat'ls	Admin Supp.	Supv. Supp.	TOTAL
Centralized Group	29	8	240*	-	35	10	3	325
Traveling Instructors	52	7	50	24	38	10	5	186
CBT at Worksite	3.8	10	-	-	25	3	0.5	42.3
Structured OJT	49	-	-	-	40	3	4	96

*Based on Average $750 Round-Trip Ticket, Avg. 5-day stay, Avg., $100 per day T&L

Figure 15-14 Unit Cost Table

	Year 1	Year 2	Year 3
Centralized Group-Paced	$368,550	$464,425	$466,700
Traveling Instructors	$ 76,632	$118,110	$178,002
CBT at Worksite	$ 8,714	$ 20,135	$ 50,633
Structured OJT	$ 29,664	$ 60,960	$114,912
TOTAL	$483,560	$663,630	$810,247
+ Delivery Volume Forecast (from Spreadsheet 2)	2062	3175	4787
= Cost per Trainee Day	$ 234.51	$ 209.02	$ 169.26

Figure 15-15 Total Delivery Cost

We have only calculated total costs for the sake of simplicity, but you can and should calculate costs for each column of the unit cost table to determine

- Number of instructors required
- Number of classrooms required
- Travel budget
- Etc.

By shifting to a different delivery mix, we have dramatically reduced cost per trainee day. However, we are spending a lot of money on developing CBT and structural OJT. You will need to compare these costs with development costs and weigh your trade-offs. You can see why the spreadsheet system is so important—change any one of your assumptions and you have to recalculate all the numbers.

SUMMARY

In this chapter we gave you a roadmap for developing a quantitative three- to five-year delivery plan. The steps in this process are as follows:

☐ Forecast delivery volume needed.

- Review population segmentation plan.
- Obtain or develop population forecast data.
- Obtain or estimate training days needed per person.
- Calculate delivery volume needed.

☐ Create three- to five-year delivery plan and resource requirements.

- Delivery volume history
- Resource consumption history
- Comparing needs and history
- Unit cost history
- Delivery strategy mix
- Unit cost assumptions
- Delivery scenario assumptions
- Delivery plan
- Resource costs.

16

STAFFING STRATEGY AND PLAN

The quality and effectiveness of your training organization will be limited by the quality, expertise, and professionalism of the training staff. The training staff must combine subject-matter expertise, knowledge of real conditions in the client organization, training expertise, administrative and managerial skill.

No single source can provide the needed mix of talents. Truly outstanding training organizations have a mixed staffing strategy drawing some people from the line and staff organizations they serve, some from the ranks of training professionals, and some subject-matter experts and consultants from outside.

The only two methods available for acquiring expertise are to recruit from outside your organization or to develop expertise internally. The mix of skills required for a top notch training organization is sufficiently complex that you will generally have to do both.

In this chapter, we identify the various types of talent needed to staff a modern training organization and discuss various approaches to acquiring and maintaining the necessary amount of staff with the appropriate mix of talents.

STAFFING STRATEGY

The progression of activities to develop a first class staffing strategy and plan is as follows:

1. Identify key responsibilities and tasks for each training function.

2. Identify important skills, knowledge and experience per responsibility.
3. Design jobs.
4. Establish selection and development criteria and strategies.
5. Define resource pools and rotational and career progression policies.

Steps 1 and 2 Identify Key Responsibilities and Tasks for Each Training Function and Important Skills, Knowledge, and Experience per Responsibility

Different training functions require different expertise. Training materials development requires a very different set of skills from instruction. In this section, we overview the skill sets needed for the various training roles. For a more comprehensive list of competencies with explanations of each, we recommend that you acquire a set of International Board of Standards for Training, Performance, and Instruction. No such list can ever be complete. You must look at your own situation and develop your own lists using these references as a guide.

To avoid making this discussion too long and cumbersome, we include only those responsibilities and tasks that are somewhat unique to the training function. There are many tasks such as word processing and bookkeeping found in the typical large training department that are not unique, so we leave them out for simplicity. However, it is critical that you do not overlook the importance of these roles to the overall staffing plan for the organization.

We focus here on responsibilities, tasks, and skills in the following areas:

- Needs analysis and curriculum architecture design
- Development and maintenance of training materials and systems
- Delivery of training
- Results measurement and evaluation
- Management of the training function.

Needs Analysis and Curriculum Architecture Design The chart in Figure 16-1 shows the principal responsibilities, tasks, skills, and knowledge required for needs analysis and curriculum architecture design.

Development and Maintenance of Training Materials and Systems The chart in Figure 16-2 shows the principal responsibilities, tasks, skills, and knowledge required for development and maintenance of training materials and systems. Some training departments will not require all of these depending on the jobs, tasks, and subject matter to be taught.

Delivery of Training The chart in Figure 16-3 shows the primary delivery

RESPONSIBILITY	TASKS	SKILLS/KNOWLEDGE
1. High-level functional analysis /job analysis	1. Segment function (e.g., Sales) into subfunctions or jobs 2. Analyze subfunctions or jobs to determine responsibilities, tasks, performance measures, typical performance deficiencies, causes of performance deficiencies 3. Analyze responsibilities and tasks for required skills and knowledge 4. Assess training needs	• Job analysis • Performance analysis • Group interviewing/ facilitation • Individual interviewing • Documentation and presentation skills • Analytical ability
2. Change analysis (new systems, products, policies, regulations, etc.)	1. Identify functions and jobs affected by the change 2. Identify tasks affected for each function/job 3. Identify changed skill/knowledge requirements 4. Assess training needs	• Job analysis • Performance analysis • Group interviewing/facilitation • Individual interviewing • Documentation and presentation skills • Analytical ability
3. Performance problem analysis (e.g., quality problems, low productivity, errors)	1. Define problem 2. Determine who is involved 3. Analyze causes of problem 4. If training is all or part of the solution, estimate cost vs. benefit 5. Recommend training and nontraining solutions	• Job analysis • Performance analysis • Group interviewing/facilitation • Individual interviewing • Documentation and presentation skills • Analytical ability
4. Curriculum architecture design	1. Establish design criteria and constraints 2. Design overall curriculum structure 3. Sort training needs into modules within the structure 4. Prepare specifications for each module 5. Design typical learning paths	• Knowledge of instructional systems design • Knowledge of various types of instructional strategies (e.g., self-paced, structured OJT, CBT) • Subject-matter knowledge • Creativity
5. Project management	1. Develop a detailed project plan including resource and time requirements 2. Control project progress 3. Prepare project reports	• Planning skills • Estimating skills • Basic supervisory skills • Experience with needs analysis and curriculum design projects

Figure 16-1   Needs Analysis and Curriculum Architecture Design

RESPONSIBILITY	TASKS	SKILLS/KNOWLEDGE
1. Job analysis/task analysis/ performance analysis	1. Develop a task list 2. Identify performance requirements 3. Analyze a task for procedure and skills and knowledge required 4. Analyze target audience capabilities 5. Develop entry requirements for training 6. Develop training objectives 7. Prepare analysis report	• Task analysis • Performance analysis • Group and individual interviewing • Performance observation • Documentation and presentation skills • Analytical ability
2. Instructional design to accomplish training objectives	1. Select instructional mode(s) (e.g., group-paced, self-paced, OJT, CBT, laboratory) 2. Design sequence of instructional activities to achieve learning objectives 3. Develop specifications for each instructional activity (e.g., lecture, case problem, lab exercise, simulation) 4. Prepare design document 5. Document the outcome of 1, 2, and 3	• Learning theory • Instruction design alternatives • Knowledge of instructional media and modes • Creativity • Documentation and presentation skills
3.* Prepare written training materials and graphics (instructor guide, trainee materials, slides, overheads)	1. Write instructor guide 2. Write trainee materials 3. Develop graphics 4. Develop tests 5. Develop materials for case problems and other exercises 6. Developmentally test	• Writing skills • Graphic arts skills • Test design • Instructional design • Learning theory • Editing/page layout
4.* Develop computer-based training modules	1. Develop instructional frames/screens 2. Develop trainee response contingencies and branching logic 3. Develop tests 4. Code 5. Developmentally test	• Learning theory • Frame design • Branching • System design • Coding • Creativity • Coding of authoring system

Figure 16-2 Development and Maintenance of Training Materials and Systems

5.* Develop instructional videotape	1. Develop script treatment 2. Develop storyboard 3. Write script 4. Design sets, props 5. Recruit talent 6. Shoot 7. Edit 8. Developmentally test	• Script writing • Production skills • Camera operation • Directing skills • Creativity • Learning theory
6.* Develop lab or simulator exercises	1. Plan exercises 2. Design and build lab or simulator 3. Develop instructor and trainee materials for exercises 4. Try out exercises 5. Developmentally test	• Learning theory • Technical knowledge of equipment operation, construction, trouble-shooting, repair • Testing
7. Conduct pilot test	1. Prepare instructors to teach if appropriate 2. Select pilot trainees 3. Prepare evaluation instruments 4. Observe instruction 5. Debrief trainees and instructors 6. Prepare pilot report including recommendation for changes	• Evaluation techniques • Management of instruction • Trainer training • Interviewing skills
8. Project management	1. Develop detailed project plan including resources and time requirements 2. Assemble and direct project team 3. Control project progress and quality or work 4. Conduct project committee meetings 5. Prepare project progress and completion reports 6. Select and manage outside contract resources	• Planning skills • Estimation skills • Use of project management tools • Basic supervisory skills • Experience with instructional development projects • Leadership skill

*Note: Responsibilities 3 through 6 can be accomplished simultaneously if necessary and appropriate.

Figure 16-2 (continued)

responsibilities, tasks, skills, and knowledge required for delivery of training. Again, some training departments will not require all these depending on the nature of training to be provided.

Results and Evaluation The chart in Figure 16-4 shows the principal responsibilities, tasks, skills, and knowledge required for results measurement and evaluation of trainee performance and attitudes.

RESPONSIBILITY	TASKS	SKILLS/KNOWLEDGE
1. Conduct group-paced classroom instruction	1. Lecture 2. Conduct discussions 3. Administer exercises and casework 4. Administer tests 5. Diagnose learning difficulties 6. Coach individuals and groups 7. Test understanding and reinforce learning	• Presentation skills • Discussions skills • Group facilitation • Diagnosing learning difficulty • Coaching • Subject-matter expertise • Field experience • Interpreting test results • Observing behavior • Giving feedback • Group dynamics • Assertiveness
2. Conduct laboratory or simulation exercises	1. Set up and test lab or simulator 2. Give directions to trainees 3. Monitor performance 4. Provide coaching 5. Assess performance 6. Give feedback 7. Maintain/troubleshoot/ repair lab equipment or simulator	• Presentation skills • Subject-matter expertise • Safety requirements • Observational skills • Coaching skills • Giving feedback • Technical skills as necessary to operate, maintain, troubleshoot, repair equipment
3. Administer self-paced or computer-based training in a classroom	1. Orient trainees to materials and equipment 2. Diagnose learning difficulties 3. Provide coaching 4. Administer tests 5. Give feedback	• Interpersonal skill • Subject-matter expertise • Coaching and problem solving • Test interpretation

Figure 16-3 Delivery

Managing the Training Function The chart in Figure 16-5 shows the principal responsibilities, tasks, skills, and knowledge required for managing the training function.

Step 3. Design the Training Jobs

Job design involves assessing the work to be performed, the responsibilities, tasks, skills and knowledge outlined in the previous step and determining how you will organize these into discrete jobs for which people can be recruited and trained. Each job should be described in terms of its mission, key responsibilities, tasks, performance measures, skills and knowledge required, background, experience, and personal traits. The example in Figure 16-6 shows a job design for an instructor of office automation sales.

RESPONSIBILITY	TASKS	SKILLS/KNOWLEDGE
1. Determine trainee satisfaction	1. Determine satisfaction criteria 2. Develop survey instruments 3. Develop administration system 4. Interpret results	• Measurement theory • Survey design • Statistical analysis • Interpersonal/consulting skills
2. Determine trainees' mastery of learning objectives	1. Support test development 2. Perform statistical analysis of test data 3. Interpret results 4. Develop administrative system	• Measurement theory • Testing theory • Statistics • Test design alternatives
3. Determine transfer of skills and knowledge to job performance	1. Develop evaluation strategy 2. Develop survey instruments and/or interview guides 3. Conduct interviews 4. Observe performance 5. Critique work products 6. Develop administrative system	• Measurement theory • Evaluation techniques • Performance analysis • Survey design • Interview skills • Statistical analysis • Subject matter expertise
4. Determine value of training received or cost of not training	1. Devise evaluation/assessment strategy 2. Determine performance differential due to training 3. Estimate the value of performance differential	• Performance analysis • Economic analysis
5. Administer Results measurement system	1. Collect data 2. Store data 3. Prepare standard and special reports 4. Interpret results	• Clerical skills • Measurement theory • Statistical analysis

Figure 16-4   Results Measurement and Evaluation

Jobs described in this way provide much more information for selection and development than the typical job description. This description also leaves little to the imagination of what will be expected of potential employees or how performance will be measured.

The best way we know to develop these job designs is in a group process involving several people who know the subject matter requirements, the instructional requirements, and the field situation. A good facilitator can push through one job design every two hours with the right group participants.

The first step is to organize all the work loosely into jobs and then do the detailed design of each job. As with all design situations there are trade-offs. For example, do we have the instructor maintain the laboratory equipment or do we have a laboratory technician? Does the instructor perform updates and maintenance on the course materials or is this done only by the instructional design and development group? The group should be able to push through all these decisions and develop a solid written job design for each job.

Step 4. Establish Selection and Development Criteria and Strategies

It is generally impossible to recruit people into most jobs who come with all the required skills, knowledge, experience, and personal traits. You will have to look at each job and sort out which attributes you will select for and which ones you will train for. For example, in the case of the office automation instructor, you could probably find candidates in the field sales force who possess all the attributes except instructional skills. You can train for those. Going the other way, selecting for instructional skills and providing training and development to acquire all the rest would be difficult and expensive.

RESPONSIBILITY	TASKS	SKILLS/KNOWLEDGE
1. Managing Work	1. Strategic Planning	• Forecasting • Elements of strategic planning • Elements of comprehensive training systems • Strategic planning process • Financial investment analysis
	2. Annual Planning/Program Planning	• Components of a complete annual plan • Planning process • Resource estimating and budgeting
	3. Project Plannning	• Project planning • Project management • Estimating and budgeting
	4. Monitoring Work and Controlling Results	• Knowledge of key result areas • Definition of result indicators • Performance analysis skills • Conceptual knowledge of work functions being managed, e.g., Instructor Delivery
	5. Organizational Interfaces	• Knowledge of training processes • Customer/supplier interface definition • Negotiation skills

Figure 16-5 Managing the Training Function

RESPONSIBILITY	TASKS	SKILLS/KNOWLEDGE
2. Managing People	1. Personnel Planning and Selection	• Personnel planning concepts • Estimating and forecasting skills • Interviewing and selection screening
	2. New Personnel Orientation and Training	• Coaching • Leaning plan development • Knowledge of available training and development opportunities
	3. Performance Support	• Performance managment concepts • Establishing meaningful expectations with subordinates • Monitoring performance against expections • Giving feedback • Coaching • Preparing formal performance appraisal • Performance problem solving
	4. Career Development	• Knowledge of available career development strategies • Career development methodology
	5. Compensation	• Knowledge of compensation system • Knowledge of marketplace competitive salary ranges
	6. Communication Needs	• Diagnosing information requirement of key constituencies • Knowledge of available communication strategies • Effective use of communication professionals
3. Managing the Environment	1. Organizational Structuring	• Theory of organizational design • Consensus building • Participative problem solving/design
	2. Job Design	• Job design theory, concepts, and methodology • Participative problem solving/design
	3. Workflow/Management Systems	• Systems and process analysis and design • Performance analysis

Figure 16-5 (continued)

Job Title: Instructor: Office Automation Sales

Mission

The mission of this job is to prepare new account executives to sell office automation systems and equipment by providing instruction in the following areas:
- Systems selling
- Specific office automation systems and equipment

Responsibilities and Tasks	Importance	% of Time
1. Classroom instruction	1	36
• Lecture		
• Discussion		
• Facilitate sales role plays		
• Coach		
• Administer tests		
• Assess skills and knowledge		
2. Laboratory instruction	2	35
• Lab setup		
• Introduce lab		
• Coach		
• Assess skills		
3. Liaison with Product Managers	3	7
• Track new product plans and release dates		
• Obtain field experience data		
4. Liaison with Field Sales	4	7
• Track sales experience		
• Obtain feedback on trainee performance		
5. Course Maintenance	5	10
• Develop list of required or desirable content or design changes		
• Negotiate maintenance plan with course development group		
• Support instructional designer and writers		
6. Administrative	6	5
• Prepare reports		
• Attend staff meetings		
• Organize and plan own schedule of work		

Performance Measures	Weight
1. Trainee mastery of objectives	50%
2. Trainee satisfaction	10%
3. Field Sales satisfaction	25%
4. State of maintenance of the courseware and lab	10%
5. Completeness and timeliness of reports	5%

Figure 16-6 Sample Job Design

Technical skills and knowledge
- Systems selling
- Features, benefits, and weaknesses of our systems and equipment
- Features, benefits, and weaknesses of competition's systems and equipment
- Operation and maintenance of our systems and equipment
- Knowledge of customer business environment and requirements for office automation

Instructional skills
- Lecturing
- Discussion leading
- Managing and scoring role plays
- Managing and assessing lab performance
- Testing and test interpretation
- Coaching

Business knowledge
- Industry structure and trends
- Basic business economics
- Knowledge of product development, manufacturing, distribution, sales, service process
- Knowledge of all sales support functions

Personal skills
- Assertiveness
- Interpersonal communications
- Analytical skills

Experience and educational
- At least two years of college
- At least two years in the field successfully selling our office automation systems and products

Figure 16-6   (continued)

Figure 16-7 illustrates some of the common staffing strategies for various types of training jobs.

Step 5. Define Resource Pools and Rotational and Career Progression Policies

Most large training departments use mixtures of the aforementioned staffing strategies. If you have a large organization with perpetual recruiting needs, it will be worthwhile to establish your resource pools. For example, a sales curriculum council made up of regional sales managers and the national account manager might be asked to maintain a list of candidates for sales instructor from their top-performing sales executives. If you elect to use contract resources for course development work, it is worth developing relationships with a list of organizations and individuals that you regularly draw on to reduce the orientation requirements and minimize risk.

Job	Alternative Staffing Strategies
Instructor	1. Recruit top performers from the field, train them in instructional skills, rotate back in one to three years to avoid loss of current field knowledge and protect careers of high performers 2. Recruit top performers from the field for permanent assignment; provide short-term field assignments every year or two to keep field knowledge fresh 3. Use outside experts on contract such as consultants, university faculty, recent retirees, etc.; train them on your business and instructional skills if necessary 4. Use top performers from the field as part-time instructors, train them in instructional skills

Performance Analyst or Instructional Designer	1. Recruit experienced analysts/designers for permanent assignment
	2. Select internal employees with necessary talent and expect to take two years to train and develop them
	3. Recruit graduates of advanced instructional technology degree programs and expect to take one year to train and develop them
	4. Use contract resources from outside the company
	  • Freelancers
	  • Consulting firms
	  • Faculty

Specialists in Measurement, CBI, Expert Systems, Video, etc.	1. Use outside experts on contract 2. Recruit experienced experts and train them in your business 3. Select internal candidates and make a long-term, multiyear commitment to training and developing them
Development Project Managers	1. Promote analysts/designers with management potential and provide training in project management and basic managerial skills 2. Recruit experienced development project managers 3. Select experienced project managers and train them in instructional systems development
Training Managers	1. Promote from within the training department and provide management skills training and development 2. Recruit experienced managers from within the business and train them in the training disciplines (may be rotational or permanent assignment) 3. Recruit experienced training managers from outside

Figure 16-7 Alternative Staffing Strategies

When you make an individual an employee of the training department, you have an impact on his or her career. If you take top performers from the field who have potential for advancement, there should be a strict rotational policy to keep these people in their career progressions, or they will die on the vine or quit to work for another company.

Training analysts, designers, and other specialists may have limited long term career opportunities within your company. A few will be promoted, some will stay content to perform well in the same job for many years, but most will seek greener pastures after between two and ten years with other training departments, as freelancers, or with consulting companies. Do not fight this. Provide as many opportunities and as good an environment as possible, and then accept the inevitable turnover. If the rate of turnover in your organization is unacceptable, look at your opportunities, consequences, compensation, etc., and make them better. You cannot keep the best if you do not provide the best situation.

Training managers in the best training departments are a mix of up-from-the-ranks instructional designers and instructors, rotational managers from the field, and training managers recruited from other companies. A wide spectrum of backgrounds and experience makes for a strong management team. The management team must have a strong appreciation for both the customer situation in the field and for the arts, discipline, and technologies of training.

STAFFING FORECAST AND PLAN

In addition to determining the types of jobs you need to fill, skills and knowledge required, and the detailed job designs for these positions, you also need to know how many of each type of person you will need. You need to develop a staffing forecast and plan.

Staffing Forecast

To determine your level of need for staffing, you can develop a spreadsheet or form following the format shown in Figure 16-8. This chart will provide you with the total number of professional staff, support staff, and management staff needed to carry out the work of each function. To calculate this, you first determine the total number of professionals required for each functional area (more information on how to do this is contained in subsequent paragraphs). Then you multiply that number by the support staff ratio for that functional area to determine the amount of support staff needed, and multiply the number of professionals by the management ratio to determine the amount of management staff needed.

Chapter 14 dealt with determining the total number of professionals needed for course development (functional area A), and chapter 15 dealt with the total number of professionals needed for delivery (functional area B). To determine the number needed for functional area C, "Planning, Needs Analysis, and Curriculum Architecture Staffing

	YEAR 5
	YEAR 4
	YEAR 3
	YEAR 2
	YEAR 1

Functional Area	Staffing Needs		Support Staff Reqirements	Support Staff Ratio	Mgmt. Staff Ratio	Mgmt. Staff Reqirements
	Type	#				
A. Course Development Resource Requirements	SMEs, 10s		x 1:3 =		x 1:8 =	
B. Delivery Resource Requirements	Instructors		x 1:6 =		x 1:12 =	
C. Planning, needs analysis, and curriculum resource requirments	Professionals		x 1:3 =		x 1:5 =	
D. Evaluation resource requirements	Professionals		x 1:3 =		x 1:5 =	
E. Special projects resource requirements	Professionals		x 1:3 =		x 1:8 =	
TOTAL						

Figure 16-8 Annual Staffing Forecast

Requirements," you can use the following procedure. First, identify the types of work done in the functional area. For example, in this area you might have the following types of work.

A. Needs analysis and curriculum architecture

   1. New needs analyses and curriculum architectures for a job functional area

   2. Change-driven needs analyses and curriculum updates for a job functional area

   3. Curriculum architecture maintenance

   4. Updating core needs analyses (every two to three years)

B. Planning

   1. Developing and updating strategic plans

   2. Developing annual plans and budget

   3. Conducting special planning studies (e.g., investigating the potential for using expert systems as a delivery technology).

TYPE OF WORK	CURRENT	YR 1	YR 2	YR 3	YR 4	YR 5
a1	0.5					
a2	0.5					
a3	0.2					
a4	0.2					
b1	0.5					
b2	0.5					
b3	0.3					
:						
:						
:						
:						
TOTAL	2.7	3	3.1			

Numbers represent person years

Figure 16-9 Estimating Professional Resources

For each type of work, you would then estimate the amount of work in person years to determine the total resources needed. The table in Figure 16-9 can be used to make these estimations. The basic method is to figure out year zero (current year) and then project from there.

The total from this chart is then carried over to Figure 16-8 as the number of professional resources required for the functional area being dealt with. This same procedure and estimating table is used for functional area D, "Evaluation Resource Requirements," and functional area E, "Special Projects Resource Requirements."

For your information in completing these tables, typical types of evaluation work are

- Designing and interpreting student opinion surveys
- Designing and analyzing mastery tests
- Designing and interpreting follow-up surveys
- Conducting value analyses (ROI)
- Conducting special studies.

We have seen groups as large as twenty-seven assigned to doing just evaluation. More information about evaluation work is given in chapter 24.

Generally, the easiest way to estimate what is going to be done relative to special projects is to look at what has been done over the last five years and then average that and project that average, as shown in Figure 16-10. If you have evidence that suggests you will be doing more special projects (e.g., you are going to be getting into the performance consulting business), then you can factor an increase into your average.

YEAR	RESOURCES	
- 5	2	
- 4	3.5	
- 3	3.5	ACTUAL
- 2	4	
- 1	3.5	
Current Year 0	4	
1	3.5	
2	3.5	
3	3.5	AVERAGE
4	3.5	
5	3.5	

Figure 16-10   Estimating Special Projects Resources

Forecast Roll-Up

When you have calculated the number of professionals and their attendant support and management staff (see Figure 16-8), you can then roll it all up into an overall forecast, shown in Figure 16-11.

The final step when you have these numbers is to figure out the dollar cost for each of these years. To do that, determine a loaded cost factor for each resource type and multiply that number by the number of people in the category and sum it all up. This can be done using the same format as in Figure 16-11. Note that your loaded cost factors should include increases in salaries and benefit cost over the next five years.

The general formula for this is

The amount of work
drives the number of people,
which drives the number of dollars spent.

RESOURCE	Year 1	Year 2	Year 3	Year 4	Year 5
• Subject-Matter Experts • Instructional Designers • Instructors • Other Professionals					
TOTAL PROFESSIONALS					
TOTAL SUPPORT STAFF					
TOTAL MANAGEMENT					
TOTAL HEADS					

Figure 16-11   Five-Year Staffing Forecast Roll-Up

You can work this backwards, too. You can say, "I have x dollars, so y is the number of people I can have, so z is the amount of work that will be done." This is useful when facing budget cutbacks.

SUMMARY

The purpose of this chapter is to help you identify the number and types of people you need to carry out the training work. The steps in this process are as follows:

☐ Identify

- Key responsibilities

- Tasks

- Skills and knowledge

- Experience requirements for each training function
  - Needs analysis
  - Curriculum architecture design
  - Development of training materials
  - Development of training systems
  - Delivery of training
  - Results measurement and evaluation
  - Support services
  - Management of training
  - Planning

☐ Design jobs, including

- Title

- Mission

- Responsibilities and tasks

- Relative importance of responsibilities and tasks

- Percentage of time spent on each responsibility area

- Performance measures

- Skill and knowledge requirements

- Educational requirements

- Experience requirements

☐ Establish selection and development criteria and strategies.

☐ Define resource pools and rotational and career progression policies

☐ Forecast number of staff needed for next five years

- Professionals
- Support staff
- Management

☐ Calculate dollar cost of forecasted staff.

FACILITIES STRATEGY AND PLAN

While a good training facility will not guarantee good training, inappropriate or poor facilities will almost certainly get in the way. Your training facility and how well it is designed and equipped sends a signal to trainees and to your customers about how the company feels about training and the development of its most important asset.

We have seen clients with multimillion dollar budgets building high-tech products costing several million dollars apiece whose training facilities were small, dark, dirty, cluttered, hot, and poorly equipped and whose employees were convinced that the company could care less about how well they did on the job, because the company could obviously care less about how they learned to do it. You can not afford to send this kind of message. You need the best facility you can possibly afford, and even if it is not world class, make sure it is clean, organized, well lighted, and well vented.

There was a lot of construction of corporate education centers in the 1960s and 1970s. But the culture was against it in the 1980s—the mood was for downsizing and giving less attention to corporate education and training. We are seeing a resurgence of interest in this area now. An impressive corporate education center sends a signal to employees, customers, and the world that your company thinks education is important. It also provides a focal point for the educational activities of your company.

There are certain types of training, such as hands-on laboratory practice, that cannot be done without a training facility. An example is a telephone company training facility that has poles set up to practice climbing, cables and dummy manholes for splicing, practice buildings for running and connecting wires, telephone switching systems, etc.

In doing your facilities strategy, you must recognize that trainees are people, and if they are going to be staying at a training facility, you must pay attention to their recreational and other human needs and decide whether you are going to design the training facility with living space. If not, you will need to locate it close to a hotel.

The problem with building a training center with living space is that once you have it, there is a lot of pressure to keep it filled to justify the expenditure. If you are not careful, then the training department becomes responsible for filling space and not for providing training when and where it is needed. As a general principle, it is better to undersize than oversize. It is easier to rent hotel space than to fill it.

Issues in locating the training facility include

- Trainee travel policies
- Proximity to transportation hubs
- Proximity to expert resources.

Whether you need one classroom or a hotel-type corporate education center with living space, this chapter shows you how to develop and plan your facilities strategy.

FACILITIES STRATEGY

The issues that drive your facilities strategy include

- Aggregate demand
- Trainee geographical distribution
- Statistical distribution of delivery volume by course and geography
- Delivery strategy mix
- Joint use by more than one training department.

Other concerns that affect your facilities strategy include

- Potential alternative uses (e.g., conference services)
- Living arrangements
- Dining arrangements
- Trainee recreation
- Trainee travel policies
- Proximity to transportation hubs
- Proximity to expert resources
- Facility fill rates.

Your broad strategy formation will fall somewhere between the extremes of having your training all in one location or providing training at every employee location. You will end up with two kinds of facilities plans:

- Global strategic plan—showing the quantitative mix of facility types and sizes by location

- Individual facility or location plan—projecting the capacity and features required for a specific location over the planning period and facility increment and tactics required to meet the requirements during development.

In this chapter, we are primarily interested in broad strategy formation and the global strategic plan. Developing detailed individual facility or location plans is beyond the scope of this book.

Broad Strategy Formation

Step 1 Review your answers to the issues and drivers listed in the previous section.

Step 2 Identify the types of facilities that could be used to meet the needs, such as

- Centralized corporate training center
- Regional corporate training center
- Local training center
- Rented hotel conference rooms or conference center space
- Conference rooms in company office building
- Training space in plants or other company facilities where trainees normally work
- Satellite TV networks
- Training center on wheels.

Step 3 List the types of training to be provided and identify one or more possible facility type, for each training type as shown in Figure 17-1. There may be other categories for types of training or facilities. These are only meant as examples.

Step 4 For each type of training, quantify the demand by geographical location. For example, if you have a relatively small number of executives and middle managers, you may want to bring them all together in one location. If you have lots of widespread executives and middle managers, you may want to supplement your plan with a satellite

Facility Types (from Step 2)--->	A	B	C	D	E	F	G	H
• Executive & Middle Mgmt. Development	X	X		?			X	
• Generic Management Skills	X	X	X	X	X	X	X	
• Lab-type Technical Training	X	X	X			X		X
• Low-volume, Hi-cost, Equip. Intensive	X	X						?
• Hi-volume, non-lab Job Skills			X	X	X	X	X	

Figure 17-1 Facility Types by Training Types Matrix

network which gives you a single class with worldwide distribution and does not require executives to travel.

Generic management skills can generally be taught anywhere. The question becomes the economics of travel and class size (which translates into instructor efficiency, classroom efficiency and timeliness of training). For example, consider a basic supervisory skills course. If you have a demand in the metropolitan Chicago area of 360 seats per year and each class can handle fifteen students, you can run twenty-four full classes. This equals two classes every month. There is no point in shipping students someplace for training that is given this frequently. On the other hand, suppose you have thirty-six students in Springfield. You could run two full classes and one half class in Springfield which means at best you can schedule one class every four months. It is questionable whether you would choose to teach in Springfield, because you do not want to have a new supervisor waiting four months to get basic skills training. Most likely, you would send that person to Chicago.

You are trying to identify those locations where demand will support a delivery site and then aggregate demand into that site from the surrounding regions where you cannot justify local delivery.

For lab and shop types of technical training, such as

- Training auto mechanics from dealerships

- Repair training for office equipment

- Installation training

- Training requiring expensive simulators,

you should take the following steps:

1. Add up the cost of a fully equipped lab.

2. See how many labs are required to satisfy the total demand (including running more than one shift, if necessary).

3. Place that number of labs at locations that minimize trainee travel and living expenses.

You can also take a look at a map of the distribution of trainees and see if there is any place where you have expensive travel, and investigate if you need to put in a lab at that location. You want to work the trade-off between travel expense and lab expense. You should also consider whether it is feasible to equip a lab on wheels and ship it around to concentrations of trainees instead of sending the trainees somewhere.

For low volume, high-cost equipment training such as

- Gas turbines
- Nuclear power plants
- Flight simulators for high-performance aircraft,

your considerations are basically the same as for the lab type, but your choices are narrower. Basically, your choice is between one centralized location versus regional locations, depending on how much demand there is and where the demand is located.

For high-volume, nonlaboratory job skills training, you would follow the same logic steps as for generic management skills except you do not have to consider centralized and regional training or training on wheels because the high demand means you can afford more widely scattered locations.

Out of all this comes a set of decision rules to follow in deciding where training is delivered. A decision model like the one mapped in Figure 13-2 can help you in calculating the trade-offs of these various alternatives.

Global Strategic Plan

You must look at all this information and decide what is needed in terms of facilities. For example, you may have enough justification to build a new corporate education center in your headquarters city, and/or you may build regional training centers in New York, Chicago, Los Angeles, Paris, Hong Kong, and Buenos Aires. You may decide that within the United States you will have a satellite TV network that connects fifty major administrative locations throughout the world. You may also decide to have a fleet of tractor trailers capable of transporting training labs for fourteen different programs. Within the United States, this fleet will be centered at the regional training centers in New York, Chicago, and Los Angeles. You may decide that all other training will be in training space in the plants or other company facilities as well as rented hotel or conference space. If you are not as big as all this, you just scale these decisions down to meet your need.

After you have made these choices, you can look at the training delivery forecast over the next five years and forecast the amount of training to be delivered at each location for each type of training. You can do this by identifying where the trainees come from and allocating trainees to the most convenient and efficient locations for the highest number of trainers.

One way to look at your demand and facility decisions is to analyze your present capacity compared to demand, as shown in Figure 17-2. The existing capacity versus demand shows that you are obviously out of space in less than a year. You should have seen this coming, but now what do you do? Your choices are either

1. Add to the existing center.

2. Build a new center for technical training and keep the existing center for executive and management development, professional orientation, and other miscellaneous training activities.

The impact of these choices is also shown in Figure 17-2.

The general principle here is that with growing demand, capacity and demand are never in balance except at any one point in time. You need to do an economic analysis to determine the incremental amount of growth for capacity that will make the best use

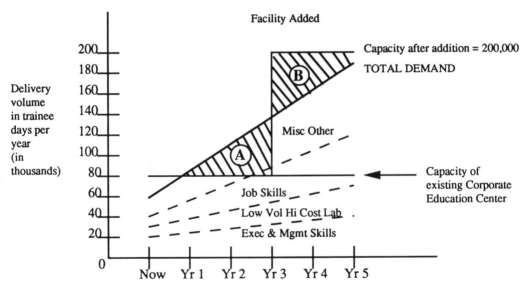

Ⓐ During this time, the load is higher than the capacity, so you will need to use rented quarters.

Ⓑ During this time, the load is under capacity, so you will need to advertise your training center for conference space and other alternate uses.

Figure 17-2 Analysis of Existing Capacity versus Demand

of the company's financial resources. To do this, you will need to bring in your company's financial wizards to help you analyze the trade-offs between costs and benefits for increasing your training capacity.

Suppose you still have to decide whether to add onto the existing center or build a new center but you want to start lab training now. You may ask, "Can we rehab the existing corporate education center to put labs in now?" The answer to this questions is most likely yes, but that cuts the capacity of the existing center even further when you convert the space. The choices you face now are

- Go ahead and rehab the existing corporate education center.

- Plan an addition to the existing center equal to the amount of lab space converted.

- Find final temporary quarters for executive and management development and miscellany.

- Start constructing a new executive and management development center.

You can keep on imagining various different alternatives to solve the problem and analyzing their advantages and disadvantages. Ultimately, you will make some basic choices with the help of some financial analysts.

Once you have made your basic choices, you can go back and add some more detail to the requirements, such as

- Number and size of classrooms

- Number and size of labs

- Number and size of breakout rooms

- Number of administrative offices, by size

- Number of conference rooms for training staff

- Computer center

- Facilities for producing, staging, and storing training materials

- Shops for constructing and repairing lab equipment and audiovisual and other equipment

- Storage for lab and audiovisual equipment

- Trainee break rooms and lounges

- Reception center

- Library

- Central files.

You should do this for every location in your geographical domain. Then you can determine if you should buy these things and calculate the capital investment over a five-year period for building, land, furnishings, and equipment. You should also estimate your operating expenses for utilities, taxes, building operation, rental space, etc. All of this gets ground into the resource requirements for the whole strategic training plan.

SUMMARY

Your overall facilities strategy is an important part of the resource requirements and strategic plan if you want to have a world class training system and send a message that you value education. Your facilities strategy should include three major elements:

☐ Broad strategy formation
- Review issues and drivers.
- Identify potential facility types.
- Match facility types to training types.
- Quantify training demand by geographical location.
- Identify location where demand will support a facility.

☐ Global strategic plan
- Specify locations, types, and overall sizes of facilities.
- Do cost analysis for various options.

☐ Individual facility specifications
- Number, size, and types of rooms
- Equipment needs
- Filing and storage needs
- Etc.

SUMMARY OF OVERALL RESOURCE REQUIREMENTS

Ultimately you need to take all the work you have done in chapters 10 through 17 and roll it up into one realistic set of scenarios to present to executives. As with the previously described development and delivery scenarios, you should have

- One complete scenario that represents the status quo

- One scenario for meeting all the needs you can economically justify

- One or more realistic scenarios in between these two.

The way this overall roll-up should work is shown in Figure 18-1.

Figure 18-2 provides a format for rolling up all these various elements. All the data you need comes from the charts and worksheets you developed in chapters 10 through 17. (Some of the cost calculation data for this roll-up was covered in chapter 7.)

Do a roll-up chart for each year in your planning period as well as for each scenario you develop. (Evaluation and support are covered in more detail when we discuss phase 3.) This will become an important part of your presentation to executives. It is the culmination of all your phase 2 work.

Documenting and Presenting the Plan

After going through all this detail in chapters 10 through 17 it should be obvious that you made hundreds of small and not so small decisions and judgments along the way. It is crucial that all this be documented—not just the final result, but the trail to getting there. Otherwise, only the people who developed the numbers are capable of going back

Types of Resources	Requirement Categories	Overall Requirements
• Staff • Facilities • Equipment X • Materials etc.	• Governance • Planning • Needs Analysis • Curriculum Design = • Course Devel./Acq. • Delivery • Evaluation • Admin Support	Forecast of capital and expense dollars (Scenario 1, Scenario 2, Scenario 3, etc.)

Figure 18-1   Formula for Overall Resource Requirements

SCENARIO:_____
YEAR: _____

	STAFF			EXPENSES	TOTAL
	Person Yrs A	Loaded Salary B	Staff Cost C	Fac, Equip D	E
GOVERNANCE					
PLANNING					
OPERATIONS:					
•Needs Analysis					
•Curriculum Design					
•Course Development					
•Delivery					
EVALUATION					
SUPPORT					
TOTAL			$	$	$

A x B = C
C + D = E

Figure 18-2   Overall Summary of Resource Requirements

and making any adjustments or explaining how the numbers were derived, and even those people may have great difficulty going back three to six months later and reconstructing the trail of bread crumbs.

This plan is not a once in a lifetime plan. You will want to update it at least once a year with new assumptions. We recommend the following practices for reconstructing your trail in the future.

• Take and distribute detailed and thorough minutes at every meeting.

• Develop your various scenarios using spreadsheets, and make sure the spreadsheet system has thorough user documentation so someone other than the originator can use it.

- Have all assumptions for each scenario you develop written down as well as any special considerations.

- Keep a running log of activities for creating the plan.

In addition to this detailed documentation (which should be kept by the project manager), there should be a summary of the plan that contains all the elements required by executives and others who need to know what the plan is as well as what issues dealt with. One side note—it is always a good idea to keep a list of the names of all the people who have contributed to the plan and to credit them for their contributions in the documented plan.

Once all this is documented, you need to put together a formal presentation for the executive and advisory groups to review. A half day is a good limit for presenting the plan to an executive advisory board. Unless you are dealing with a small training department, an hour or two is not enough time.

In your presentation, go back to the beginning and reemphasize the training implications of business challenges and how this plan is structured to make sure training is supporting the important business goals (Chapter 4). Another factor worth emphasizing is the importance of resource continuity. In a large training system you cannot gear up and down by large ratios on an annual basis and expect to have high quality training products that make a difference. Present enough of the trail you followed in developing the scenarios to make it clear that you are not picking numbers out of thin air, but do not get bogged down in the details of all the formulas. It is also worth making a big deal about the conservativeness of the assumptions that you used throughout the development of the numerical plan. In addition, it is extremely important in presenting the numbers to compare what is being proposed with what is actually needed. You should always keep that "need line" visible on the charts. Otherwise, it may look to others like you are trying to build an empire. Finally, you want to be sure that you present features and benefits as well as impediments to implementation and what must be done to overcome those impediments.

We recommend that at the presentation of the plan you provide each person present with a copy of the documented plan and then use overheads to take them through the portions that are relevant to their decision-making process. A typical agenda for a meeting like this is shown in Figure 18-3. As always, it is important to be well prepared and professional. Notify everyone in advance in writing, reserve the room, have materials ready, etc. This is a critical meeting for the future of your training department.

SUMMARY

When you have completed the work in chapters 11 through 17 you are ready to

- Project Purpose and Background

- Summary of Phase 2 Process Steps
  - Needs analysis
  - Curriculum design
  - Development strategies and plan
  - Delivery strategies and plan
  - Facilities
  - Staffing

- Presentation of Scenarios
  - Description
  - Data sources
  - Assumptions
  - Implications
  - Features and benefits
  - Impediments
  - Costs

- Discussion and Commitment

Figure 18-3   Typical Agenda for Phase 2 Executive Review

☐ Summarize overall resource requirements (alternative scenarios)

☐ Complete your documentation of the plan

   • Detailed

   • Executive summary

☐ Present the alternative scenarios to the executive review boards.

19

INTRODUCTION TO PHASE 3: OTHER TRAINING SYSTEMS

When we explained the overall training system in chapter 5 we pointed out that there are five major systems in the overall training system, including:

- Governance

- Planning

- Operations

- Results

- Support.

Phase 1 dealt with laying the groundwork for your training system, and phase 2 dealt with the various elements of the operations system, because operations is the central part and the biggest resource eater in your training system. In phase 3, which we deal with in this section of the book, the focus is on governance, planning, results, and support and their associated processes (see Appendix C).

To begin looking at phase 3, we suggest you go back to chapter 5 and revisit your evaluation of these systems in the context of the new plan you have been developing. Then you can identify which of the governance, planning, results, and support systems need major design and development work to support the new plan effectively.

You will then need to prepare a set of specifications and macro systems design and rationale for each system and process. Estimate what all of this would cost to develop over what period of time, and put it into your overall resource requirements (see chapter 18).

All systems and processes are important in one way or another to the successful functioning of the training system as a whole. In most cases, the customer for the system or process is the internal training department. So, following the TQM approach, with every phase 3 process you need to

- Identify your customer(s).
- Define the customer requirements for the system or process.
- Define or design the process.
- Establish performance measures for the process.
- Bring the process under control.
- Embark on continuous improvement.

Every one of these processes should be documented and have performance measures with regular data collection, allowing all people involved in the process to control the quality of the process and engage in continuous, quantitative process improvement.

We cover the specifications for all of the phase 3 systems and processes in chapter 5 and Appendix C. Not all of them are covered in this section. However, some of them are of such strategic significance that it is important to address them in more detail here:

- Organization of training
- Governance or advisory structure
- Supervisor/manager support system
- Financing and financial accountability
- Measuring results.

Although we do not cover administrative support systems in detail in this book (except for Appendix C), be sure you do not overlook their importance to your system. Such systems include

- Information systems
- Registration and scheduling
- Communications
- Production support
- Technologies
- Specialists
- Administrative manuals

- External resources.

Two other administrative systems (staffing and facilities) were dealt with in Phase 2 (Chapters 16 and 17).

Organization of Training   This is a strategic issue because it affects the linkage and communications channels between the training department and its customers. It affects the ability of the training departments to recruit and support specialized expertise in instructional design and other training and education specialties. It also affects the ability to establish and manage the training processes. It affects the efficient and effective teaming of subject-matter experts with instructional specialists. It affects the ability to measure and control results. It is also an issue that everyone is interested in and has opinions about. So we weigh in with our opinions. In chapter 20, we provide an approach to defining an organization structure and some pros and cons of different structural choices.

Governing or Advisory Structure   This system formalizes the partnership between the training department and its customers. It provides a systematic method or forum for joint decision making as well as for the identification and prioritization of needs, strategies and plans for meeting those needs, resources to be allocated, and assessment of the effectiveness of the training and education system. Without a formalized advisory structure, the training departments are usually subjected to the conflicting wants and whims of individual executives and managers, who represent various facets of the customer world. There is no forum in which to debate and reconcile conflicting priorities, needs, or plans, which leaves training in a no-win position. The type of strategic training plan we have been advocating in this book has little chance of succeeding without the support of an overall executive training advisory group. The needs analysis and curriculum design and development approach has little chance of succeeding without curriculum advisory groups. Coordination of training systems and processes across multiple training departments has little chance of success without the training administrative council. Chapter 21 provides more detail on the governance or advisory structure and its processes.

Supervisor/Manager Support System   The supervisors and managers in the line and staff organizations that are customers of training have critical roles to play in the overall training systems, including

- Developing individual training plans with subordinates
- Developing training plans for their organizational unit
- Preparing subordinates for training
- Making sure that the lessons learned in training are appropriately applied on the job

- Providing coaching to further strengthen and reinforce on-the-job application
- Identifying unmet training needs
- Providing evaluative feedback to the training department on the training system.

Managers and supervisors are not born with the skills and knowledge to do all of this. To do it effectively, they have to be provided with job aids and training expectations and feedback. If this is not done you can have the world's finest training department with the best staff, all the money needed, and the best equipment, and training will only achieve a fraction of its potential payoff. Chapter 22 deals with the supervisor/manager support system.

FINANCING AND FINANCIAL ACCOUNTABILITY

As we have seen throughout this book, good training is expensive and represents a major investment of corporate resources. To manage that investment effectively and to maximize the business return on investment, you must to have an appropriately designed system for financing the effort, making the appropriate investment decisions, tracking expenditures, and holding the spenders accountable. It is almost a cliché that when times get tough, the first thing that gets cut is training. Large, arbitrary cuts in training finances defeat a company's ability to sustain a world-class training system that will support the company's business goals. The financing system has to be robust enough to withstand uninformed executive overhead cost cutting. Chapter 23 provides an overview of the different ways of solving financing problems and some of the pros and cons of each.

MEASURING RESULTS

Without results measurement, any process is out of control. The measurement of training results is especially important, since the effectiveness of training has a potentially major impact on business success and is a consumer of lots of resources. Some of the important results areas include the following:

- What percentage of important training needs is being met?
- What is the satisfaction level of the training customers?
- Are the trainees actually mastering the required competencies?
- Is there substantial application of the learned competencies back on the job?
- What is the return on training investment?

To have true control of your training systems, a formalized measurement system is needed to measure and report results in each of these areas. Chapter 24 provides more detailed descriptions of the results areas and a measurement system approach to measuring those results.

20

ORGANIZATION OF TRAINING

The way the training organization is structured is an important strategic issue. It can also be a political and emotional process, as people struggle to retain power, gain new territory, or keep control of issues and people that are important to them.

There is no organization structure for training that is best for all situations. In fact, as conditions change and evolve in your company, the training structure should evolve to fit the new conditions. Part of your strategic training plan is the planned evolution of the organization of training.

The old architects' maxim, "Form follows function," applies to the design of organizations. The organization structure is form. What it is supposed to accomplish is function. The structural design should be driven by your strategic vision and goals and by the quantitative plans you have developed for the amounts of work to be performed and resources to be organized to accomplish the work. The purpose of this chapter is to present some guidelines and objective methods for developing a viable organization structure that will enable you to meet needs without ruffling too many feathers.

Some of the questions you should address in this process include

1. What training responsibilities will be delegated to training departments, and what responsibilities will be retained by line managers?
2. To what degree is it appropriate to centralize certain training responsibilities?
3. How will the organization support the specialized expertise needed to achieve strategic training goals, such as computer-based product training?
4. How will the organization facilitate management control of training results and training costs?

5. How will the organization facilitate clear communication between training units and their user groups?

6. How can we best avoid expensive duplication of training materials development?

7. How can we structure the training function to get the biggest return for our training investment?

8. What structure will best assure responsiveness to changing user needs?

Your answers to these questions will in part determine how you should structure your training organization.

GUIDELINES

There are some guidelines that have been evolved from watching the evolution of training organizations over the last eighteen years. These are not absolutes, just things to consider based on our observations of many successes and failures. Any organization structure can be made to work, but some work much better than others.

1. Create a position for a high level training officer. Every organization of any significant size should have a high-level training officer who has responsibilities broad enough to provide leadership and to oversee training across the entire organization and represent training issues in executive circles. Motorola has a President of Motorola University, Ameritech has a Vice President of Education and Training. There are many other examples.

2. Do not make the training departments too big. In a large corporation, do not try to force all training into one huge training department. Giant training departments that try to be all things to all people get unwieldy, bureaucratic, and unresponsive to their users.

3. Training departments should be large enough to support the specialized expertise needed to fulfill their responsibilities. Modern, high-quality training may require specialized expertise in

- Performance analysis and training needs analysis
- Curriculum architecture design
- Instructional design and development
- Testing, measurement, and evaluation
- Computer-based training
- Video and audio scripting and production

- Expert systems.

Small training units scattered all over the corporate landscape never achieve the critical mass necessary to support all these specialties.

4. Centralize curriculum architecture and common instructional materials development. A common curriculum architecture for a function such as marketing or sales provides the framework on which to hang all the needed training materials. With a common curriculum architecture, the needed modules can be developed once and used by everyone. There is no need for each business unit or division to develop its own basic selling skills course. The centralization of development and procurement is worth millions per year to a major corporation.

5. Establish one organizational unit to provide leadership in the areas of instructional methodology, technology, and procedures. Corporations with multiple training departments each espousing different methods, standards, and procedures have great difficulty sharing curriculum, course materials, administrative systems, and the like. One of the competitive advantages of size is the potential for synergy and sharing among organizational units. We see far too many training units who maintain a posture of arrogant competition and "not invented here" with respect to training units in sister plants or other departments of the same company. The corporate training unit headed by the company's top training officer should have the responsibility of leading all the training units to a common instructional discipline and a spirit of sharing and synergy among the units. In addition, every large training department should have one organizational subunit charged with instructional methodology leadership and consulting within the department. The subunit should be linked closely with similar groups in other training departments.

6. Do not try to mix instructional design and training materials development and instructing in the same jobs. Developing instructional materials should follow a systematic development project plan and process. Interrupting development work to teach can have strong negative effects on the development projects, particularly if the people involved have a heavy teaching load. One exception to this rule is that it is a good idea to use active instructors as technical advisors to the development team. This role can be handled as part of a busy teaching schedule and can make a substantial contribution to the development effort. It is particularly important to involve some of the instructors who will teach the course when it is ready to deliver.

We have found that problems are more likely to occur when development and delivery report up through long chains of command before they come together under a common manager. The best arrangements involve a manager with a defined curriculum area (e.g., the sales curriculum) who has several development supervisors and several delivery supervisors. This allows one level of supervision to specialize in either development or delivery and provides a manager who can resolve conflicts without a long escalation chain and who can represent the total curriculum area to the clients.

DESIGNING THE MACRO ORGANIZATION STRUCTURE

The macro organization structure describes the overall organization structure for a business or business unit. Figure 20-1 shows a macro organization structure for the fictitious UMC Corporation.

For a large organization, such as a major corporation, the first major decisions in designing the macro organization structure should answer these questions:

- How many training organizations will there be?

- To whom will they report?

- What are their missions and responsibilities?

- How will they be linked together to achieve synergy and avoid unnecessary duplication?

- How will they be linked together to best serve the training client?

The general approach to answering these questions is to

- Develop a set of alternatives.

- Develop a list of criteria for comparing the alternatives.

- Compare the alternatives and choose one or two for recommendations to executive management.

- Make your recommendation to executive management.

- Design the final structure based on executive feedback.

The best method we have found for doing this is to use a group process involving training directors and others who have a major stake in the outcome. Have a neutral facilitator lead the group process. One rule to remember is that there is no organizational structure that simultaneously maximizes all the criteria. Compromises will have to be made.

Figure 20-2 provides a sample criterion evaluation sheet for comparing alternative structures. In this example, alternative B scored 180 out of a possible 234 points. This method is not foolproof, but it does take some of the emotion out of the decision making by comparing organizational alternatives against a list of important criteria. Weighting the criteria is useful since they are never all equally important. Of course, you should develop your own list of criteria and establish your own weights.

One way of using this rating sheet is to have each individual on the design team

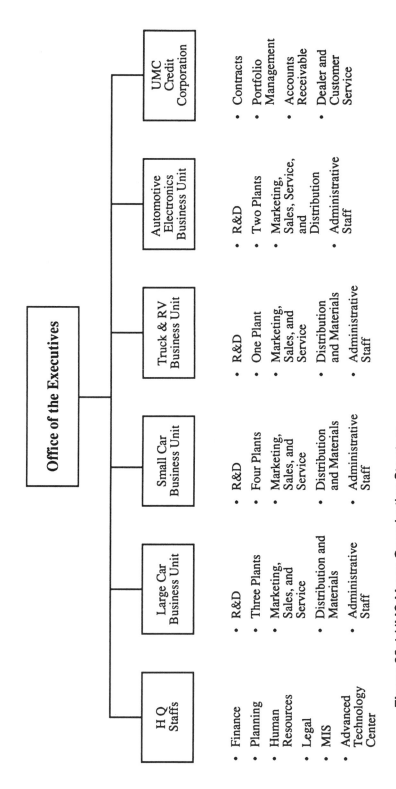

Figure 20-1 UMC Macro Organization Structure

315

fill out the rating sheet after agreeing on the criteria and weighting. If there are major differences in scores on individual criteria, these should be discovered and opportunity be given for individuals to change their ratings. Then sum the scores for the alternative. If you are lucky, one alternative will be an obvious winner.

Comparison of the ratings among competing alternatives may suggest further alternatives which combine some of the best features of the original alternatives and avoid some of the worst faults. The best structures we have seen have been developed this way. The first set of alternatives almost never includes the best design that could be created.

Figure 20-3 shows a logical macro training organization structure alternative.

This structure has a strong corporate training organization to provide leadership to the training function throughout the corporation and to provide development and delivery of training most effectively and economically done centrally. The business units each have a training department to deal with training best done at the business unit level such as product-specific training. Similarly, each plant has its own training unit to deal with the right volume training needs at the plant. The UMC Vice President of Education and Training has direct control of the corporate education department and the corporate training staff and indirect supervision of the business unit and credit corporation training directors.

DESIGNING THE MICRO ORGANIZATION STRUCTURE

The micro organizational structure defines the organization within an individual training department. Key questions to be answered by this design include

- What types of subfunctions and jobs are needed to fulfill the department's mission and responsibilities?
- What is the best structure to house these subfunctions and jobs to assure responsiveness to client needs, quality, and economy?
- What are the key interfaces to the world outside the training department?
- What is the internal work and information flow?

The chart in Figure 20-4 provides a partial list of the subfunctions and types of jobs at the working level.

The design procedure follows the same basic steps as the macro organization design:

1. Identify subfunctions and jobs.
2. Develop structural alternatives.
3. Identify comparison criteria and weightings.
4. Compare alternatives and select one for recommendation to management.
5. Adjust design depending on management feedback.

Criteria	(1-10) Weight	(1-3) Score	Weighted Score
Alternative _____ B _____			
1. Responsiveness to client needs	10	3	30
2. Least overall cost	8	2	16
3. Commonality of training methods and procedures	5	1	5
4. Internal communications within training	5	1	5
5. Support for specialized expertise	6	2	12
6. Provides vehicle for instilling corporate values and culture	7	3	21
7. Avoids duplication of instructional materials development	7	2	14
8. Provides a means for delivering high-cost, low-volume training (such as for plant engineers)	9	3	27
9. Provides for a high-level corporate training officer	8	3	24
10. Fits corporate organizational philosophy (e.g., centralized vs. decentralized)	4	2	8
11. Linkage to client/customer organizations	9	2	18
Total			180
Maximum Possible			234

Figure 20-2   Evaluation Sheet for Organizational Alternatives (Example)

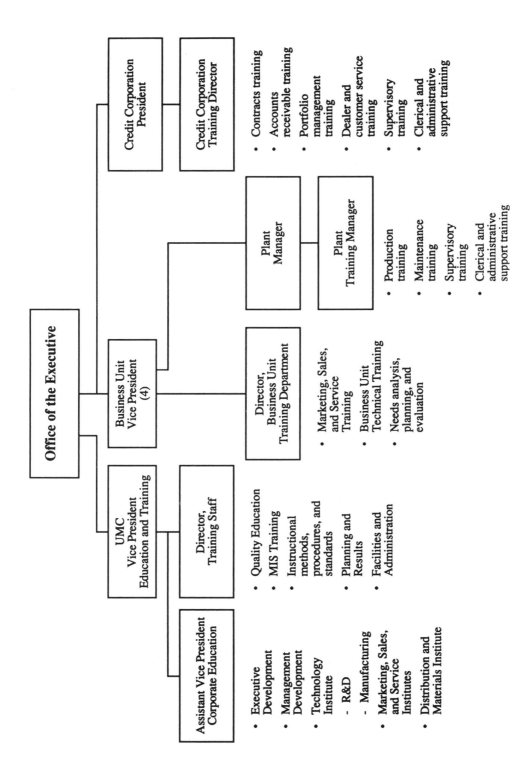

Figure 20-3 Example Macro Training Organization Structure

Subfunction	Jobs
Needs analysis and curriculum architecture design	<ul><li>Analyst</li><li>Instructional designer</li><li>Typing and graphic arts</li></ul>

Instructional materials development and maintenance	<ul><li>Analyst</li><li>Instructional designer</li><li>Content expert</li><li>Writer</li><li>Media specialists
	  - Video
	  - Computer-based instruction</li><li>Editor</li><li>Typing and graphic arts</li></ul>

Delivery	<ul><li>Instructor</li><li>Administrator of self-paced instruction</li><li>Administrative clerical support</li><li>Registration clerk</li><li>Scheduler</li><li>Lab technicians</li></ul>
Evaluation and Results	<ul><li>Measurement specialist</li><li>Analyst</li><li>Clerical support</li><li>Programming support</li></ul>
Planning	<ul><li>Planner</li><li>Clerical support</li><li>Programming support</li></ul>
Facilities Management	<ul><li>Food service staff</li><li>Cleaning staff</li><li>Building engineer</li><li>Maintenance technician</li></ul>
Materials Management	<ul><li>Reproduction clerk</li><li>Shipping clerk</li><li>Stockroom clerk</li><li>Inventory clerk</li></ul>

Figure 20-4   Training Organization Substructure over Jobs

The internal micro design of the training department should be done by a design team made up of people who will have to live in the department and led by a neutral facilitator. The same approach to developing a weighted criterion list and scoring chart can be used as described earlier for the macro organization design.

The example micro structure shown in Figure 20-5 (or some variant of it) has been found to work well across a wide variety of organizations from manufacturing to insurance.

SUMMARY

Designing the training organization structure to support a large organization is not a trivial task. The structure can have a major impact on the effectiveness of training in meeting the needs of the business and the overall cost of meeting those needs. Organization structures can be political and emotional issues. Going through a structured design and review process like the one described in this chapter, with objective criteria to compare the alternatives, will help take some of the emotion out of it. A neutral design consultant to facilitate the process and help suggest and compare alternatives will also help. The process is as follows:

☐ Evaluate organizational alternatives.
☐ Design the macro training structure.
☐ Design the micro training structure.

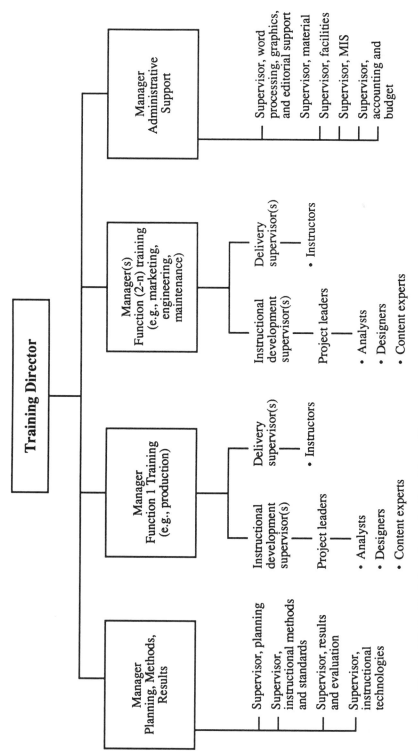

Figure 20-5 Training Organization Micro Structure

321

21

GOVERNING OR ADVISORY STRUCTURE

People often ask us what is the one most important ingredient in a successful training system. We always answer without hesitation that it is the governing or advisory structure. In our strategic planning for training workshops, we always recommend to participants that if they do not follow any of our other suggestions, they should not fail to implement this one.

What is it about the governing structure that is so important? One of the maxims of the modern excellence and quality movements is the notion, "The customer is king." The governing system is a structural, proven way to actualize this maxim for training. The customer for the training department is all the internal and external organizations and people served by them. The governing structure provides the mechanism for these customers to partner with the training department in exercising control over the training they receive.

If you accept the thesis that training only exists to enhance the business performance of organizational units and individuals, then you must accept that the training users have an enormous stake in what training is provided. The training customer has a legitimate interest in

- What programs are provided
- How and where they are delivered
- Availability and timeliness of training
- Relevance of the content to organizational and individual performance
- All the associated costs.

The governing structure provides a system of representation for these training customers to share in making training decisions to further their own legitimate interests.

We know many training directors and training managers who have resisted this concept of letting the customer make critical training decisions. They seem to fear that their budgets will be cut, that they are giving up authority and power over their own department, or that the customer groups will make unwise decisions. Our experience is that these fears are groundless. The training departments that operate under a strong governance system generally enjoy a higher reputation inside their companies and in the training community at large, they grow to meet real needs, are protected from arbitrary cuts in tough times, and have influence across the entire organization. The influence gained is much more potent than exercising autocratic power over the training department.

The governing or advisory structure provides the mechanism for a synergistic partnership between the training department and those it serves, enabling much higher levels of performance and achievement by both parties than either could achieve with an arm's-length provider/customer relationship.

BSCTE, THE HISTORY OF A SUCCESSFUL GOVERNING STRUCTURE

When Ray Svenson joined the Bell System Center for Technical Education (BSCTE) in 1972 as Manager of Planning, Methods and Results, the beginning of a fully articulated advisory structure was already in place. He tells the following story about the development of the full-fledged advisory structure at BSCTE.

Board of Advisors

The Board of Advisors consisted of some of the most respected engineering vice presidents from the operating telephone companies and assistant vice presidents of engineering from AT&T Headquarters. They met twice a year to review our goals, help set priorities, vote a budget, and set our tuition rate.

I'll never forget my first meeting. We proposed a course development budget of $1 million. This was an increase of about 30 percent over the previous year. They looked at the priorities, decided that we had to do more, and forced an additional $150,000 on us. It was all we could handle without the growth rate throwing us out of control. As in all succeeding board meetings I attended, there was a debate between the conservatives, who felt we should go slow to control spending and the hawks who saw training as a crucial element of success in the company's technological revolution. The final result was always a balance between the conservative and hawk positions, but it was a result all could accept and support.

If we and our executive bosses at AT&T had set the budget, everyone would have called us wrong. The conservatives would have accused us of empire building, and the hawks would have accused us of going too slow and obstructing progress. Instead, the size of the operation was doubled every three years from 1968, when AT&T opened, until 1984, when AT&T broke apart. Every step of growth was fully supported by a powerful cadre of executives who were not and never had been trainers.

Chuck Sener, the founder of the BSCTE, set up the board of advisors with more members from the operating companies than from AT&T Headquarters. The operating companies were our true customer. They paid our bills and benefited from the training we provided. They therefore deserved to dominate the decision making. AT&T was in effect our supplier. They represented the cornucopia of new technology, new methods, and new systems. They played an extremely valuable role on the board since they could usually see farther over the technical horizon than the operating heads.

Steering Committees

Another feature of the early BSCTE governance structure was the steering committees which were organized to guide the development of new courses. The steering committees were composed of middle managers from the operating companies and AT&T who had a direct stake in the course being developed. They would meet four or five times during the development of a new course to provide customer input and direction.

The first meeting was usually a review of the purpose, concept and scope of the course as well as the development project plan. If the project was off target from the users' point of view, it could be redirected from the start before any real resources were consumed. As the project progressed, these committees provided useful input on priorities for tasks to be taught and other content of instruction. They were invaluable for identifying and providing access to sources of information from the field, from AT&T, and Bell Labs. They reviewed drafts of training materials for accuracy of content and conformance to company policies. They helped recruit students for the pilot and early sessions of the course. They helped recruit top talent from the field to serve as instructors. And they went home and presold the course to the user organizations.

It is a training director's dream to have managers in the field driving demand for new courses. The steering committee system built in quality from the user's point of view and stimulated tremendous demand for the training.

Curriculum Planning Councils

By 1973, the course development program had expanded to the point where we were developing dozens of new courses per year, with course development budgets and workload doubling every two to three years. The board of advisors was increasingly drawn into strategic planning and overall governance issues and becoming less and less able to sort out priorities among competing new course development projects. It became apparent that we needed an advisory level between the board of advisors and the steering committees.

Out of this need was born the concept of the curriculum advisory council. The councils provided a level of governance over a family of courses or curriculum relating to a functional technical discipline in the operating telephone companies. These functional disciplines were our major training market segments. They had names like Outside Plant Engineering, Central Office Engineering, Technical Planning, Network Administration, and Commercial Forecasting.

Between 1973 and 1978, approximately fifteen curriculum advisory councils were formed. The councils were made up of fourth-level managers, two levels below the board of advisors. They were chaired by the AT&T staff manager with responsibility for support of that technical discipline and the remaining members, usually six to eight, were from the operating companies. Each member represented approximately three operating companies.

Preproject Studies

At about the same time that we created the curriculum advisory councils, we introduced a requirement that no new course development project would be funded without first completing a preproject study. The purpose of a preproject study was to investigate the business benefit versus cost of developing and delivering a new course. It took a few weeks of an investigators time, starting with a one page or one line request for a course, to answer the following questions:

- What is the problem?

- What is it costing the company?

- What is causing the problem, lack of skill and knowledge, or other factors?

- If training is a legitimate solution, what is the cost/benefit ratio?

The curriculum advisory council became a wonderful mechanism for generating and screening the initial list of problem statements, voting priorities for preproject studies, reviewing the results of preproject studies,voting priorities for course development, and recommending a course development budget to the board of advisors. The initial screening process based on the knowledge of the council members rejected about 25 percent of the list of requested courses, an additional 25 percent were rejected through preproject analysis, and the remaining 50 percent were subjected to prioritization for budget allocation. Very few courses made it through this process that were not winners when they were developed and put on line.

In spite of this ruthless paring of the wish lists, this curriculum planning process became a powerful engine that continued to put upward pressure on the course development budget. Each of these councils was lobbying with the board of advisors for their program, priorities and budget. This upward pressure kept the development budget growing at an exponential rate throughout the 1970s. This was another training director's dream—line managers lobbying with executives in support of their course development budget. All we had to do was run the planning process, serve as staff support to the curriculum advisory councils and board of advisors, tell the councils whom to lobby with, present the options to the board, and stand back and accept the results.

In addition to this front-end planning role, the curriculum advisory councils were expected to appoint the steering committees or project committees for course development projects, review results of the curriculum under their jurisdiction, and prioritize and recommend a course maintenance budget.

Curriculum Architecture

By about 1975 to 1976, we had populated some of the curricula with enough courses that the questions of overlapping content, gaps, and logical sequences of courses could not be ignored. The solution was the development of a curriculum architecture for each major discipline. These were created through curriculum studies, by analyzing the work to be done by the target audience and the broad mix of skills and knowledge required and chunking the required training into logically related sequences of courses with minimal overlaps or gaps. The curriculum advisory councils sponsored the curriculum studies and used the resulting curriculum architectures as a menu for preproject priorities and course development priorities.

Departmental Advisory Boards

Along the way, another level of advisory boards was created between the board of advisors and the curriculum advisory councils. These were departmental advisory boards at the fifth level of management, and they had titles like Engineering Education Advisory Board, Network Operations Training Advisory Board, and Forecasting Training Advisory Board. This helped sort out priorities between the curriculum advisory council level and the board of advisors. I believe to this day that they were a mixed blessing. They contributed one more layer of political support which was sometimes very helpful, but they also added another layer of bureaucracy that was not really essential to effective decision making.

Administrative Coordinators

The final advisory group that contributed to the success of BSCTE was called the Lisle Coordinators. (BSCTE was located in Lisle, Illinois). These were our administrative interfaces with our customers, the operating telephone companies. In most cases, they were the heads of engineering training for their company. This group met with us twice a year to work through issues of training administration such as policies and procedures for registration, scheduling, cancellation, financial transactions, and transfer of courseware.

Meeting Management

By the late 1970s, on any given week there were usually one or more of the advisory groups meeting at the training center. Their participation kept the program vital and responsible to user needs, sold the budget year after year, and supported construction of courses.

These groups were always treated like our owners and customers. We usually provided a social hour and dinner the night before the meeting for informal discussion of issues. The meetings were run with pre-prepared agendas and materials mailed in advance. Meetings were decision oriented, not a show-and-tell by the training organization. Members were generally not permitted to delegate attendance to subordinates. Our absence rate was very low, and we had some of the best managers in the business on our councils and boards.

The dynamics of this type of system can get a little rough and tumble, since good managers will not keep quiet about important problems and issues and since different interest groups have different needs they want met. Based on my experiences at BSCTE and with many subsequent clients, I believe that representative systematic group decision making based on systematic analysis of needs is far superior to under-the-table politics which often leads to supplier and customer alienation."

BUILDING YOUR OWN ADVISORY STRUCTURE

You will need to design a structure that fits your own organization and your own needs. For a small, narrowly focused training system such as might be found in a small- to medium-sized manufacturing plant, one advisory committee supported by project committees is probably enough. For a major corporation like AT&T, IBM, or GM, the governance structure will need to have wheels within wheels within wheels.

Sample Governance Structure, UTX Corporation

The chart in Figure 21-1 shows the governance structure for UTX, a fictitious medium sized manufacturing company.

The following sections provide charters for the UTX governance groups. You can develop charters for your own governance groups by simply editing these to fit your own situation.

The purpose of the UTX training governance structure is to formalize the partnership between training and line management for overall direction and resourcing of the training function to meet important business requirements. It also serves to coordinate and unify the training system across the corporation.

The training governance structure includes

- An executive training advisory board
- Functional curriculum advisory councils
    - Marketing and sales curriculum council
    - Engineering curriculum council

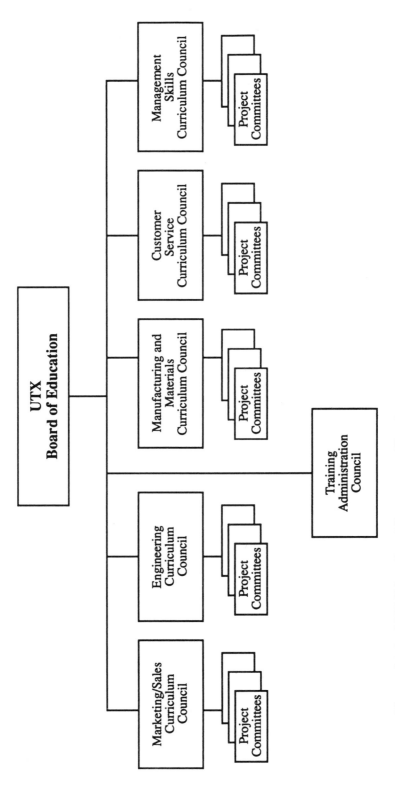

Figure 21-1 UTX Educational Governance Structure

- Manufacturing and materials curriculum council
- Customer service curriculum council
- Management skills curriculum council
- Others as determined by the training advisory board
- Training administration council

These councils represent all business units and all levels of training.

Executive Training Advisory Board

Mission   The mission of the executive training advisory board is to support, advise and oversee the management and operation of all UTX training to ensure that training is properly focused and resourced to meet important business needs.

Roles
The roles of the board include:

- Review and concur in overall mission and philosophy statements for training.

- Review and approve strategic training plans.
  - Corporate education
  - Each business unit.

- Review and approve annual objectives and budget for corporate education.

- Establish priorities across programs identified by subsidiary curriculum advisory councils.

- Review annual results compared to objectives.

- Review progress toward strategic goals
  - Corporate education
  - Each business unit.

- Review and approve overall policies for training and education within UTX.

Membership

The executive training advisory board is chaired by the CEO, who will appoint the other members with recommendations by the training director.
The recommended initial group includes

- David Braun, CEO, Chairperson

- Jane Steele, VP Corporate Support

- Daniel Valdez, VP Sable Products

- Kim Soon, VP Industrial Products
- Cynthia Van der Zant, VP International
- Maria Suarez, VP Human Resources
- Chuck Little, VP Quality
- Two of the four VP/GMs
- John Stockton, Training Director, Secretary

Meetings

The board should meet at least twice per year. Members unable to attend may not delegate attendance to subordinate manager. The secretary shall supply an agenda in advance to allow proper preparation by board members and will prepare and distribute minutes promptly following each meeting.

Typical Agenda Items: UTX Executive Training Advisory Board

First (of two) meetings of the year

1. Review last year's results
   a. Training delivered
   b. Income and expense
   c. Training developed
   d. Budget conformance
   e. Utilization of staff and facilities
   f. Training effectiveness data
   g. Special problems or issues dealt with
   h. Results compared to any other objectives that were set
2. Review strategic plans
   a. Five-year projection of course development requirements
   b. Five-year forecast of delivery requirements
   c. Long-range goals and objectives
   d. Facility plans
   e. Staffing strategy
   f. Changes in mission or basic philosophy
   g. Revision of development or delivery strategies
3. Review recommended policies or policy changes

4. Review and approve major decisions requiring board action (e.g., construction plans for new training center)

5. Conduct presentations on projects or programs by the training staff for information and education of the board.

Second (last) meeting of the year

1. Establish priorities for development of new training programs for next year.

2. Review and approve major training department objectives for the coming year.

3. Review and approve training development budget.

   a. Needs analysis and curriculum architecture design

   b. New courses

   c. Course maintenance

4. Review and approve training delivery budget (and tuition level, if appropriate)

5. Discuss special problems or issues and make decisions, if appropriate

6. Presentation for information and education of board members, if time permits.

UTX Curriculum Advisory Councils

Mission   The curriculum advisory councils will, for the content areas within their jurisdiction, approve an overall curriculum architecture, determine priorities on programs to be developed, and oversee the delivery of training.

Jurisdictions   UTX curriculum advisory councils will be established to have jurisdiction over the following content areas:

- Marketing and sales curriculum council

- Engineering curriculum council

- Manufacturing and materials curriculum council

- Customer service curriculum council

- Management skills curriculum council

- Others as determined by the training advisory board

Roles   The curriculum advisory councils will have the following specific roles:

- Develop a list of functions describing their jurisdiction.

- Review and approve an overall curriculum architecture for their functional jurisdiction.

- Identify unmet training needs.
- Establish priorities for formal training needs analysis.
- Review recommendations of formal training needs analysis studies.
- Establish priorities for developing new training programs.
- Establish priorities for maintenance and upkeep of existing courses.
- Review and approve recommendations to discontinue courses.
- Review reports of efficiency and effectiveness of training.
- Establish priorities for formal follow-up evaluation on specific courses.
- Assist in the recruitment of subject-matter experts for
  - Training development teams
  - Training development project committees
  - Instructors.

Membership   The executive training advisory board will appoint the chairperson for each of the councils. The chairperson will appoint the remaining members with advice from the training director.

Membership should consist of upper-middle managers who are able to represent their organizational unit and commit resources. Total membership for each council should not exceed ten.

Meetings   Meetings should be held at least twice per year and be timed to provide necessary input to meetings of the executive training advisory board. Members unable to attend may not delegate attendance to subordinate managers but may delegate to peers.

The chairperson should supply an agenda in advance to allow proper preparation by council members. The manager representing the training department will serve as secretary and prepare and distribute minutes promptly following each meeting.

TYPICAL CURRICULUM ADVISORY COUNCIL AGENDA

New Courses

1. Make and review a list of proposed training courses.
2. Review each item in the list for the following:
   - What is the problem, who is involved, etc.?
   - What evidence exists that the problem or need is real, and what is its extent?

- What are the stakes involved?
  - Costs
  - Safety
  - Corporate image
  - Market share
  - Etc.
- What evidence exists that the problem is due to a lack of skill and/or knowledge and that training is a part or all of the solution?
- What other studies or data are available?
- Who is the key person(s) for the training department to contact regarding further investigations?
- How does the proposed course fit into the overall curriculum?
- Discard any items from the list that seem inappropriate after discussing their merits.

3. Assign priorities for formal needs analysis:

- Ask each member to rank order the remaining projects
- Develop a composite rank order by summing the rankings of the individual members
- Discuss the prioritized list and vote on acceptance
- Decide which, if any, of these projects are so certain or urgent that development should be started without formal needs analysis
- Obtain commitment from the trainers as to the number of projects likely to be analyzed before the next meeting
- Make recommendations to executive training advisory board, if appropriate.

4. Review results of formal needs analysis studies completed:

- Are the findings and conclusions believable?
- Are the recommendations based on the findings, and are they practical?
- Who will handle nontraining issues which need resolution before training development can begin?

5. Establish priorities for development:

- Review the list of projects which are candidates for course development.
- Briefly review the stakes involved in each one.
- Vote on priorities.
- Forward recommendations to executive training advisory board.

- Determine who should chair the training development project committee for each project.

6. Review status of projects under development:

- Changes in scope or intent of the course

- Schedule

- Problems requiring council help or attention (e.g., cannot get access to experts for job task analysis).

Existing Courses

1. Review status and effectiveness of courses in delivery:

- Delivery manager or instructors present evidence they have gathered.

- Review results of follow-up studies.

- Review any informal feedback gathered by council members.

- What courses should be subjected to formal follow-up evaluation?

2. Review proposed changes:

- Which courses should be discontinued, on what grounds?

- What changes are required to existing courses?
    - For instruction effectiveness
    - For content update
    - For administrative efficiency

- What resources and costs are required to implement each change?

3. Approve course maintenance program:

- Establish priorities on the proposed changes.

- Determine the level of resources to be allocated.

- Approve a list of changes.

Special Agenda Items: First Session of a New Curriculum Advisory Council

1. Overview the meeting plan.
2. Introduce council mission.
3. Overview systematic course development process and curriculum advisory council and executive training advisory board roles in planning and control.
4. Develop a list of jobs and functions to be included within the jurisdiction of the council (i.e., identify and segment the market this council is charged with serving).
5. Review typical agenda for a curriculum advisory council meeting.

6. Begin conducting the real work of the council.

TRAINING ADMINISTRATIVE COUNCIL

Mission   The mission of the training administrative council is to provide a formal means of establishing policies and procedures relating to administrative interfaces between the headquarters and business units training organizations.

Roles   The training administrative council will review and approve administrative procedures and recommend administrative policy to the executive training advisory board in the following areas:

- Advertising of available training
- Selection and registration of students
- Training records
- Tuition charges
- Billing and paying systems
- Transfer and sale of training materials
- Delivery forecasting
- Delivery systems planning
- Facility planning.

FOLLOW-UP AFTER MEETINGS

Each meeting should have carefully documented minutes. These minutes should be prepared immediately after the meeting. Submit the minutes to the chairperson for approval and for transmittal to the committee or council members. Also send copies of the minutes to members of the other related committees, councils, and training managers to keep them informed of the work your committee is doing.

You should quietly solicit verbal feedback from members on their reactions to the meetings. Get feedback on both content and process. Review this feedback with the chairperson as input to planning the next meeting.

SUMMARY

The governance or advisory structure is the single most important ingredient in a successful training system.

☐ Implement an advisory structure with the following elements:

- Executive training advisory board
- Functional curriculum advisory councils
    - Marketing and sales curriculum councils
    - Engineering curriculum council
    - Manufacturing and materials curriculum council
    - Customer service curriculum council
    - Management skills curriculum council
    - Others as determined by training advisory board.

☐ Establish a charter for each board or council, including

- Mission
- Roles
- Membership
- Meeting guidelines.

☐ Document each meeting with formal minutes, and distribute these.

☐ Provide feedback on meetings to the chairperson.

SUPERVISOR
AND MANAGER
SUPPORT SYSTEM

Supervisors and managers play some of the most critical roles in the education and training system. Yet most organizations fail to train them for these roles and provide the necessary information, resources, expectations, and consequences for effective performance.

We have personally interviewed hundreds of employees of top American companies about their jobs and the training they receive. Here are some typical comments from these interviews:

- I can go to training programs when I need them, but I'm not sure what's available and it's usually very hard to make the time.

- The orientation program for new professionals was excellent, but I should have had it at least a year ago; over half of what I learned I've picked up the hard way.

- The plant required me to take a five-day Statistical Process Control course twelve months ago even though there was no opportunity to apply what I learned in the job I had then. Now I need it, but I've forgotten most of what I learned.

- Our local travel budget got cut this year, so the training I was to receive on using my new workstation got canceled.

- I caused some big problems in my first year as a supervisor because I didn't know enough about the labor contract.

- As a new sales representative I was assigned a senior sales representative as a "buddy" to help me learn the ropes, but she never had the time and didn't seem interested in my problems.

- The training catalog is kept locked in my manager's office.
- Off-site training is reserved as reward for good performance.
- My boss has no idea what I need to learn to improve my job performance.
- Management gives lip service to training, but what they reward us for is being visibly at work on production problems sixty hours a week.

Your company can have the finest training staffs, high quality courses, terrific training facilities, and top management support for training and still fail in its education and training efforts because the supervisors and managers of the trainees have not been effectively brought into the system. For the education and training system to have maximum impact on business performance, supervisors and managers must

- Know what tasks their subordinates are expected to perform
- Know what skills and knowledge are needed to perform these tasks
- Be able to assess deficiencies in subordinates' skills and knowledge
- Know what training is available and how to access it
- Know how to provide structured learning opportunities where no formal training is available
- Schedule time for training into the work plan
- Budget adequately for planned training
- Properly prepare subordinates for training experiences
- Reinforce training with meaningful assignments to apply what was learned
- Provide coaching to help overcome difficulties in applying newly acquired knowledge and skills
- Reward and recognize subordinates for their accomplishments in mastering new skills and knowledge
- Give constructive feedback to the providers of training
- Demonstrate by their actions the value they place on learning.

We submit to you that if we were to survey employees on the effectiveness of their supervisors and managers on these points, the mean score across the U.S. workforce would be about three on a ten-point scale.

Why is this so? Is it because our managers do not care or do not want to do a good job? Probably not. Here is our list of reasons, based on interviews with hundreds of supervisors and managers:

- They do not know what they should do; they have not had good role models themselves and no one has ever explained it to them.

- They lack some of the essential skills.

- They are under extreme pressure from their bosses and peers to focus on other things.

- They are not recognized and rewarded for training and developing their subordinates.

- They lack the essential information and tools to make good decisions.

For most managers and supervisors, missing their operating budget by 1 or 2 percent would have more serious personal consequences than missing their planned training objectives by 40 percent (if they even have a training plan with measurable objectives).

ESSENTIAL SYSTEM DESIGN FEATURES

If you want to have a world class learning culture, designing and implementing a system that will mold supervisors' and managers' values, expectations, skills, and behavior is a major strategic issue.

Stating the problem is easy compared to designing and effecting the solution. The easiest and least effective part of the solution is training the supervisor and managers in what to do and how to do it and providing them with the information and tools to do it. The hardest and most important part of the solution is creating the values and balance of consequences which are the most powerful shapers of behavior.

The diagram in Figure 22-1 shows the essential elements of the system. The goal is appropriate supervisory and management behavior. It all starts with stated values and expectations. Training information and tools are enablers. Feedback and consequences make the ultimate difference between successful behavior modification and a flag-waving corporate initiative cynically saluted as another top management fad which will soon pass.

THE GOAL: APPROPRIATE SUPERVISOR AND MANAGER BEHAVIOR

The ultimate objective is to achieve a state where all members of the organization possess the skills and knowledge they need for peak performance and continue to learn in support of continuous performance improvement and long-term development.

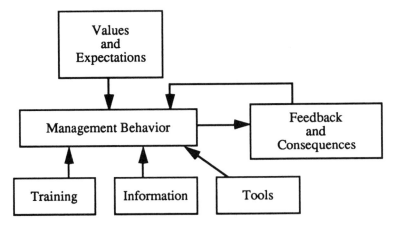

Figure 22-1 Values and Expectation Diagram

The goal of the supervisor and manager support system is a set of management decisions and behaviors that consistently support this ultimate objective. The following is a checklist of appropriate supervisor and manager behaviors:

1. Analyze training needs.
   - Build and maintain a list of tasks performed by subordinates.
   - Build and maintain a list of skills and knowledge needed to perform the tasks.
   - Assess capabilities of subordinates against the lists of tasks, skills and knowledge.
   - Develop a prioritized list of training requirements.

2. Develop training plans.
   - Develop their individual training plans with individual subordinates.
   - Develop a training plan for the organizational unit.
   - Budget time and money to support the training plans.

3. Schedule training and prepare subordinates.
   - Schedule attendance at company and other schools, timed for maximum payoff.
   - Schedule trainers to facilitate or instruct on-site classes.
   - Schedule structured on-the-job training including the expert coach.
   - Establish learning expectations and objectives with subordinates in a pre-training briefing.
   - Establish expectations and objectives with expert coaches for OJT.

- Refrain from rescheduling or pulling subordinates out of training to meet short-term expediencies of the job.

4. Follow up on learning outcomes.

   - Review any data from the training program such as mastery of objectives data.

   - Debrief subordinates after training to assess which learning objectives were achieved and to develop remedial plans for those which were not.

   - Debrief OJT coaches.

   - With the subordinates establish objectives for application of new skills and knowledge on the job.

5. Make resources available to support training.

   - Assign master performers and others with expertise to work with analysts and instructional designers to analyze the jobs and design and develop the training materials.

   - Assign master performers as instructors and OJT coaches.

   - Assign the most qualified people to serve on training committees.

   - Provide time on equipment for training purposes.

   - Develop and maintain a library of learning resources.

6. Assess effectiveness of training.

   - Review mastery of objectives results for the various training programs used.

   - Make an assessment of the value of training in terms of improved business results.

   - Give feedback to the providers of training.

7. Provide appropriate recognition and rewards.

   - Provide recognition for individuals' accomplishment of learning objectives both informally and in performance appraisal.

   - Provide recognition, formal and informal, for other contributions such as serving as an OJT coach, serving on training committees, etc.

   - Recognize and reward subordinate supervisors and managers for appropriate behavior in support of training goals and for accomplishment of their group's training objectives.

TOOLS, INFORMATION, AND TRAINING

Most supervisors and managers, unaided, will not be able to exhibit the behaviors listed in the previous sections. They probably will not possess all the skills and knowledge needed, and they probably do not have time given the pressure of other tasks. This is where tools, information, and training come into play.

Tools and Resources

Tools and resources can be devised that are real time-savers for managers and supervisors and simultaneously ensure high quality. These can take the form of job aids (paper or computerized), reference materials, and administrative and professional support.

Job Aids   Job aids include

- Job performance models that can be edited for specific jobs
- Skills assessment instruments
- Fill-in-the-blank individual training plans
- Evaluation questionnaires
- Performance tests or observation checklists to assess mastery of skills
- Typical learning paths
- Budgeting worksheets for training.

These can be provided in handbook or kit form or as a menu-driven, online, computer-based support system.

Reference Materials   Some of the typical reference materials needed include

- Catalogs of available training with complete course descriptions
- Lists of tasks, skills and knowledge
- Supervisor and manager guidelines for managing learning.

Administrative and Professional Support   The following are some typical examples of administrative and professional support:

- Administrative support
    - Scheduling training events
    - Registration of individual trainees
    - Keeping data on training records
    - Keeping files on training plans
    - Tracking results compared to plans
    - Issuing reports of results
    - Keeping up to date catalogs of training available

- Keeping data on effectiveness of various programs
- Professional support
  - Job analysis/task analysis
  - Training needs assessment
  - Support for development of training plans
  - Evaluation of training effectiveness
  - Training OJT coaches
  - Developing structured for OJT experiences.

Information

Much of the information needed is implied in the preceding lists of job aids and reference materials. There are a few critical information sets that deserve special mention:

- Individual training records

- Skills inventories for groups, organizations, and individuals

- Schedules for available training programs, including registration information.

TRAINING FOR SUPERVISORS AND MANAGERS

Even if you are able to provide a complete set of all the tools, resources, and information, most supervisors will not be able to use them effectively unless trained to do so. Basic training for supervisors and managers should include

- Orientation to the supervisor/manager role in training
  - Training mission and philosophy
  - Ultimate objective of mastery level for everyone, with expectation of continuous improvement
  - Supervisor and manager tasks
  - Expectations of appropriate supervisor/manager behavior
  - Expectation of employee roles and behavior
- Introduction to available tools, resources, and information
- Practice using the tools, resources, and information to perform key tasks such as assessment of individual training needs and development of individual training plans.

Advanced training can include

- Coaching skills for improving job performance

- Structuring OJT
- Overviews of core training programs available for subordinates.

FEEDBACK AND CONSEQUENCES

No matter how much training you provide or how good the tools and equipment are, the most powerful shapers of behavior are feedback and consequences. Most people tend to do the things for which they get the most frequent and strongest positive consequences, and they tend to avoid the things for which they get negative consequences.

The following are some types of feedback that most supervisors and managers receive and are sensitive to.

Feedback Categories

- Production data
- Quality data
- Cost data
- Timeliness data
- Customer satisfaction data (including internal customers)
- Employee satisfaction data
- Employee competence and development data
- Questions and comments from their bosses about all of the above

As you look at this list, think about situations you are familiar with. Which of these data sets are best articulated, and which have the most impact on supervisor/manager behavior? Those with the most impact are usually questions and comments from the boss and customer satisfaction. If employee competence and development data are missing, incomplete or imprecise and especially if the boss appears not to be interested in them, these questions and comments will not have much impact. The joker in the deck is that employee competence affects all the other feedback data, but the link is often not made either by the supervisor/manager or the boss.

Consequences are stronger than feedback as shapers of behavior.

Consequence Categories

- Performance appraisals
- Compensation

- Promotions
- Demotions
- Formal and informal recognition
- Special bonuses and rewards

How many organizations are you aware of in which development of people plays a significant role in the consequences perceived by supervisors and managers? Hitting production or sales targets, meeting a budget, and the like, are likely to be much more influential in the establishment of promotions and bonuses than development of people. In the most aware organizations, top management and middle management realize that human resources development is an essential ingredient to get the best production, sales, quality, and cost results. The problem is that you have to pay the price before you get the benefit. It is an investment. So to encourage subordinate managers and supervisors to develop people, managers establish what may seem like disproportionately strong consequences in the people development category.

SUMMARY

This chapter showed that

- Supervisors and managers have an important set of roles in the training system.
- They are not born with an awareness or with the skills to discharge these roles effectively.
- They are not likely to perform well, even with the awareness and skills if they do not have convenient information, job aids, and other resources to help them.
- Most of them will not conduct effective training if they do not receive a positive balance of feedback and consequences.

The training system must include a supervisor/manager support system with the following components:

- Defined supervisor/manager training roles and expectations
- Training
- Information, job aids, and resources
- Supportive feedback and consequences.

23

FINANCING AND FINANCIAL ACCOUNTABILITY

A company that fully addresses its training needs will be making a substantial annual investment in training its workforce. For a *Fortune* 100 company, this will amount to hundreds of millions of dollars per year. For most organizations, it will amount to between 5 and 10 percent of payroll, depending on whether you count the wages and salaries of the trainees while they are in training.

Good management of an investment of this size requires that a system for financing and financial accountability be created. The financing strategy should be capable of funding all the training goals and objectives that have been agreed to by management, and the accountability system should track the usage of the funds that have been created.

The financial systems are a major requirement for running the training department like a business. The major activities, as in any business, include

- Building budgets based on business needs and priorities
- Financing the budget
- Accounting for expenditures and results.

This chapter provides an overview of each of these areas and presents some of the alternative approaches.

BUDGETING

We favor a system with three training department budgets, to be reviewed and authorized by company management through the governance system described in chapter 21:

- Development budget
- Operations budget
- Capital budget.

The development budget supports needs analysis, curriculum architecture design, development and acquisition of new courseware, maintenance of courseware, and development and maintenance of administrative systems. The operations budget supports the delivery of training and any other services provided by the training departments, such as performance consulting. The capital budget supports the acquisition of capital, such as land and buildings for training, laboratory equipment, computers, and furniture.

Each manager within the training department should have his or her own budget, which may or may not include components of all three budgets. The managers' budgets must roll up to the overall department budget.

In many organizations, training costs are charged back to the departments who use the training. In these cases, each manager of a user department that uses training needs a budget for procuring training from the internal training departments and from outside sources. These budgets should be rolled up and reconciled with the training department budgets so the company has control over its entire training investment and to make sure that the training departments are not budgeting to provide more training than their users are budgeting to procure from them.

In the following sections, we deal with the training department budget.

The Development Budget

The development budget should include

- Needs analysis
- Curriculum architecture design
- Courseware development
- Course licensing fees
- Courseware maintenance
- Administrative systems development and maintenance.

As shown in Figure 23-1, the development budget is built up from several departmental development budgets.

We present a simplified development budget for a fictitious training department, UTX Corporate Education.

Let's take a look at the marketing and sales development budget shown in Figure 23-2. This budget includes needs analysis and curriculum architecture projects, projects to develop or acquire new courseware, and maintenance of existing courseware. The maintenance budget provides for keeping the existing courseware current with changes in technology, markets, competition, and products. It is calculated at 15 percent of the replacement cost of the in-place curriculum.

Budgets just like this are built for the engineering, manufacturing, and management skills curricula.

The training administrative systems development budget in Figure 23-3 supports the development and maintenance of administrative systems. For a new or rapidly evolving training department, this budget can be significant.

Each individual budget is rolled up into the UTX total development budget, as shown in Figure 23-4. The development budgets are built up from individual project budgets (e.g., the Zebra Products new courseware development shown in Figure 23-5). With each project built up like this from standard components, the components can be added across all projects and programs and reconciled (e.g., the instructional design staff salaries in Figure 23-6).

At UTX, the loaded salary of an instructional designer averages $70,000. Therefore, this budget will support the equivalent of thirty-four full-time instructional designers. If there are thirty on the staff now, that would mean a net growth of four or 12.5 percent.

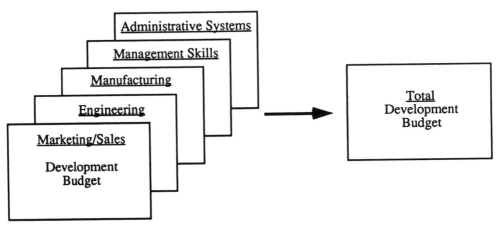

Figure 23-1 Sample Development Budget Architecture for UTX Corporate Education

Needs Analysis and Curriculum Architecture	$ (000)	%
Needs Analysis, Sable Product Line	20	
Needs Analysis, Zebra Product Line	17	
Curriculum Architecture, Product Managers	60	
Curriculum Architecture, Sales Managers	60	
	157	9.4
New Courseware Development		
Stallion Products (14 modules)	140	
Sable Products (25 modules)	250	
Zebra Products (18 modules)	180	
Account representative skills (4 modules)	120	
Product support skills (3 modules)	80	
Marketing /Sales Executive Institute	140	
	910	54.8
Acquisition of Rights to Use		
Basic selling skills	30	
Sales forecasting	25	
	55	3.3
Maintenance		
Maintenance of 260 Marketing/Sales training modules valued at $3.6 million replacement cost	540	32.5
TOTAL	1,662	100

Figure 23-2   UTX Marketing and Sales Development Budget

The Operations Budget

The operations budget should include both income and expenses for

- Training delivery
- Conference support
- Other services.

At UTX, income includes charge-backs to users for the following items:

- Attendance at training classes

	$ (000)	%
New Systems Development		
User satisfaction survey	50	
Vendor qualification system	25	
Instructor performance model and selection system	35	
	105	54
Systems Maintenance		
New features for registration and scheduling system	15	
Miscellaneous maintenance of other systems	75	
	90	46
TOTAL	195	100

Figure 23-3 UTX Training Administration Systems Development Budget

- Purchases of training materials

- Conference support

- Consulting and other services.

Expenses include a wide variety of items:

- Staff salaries
  - Instructors
  - Managers
  - Administrative support personnel
- Amoritization of capital expenditures
  - Land
  - Buildings
  - Equipment and furnishings
- Supplies
- Procured services
  - Instructors
  - Housekeepers
  - Other, such as legal
- Utilities and telecommnications
- Mail and shipping
- Travel and living expenses

	$ (000)	%
Needs Analysis and Curriculum Architecture		
Marketing/Sales	157	
Engineering	130	
Manufacturing	200	
Management Skills	60	
	547	9.1
New Courseware Development		
Marketing/Sales	910	
Engineering	650	
Manufacturing	1250	
Management Skills	325	
	3135	52.4
Acquisition of Rights to Use		
Marketing/Sales	55	
Management Skills	125	
	180	3.0
Maintenance		
Marketing/Sales	540	
Engineering	425	
Manufacturing	750	
Management Skills	210	
	1925	32.2
Administrative Systems	195	3.3
TOTAL DEVELOPMENT BUDGET	5982	100

Figure 23-4   UTX Total Development Budget

- Employee relocation expenses
- Food services

To continue our UTX example, the UTX corporate education department divides its operations budget as shown in Figure 23-7. This means that each operations area must be managed to run about a 44 percent margin of income over direct expense to cover indirect expenses. You can force income to equal total expenses by adjusting the rates charged for training and other services, assuming the demand is relatively insensitive to price.

	$ (000)	%
Development Staff Salaries	50	28
Development Staff Travel and Expenses	15	8
Subject-Matter Experts Travel and Expenses	10	6
Purchased Design services	33	18
Production Support	36	20
Administrative Support (allocation for space, furniture, support overhead, etc.)	36	20
TOTAL	180	100

Figure 23-5 UTX Zebra Products—New Courseware Development (18 modules)

	$ (000)
Marketing/Sales	550
Engineering	400
Manufacturing	725
Management Skills	275
Administrative Systems	60
TOTAL	2010

Figure 23-6 UTX Instruction Design Staff Salaries

The direct income and expense budgets include everything directly attributable to the individual operations area. Operational expenses are

- Instructional staff salaries
- Production support
- Travel and living expenses
- Purchased materials.

The indirect expenses must include everything else.

	Income	Expenses
	$ (000)	$ (000)
Direct Income and Expense		
Marketing/Sales	2830	1960
Engineering	1760	1220
Manufacturing	3030	2100
Management Skills	1370	950
Conference support	750	520
Consulting services	500	350
	10,250	7100
Indirect Expenses		3150
TOTAL	10,250	10,250

Figure 23-7 UTX Operations Budget

- Cost of training and staff space
- Computer systems operation
- Personnel office
- Registration and scheduling
- Amortization of capital
- Personnel moves
- Administrative personnel salaries, travel, and living
- Library
- Materials management
  - Procurement
  - Reproduction
  - Archives
- Facilities maintenance and operations
- Security service
- Property tax
- Marketing and advertising
- Evaluation and results measurement
- Utilities

- Telecommunications

- Mail and shipping.

The Capital Budget

Most companies have a separate budget for items that must be capitalized. These include land, buildings, furniture, equipment, etc. The training department must also segregate its capital budget. A training department capital budget might look like the simplified UTX example in Figure 23-8.

Some of the items in the capital budget are directly linked to items in the development and operations budgets. For example, the product repair labs are directly linked to the Zebra and Sable Product courseware development and delivery budgets. If you cannot get the capital to build the lab, then there is no point in developing courseware that depends on laboratory work.

	$ (000)
Training Center Addition	
Building	6000
Furniture	525
Equipment	1200
Landscaping and grounds	800
	8525
Training Laboratories and Equipment	
Sable product repair lab	225
Zebra product repair lab	285
Student workstations	525
	1025
Computer system enhancements	225
General Furniture and Equipment	
Office automation	86
Reproduction equipment	75
Furniture	100
Other	250
	511
TOTAL	10,286

Figure 23-8   UTX Corporate Education Capital Budget

The Budget Building Process

The budget is built from the bottom up for each year within the framework of the strategic training plan. Figure 23-9 shows the process used at UTX.

Involving the curriculum advisory councils and board of education in the budgeting process is one of the great secrets of obtaining adequate resources to get the job done. The curriculum advisory councils will advocate their portion of the budget to the executives on the board. This takes the training director out of the role of selling a budget. Instead, the training director is simply presenting and explaining a budget that has hopefully been presold by customers.

One last point about budget making concerns a common database for estimating. How much does the average employee relocation cost? How much time does it take to develop a three day group-paced course? What should we assume for loading factors on salaries? What is the average project manager's salary? You need to keep a database of actual expenditures to be used in building budgets. Whoever is charged with compiling the budget should analyze the actual, forecast changes due to inflation and other factors, and issue a table of estimating factors for all managers to use as a starting point in building their budgets.

FINANCING STRATEGIES

There are many different ways of financing the training system, but they all boil down to four major strategies:

- The overhead staff budget

---

1. Each department (marketing/sales, engineering, etc.) builds a list of requirements for the development, operations, and capital budgets and estimates the cost of each of the line items.

2. Department budgets are reviewed and prioritized by the appropriate Curriculum Advisory Council.

3. The training director builds a proposed consolidated budget.

4. The consolidated budget is reviewed, adjusted, and approved by the UTX Board of Education (company officers).

5. The UTX Board of Directors approves individual capital expenditures in excess of $2 million.

Figure 23-9 UTX Corporate Education Budgeting Process

- Charge-back to users
- The training tax
- The training subsidiary.

The overhead staff budget is the simplest, but it has its problems. Overhead staff budgets are generally under attack today, making it more difficult to build the size budget that is really needed. Overhead budgets are prorated back to business units or departments, who resent the prorate because it is not connected directly to value they receive. The overhead staff budget can be cut deeply during tight times by an individual staff executive without regard for the cost to the training customers in the field, who have had their training shut off with little or no recourse possible. It is fairly common for field organizations to set up their own training departments, duplicating the centralized training staff, simply because they do not trust the continuity of support.

Charging the costs of training back to the users has many advantages. It forces the training department and its customers to agree on what is needed and what it is worth. It bypasses arbitrary controls placed on overhead staff budgets. No individual can make deep cuts during tight times. The biggest objection we hear to this form of funding is that the line departments are not believers in training and therefore will not put up the money. If this is true for your organization, then you have some real homework to do with your customers.

The training tax is a kind of hybrid between the overhead budget and the charge-back approach and has some nice advantages. Motorola implemented this approach a few years ago as a means of encouraging its business units to invest appropriately in training. The way it works is that the corporation levies a payroll tax on the business units. This tax is held in escrow and can only be used by the business units for training and education purposes. The business units can use it to procure training services from the corporate education groups, business unit training groups, or outside sources. The big advantage of the system is that the appropriate level of investment in training and education to meet the strategic needs of the business is established by the executive board of education. Shortsighted cost cutting by local managers will not do them any good because they pay the tax whether they use it or not.

The training subsidiary is a strategy that sets up a training department as its own business unit with bottom-line accountability. It must successfully provide service to the other business units or go out of business. This is a variation of the charge-back strategy. The Bellcore Technical Education Center uses this strategy.

None of these strategies is right for all organizations. You will have to pick the one that suits your needs best and fits your company culture. If you plan to switch funding strategies, be sure you allow plenty of time and provide sufficient information for all affected organizations to change their budgeting process. A few years ago, Western Electric changed the financing strategy at its corporate education center from an overhead staff budget to a charge-back strategy. They did it overnight with insufficient lead time for field organizations to budget for the charge-backs. As a result, the fill rate at the corporate education center went from nearly 100 percent to the 30 to 40 percent range and stayed there for a year until the budgeting process caught up. The sad thing about an experience like this is that needed training does not get done and the major expenses continue, since the building and equipment are in place and you do not want to decimate the training staff while riding out a lull.

Development Budget Financing

Some training departments that charge back training costs get their development budget from margins in their operating budget. This only works well in situations where there is a large ongoing operation that generates sufficient income to support development or where the training department is permitted to borrow money to finance development, paying back out of future income. New, growing training departments require a development budget that far exceeds anything that could realistically be funded out of operating income.

Therefore, in most cases we favor separate development and operating budgets, separately financed. The only risk in this is that top management may misguidedly shut off new development during a lean year while continuing to support training operations. This is happening as we write at a national training center for one of the Big Eight accounting firms with the consequences that the instructional design staffs that have been built up and nurtured over many years are being decimated. Recovery will be difficult and expensive.

We have seen more examples where training departments have failed or been ineffective because they had no separate mechanism for funding a development budget. One of these was the corporate education center for a *Fortune* 100 manufacturing company. Since they had no sizable development budget, most of their courses were off-the-shelf material obtained from vendors. Very little of it was custom developed to meet the specific needs of the training customers. The customer groups kept making requests for programs they needed, but the corporate group could not deliver because they did not have a development budget except for what they could skim off of charge-backs for delivery. To add insult to injury, the field customer groups could procure the same or equivalent vendor training at a lower cost by bypassing corporate education. During an overhead value analysis campaign, the auditors found that corporate education was not contributing sufficient value to justify cost, and the company officers shut it down.

Financing Policy

After the financing strategies have been worked out, it is a good idea to document them in a financing policy. This policy should be reviewed and approved by the executive board of education and then shared with everyone who is affected. Figure 23-10 shows a sample financing policy for UTX.

FIELD BUDGETS FOR TRAINING

Every organizational unit in the business needs a training budget, even if they are customers only and not providers of training. What goes in this budget depends on the financing strategy. If everything is charged back to user organizations, then they must budget for the charge-backs.

<u>Development Budget</u>

1. A separate development budget will be prepared and financed by the pro-rated charge-back to the Business Units on the basis of employee head count.

2. The development budget will include
   • Needs analysis and curriculum architecture design
   • New courseware development
   • Maintenance of existing courseware.

3. Budgets will be reviewed by the appropriate Curriculum Advisory Council and recommended for approval to the Board of Education.

4. The Board of Education will approve the budget.

5. Business Units will express their needs, priorities, and opinions in the Curriculum Council and Board Reviews. Once the budget is approved, Business Units are required to contribute their fair share.

6. Budgets to develop training for new products are to be assessed against the product development budget.

7. Budgets to develop training to support implementation of new internal systems, such as Order Entry Systems and the like, are to be assessed against the development budget for the new system.

8. Any Business Unit or other organizational entity within UTX may contract with Corporate Education for development work that falls outside the approved budget. This would most likely occur for training needs that are unique to one Business Unit. Corporate Education is not constrained in the amount of work they may take on but must manage to balance income and expenses.

9. Corporate Education is accountable for balancing the total development budget but will not be held to estimates on individual line items.

---

continued

Figure 23-10   UTX Corporate Education Financing Policy

Operations Budget

1. A separate Operations Budget will be prepared and financed by charge-backs to the users on the basis of use.

2. The Operations Budget income will include charge-backs for
   - Attendance at centralized training
   - Training delivered in the Business Units, and distributor and customer premises by Corporate Education
   - Materials provided by Corporate Education
   - Conference space and support services provided by Corporate Education
   - Consulting and other services provided by Corporate Education.

3. Corporate Education will forecast demand, income, and expenses and propose a rate structure to the Board of Education to balance income and expense.

4. The Board of Education will approve the rate structure, which will be communicated to all interested parties.

5. Corporate Education may accept any level of demand generated by its customers and add resources as necessary to meet the demand.

6. Corporate Education is accountable for balancing the Operations budget but will not be held to estimates on individual line items.

Total Expense Budget

1. The total expense budget, consisting of the sum of the development budget and the operating budget, will be managed by Corporate Education to balance within five percent for each year.

Capital Budget

1. A separate capital budget will be prepared by Corporate Education and financed by the Corporate Capital Budget.

2. This budget will be approved by the Board of Education.

3. Individual expenditures exceeding $2 million will be approved by the UTX Board of Directors.

4. Capital recovery will occur by including amortization and depreciation expenses in the Operating Budget.

Figure 23-10 (continued)

A typical list of items for a user department training budget includes the following:

Corporate Education

- Development budget pro-rate
- Tuition at corporate education center
- Fees for on-site delivery
- Room and equipment rental for on-site delivery
- Fees for materials
- Travel and living expense of students attending corporate education courses
- Fees for consulting and other services

Other Sources of Training (e.g., Seminars)

- Tuition fees
- Trainee travel and living
- Speaker expenses
- Room rental and support costs

Administrative

- Administrative coordinator salary and expenses.

FINANCIAL TRACKING AND ACCOUNTABILITY

Every manager should be held accountable for delivering expected results within his or her agreed-on budget. This means that there must be a system in place for tracking costs as they appear in the budgets and maintaining the visibility of actual versus expected expenditures versus expected results. Just tracking monthly actual versus expected expenditures is insufficient since you could be halfway through the year, spent half your project budget as expected, but have nowhere near half the work done.

The tracking system should report monthly results by line item to each manager with a budget. It should also be capable of forecasting year end results. If the reports aren't timely or accurate, you can be in lots of trouble and not know it. As with other systems, the tracking system should definitely be computerized.

SUMMARY

Good management of a large training investment requires that a system for financing and financial accountability be created and maintained. This includes

☐ Building budgets based on business needs and priorities
- Development budget
    - Needs analysis
    - Curriculum architecture design
    - Courseware development
    - Course licensing fees
    - Courseware maintenance
    - Administrative systems development and maintenance
- Operations budget
    - Training delivery
    - Conference support
    - Other services
- Capital budget
    - Land
    - Buildings
    - Furniture
    - Equipment
    - Etc.

☐ Financing the budget
- Overhead staff budget strategy
- Charge-back to users strategy
- Training tax
- Training subsidiary

☐ Developing financing policy statement

☐ Developing field budgets for training

☐ Developing computerized financial and accountability systems
- Actual versus expected costs
- Actual versus expected results
- Reporting system.

24

MEASURING RESULTS

You can only tell if all the systems implemented are producing the desired benefits if you measure results.

A results measurement system provides feedback information which is needed by training management for planning, directing, and controlling training activities. This is important for three reasons. First, this data is an important input to establishing objectives for the training function and measuring performance against those objectives. Second, it is an important input to the planning and forecasting process, providing much of the required historical data. Third, it is the way in which management obtains reports on the overall performance of the training function.

A results measurement system also provides information which can be used by training management to report to its clients and to upper management on the impacts and progress made by the training system. (The information of interest to people external to the training department will be a small subset of the information of interest to training department management.)

The results measurement system should be as lean and simple as possible while still providing management with critical information for decision making. The purpose should be merely to provide information which indicates areas of problems, not causes of problems. Otherwise, the system would be too costly to operate.

Few organizations have a comprehensive system for measuring training results. Results measurement closes the feedback control loop on planning and training operations. Without results data, the training system is out of control. Without results you have no way of knowing whether important needs are met or to what degree, what the cost/benefit ratio of meeting these needs is, how satisfied the customers of training are, etc. Good results data help guide future planning, help pinpoint deficiencies, help with allocation of resources, and protect against arbitrary cuts in training budgets and head count.

To be most meaningful, the entire training system involving all training departments should be on a common results measurement system. Otherwise, there is no comparability of data. The results will only be useful in managing individual training units, and top management will not be able to assess the degree to which training is meeting the strategic needs of the business.

The results measurement system should be hierarchical and should serve the needs of managers and professionals throughout the organization from top to bottom. Top management should be able to assess how well the overall needs of the business are being met. A plant manager should be able to assess how well his or her needs are being met. A training director should be able to identify weak spots in the curriculum. An instructional designer should be able to assess his or her contribution to business.

A comprehensive, well designed results system is not cheap but is well worth the price. Measurement cost is a part of the cost of quality and productivity. Without measurement, there is no possibility of continuous improvement.

Here are some broad guidelines for designing results measurement systems:

- Measure only important results.

- Make data collection, storage, and retrieval administratively simple.

- Mechanize as much as possible.

- Keep standard reports simple.

- Provide access to backup reports or customized reports for diagnostic purpose or special needs.

PRIMARY TRAINING RESULTS

Training results fall in the following categories:

- Training needs met

- Organizational benefits from training needs met

- Cost of training needs met

- Quality/effectiveness of training provided

- Productivity of training resources

- Training needs not met

- Organizational cost of training needs not met (cost of nonconformance, see chapter 4).

The chart in Figure 24-1 shows an example annual training results report for the Tuscaloosa assembly plant of UMC. This chart shows that the total number of training days went up 10.6 percent at the same time the total number of employees declined 5 percent. The total cost of training went up 16.2 percent and the training cost per employee was up 22 percent. If these were the only results, management would be asking questions about runaway training costs. The value of training provided was 11.2 times the cost, however, compared to 9.24 times the cost for last year. Moreover, the cost of missed training was reduced by $36.5 million. Obviously, training is improving and providing a better overall value for the investment. There is also obviously room to improve, since the cost of training missed is still $60.3 million and the training quality index stands at 78 out of 100 points.

The plant manager and his or her staff can evaluate this report in ten minutes and decide whether they want more details on weak spots. Each department manager reporting to the plant manager gets a similar report for his or her department. A useful expansion might look like the one in Figure 24-2.

As you might expect, the most important results, namely

- Benefits of training provided

- Cost of training missed,

are the most difficult to measure. Generally, these are measured based on assessment of increased productivity gained by training. Thus, if you find that training increases productivity by 30 percent for an individual worker, you can use the other results to determine benefits of training in dollars and to calculate the cost of training missed.

SECONDARY RESULTS

The results presented in the previous section could be called primary training results. The next layer, secondary results, measure training processes such as needs analysis, development, and delivery. These secondary or process results might include

- Needs analysis and curriculum architecture process results

- Instructional materials development results

- Instructional delivery results

- Training facilities utilization

Figure 24-3 shows some of the results you may want to measure for your needs analysis and curriculum architecture processes. These numbers tell you whether your curriculum architectures are up to date and how much of the training need they cover.

Tuscaloosa Assembly Plant Training Results (Annual)	This Year	Last Year	Deviation
Number of employees	3730.0	3925.0	5.0%
• Hourly	3000.0	3200.0	-6.25%
• Professional	350.0	325.0	-6.25%
• Management	380.0	400.0	-5.0%
Number of days training provided			
• Overall	25440.0	22995.0	+10.6%
• Hourly	19023.0	18055.0	+5.36%
• Professional	3605.0	2340.0	+54.1%
• Management	2812.0	2600.0	+8.15%
Number of days training per employee			
• Overall	6.8	5.9	+15.2%
• Hourly	5.1	4.6	+10.9%
• Profesional	10.3	7.2	+43.1%
• Management	7.4	6.5	+13.4
Total cost of training ($ million)	13.36	11.50	+16.2%
Cost per trainee day ($)	525.0	500.0	+5.0%
Cost per employee ($)	3581.0	2930.0	+22.0%
Value of training ($ million)	150.25	106.3	+41.3%
Return on training investment	10:1	8:1	
Cost of training missed ($ million)	60.3	96.8	-37.7%
Training quality index (100 maximum)	78.0	67.0	+16.4%
Percent of training needs met	65%	55%	+10.0%

Figure 24-1   Sample Annual Training Results Report

Type of Training	Cost of Training Missed (Millions)
• Hourly maintenance skills	10.6
• Hourly production skills	12.8
• Quality awareness and tools	9.8
• Entry engineer skills	5.6
• Automation technology for engineers	4.3
• Materials management	3.2
• High-performance team	2.6
• Other miscellaneous	11.4
TOTAL	$60.3

Figure 24-2   Tuscaloosa Assembly Plant Significant Training Needs Missed

Function	Months Since Last Job Analysis	Percent of Job Covered	Months Since Last Curriculum Architecture Update	Curriculum Design Quality Index
Marketing	24	80	20	86
Manufacturing	12	65	10	75
R&D	36	60	24	60
MIS	10	76	8	76
Service	15	85	12	82
TOTAL COMPANY		73.2		75.8

Figure 24-3   Needs Analysis and Curriculum Architecture Process Results

The curriculum design quality index is made up of weighted factors to assess the overall quality of the curriculum for each functional area.

Likewise, Figure 24-4 shows important measurement categories for your instructional development process. Note that you are measuring by categories of development,

% of Needed Training Available for Delivery	This Year	Last Year
Overall (%)	60%	45%
Basic training (%)	70%	50%
Change-driven (%)	50%	35%
Number of days developed	1500	1100
Cost per day developed ($200)	30	25
Development quality index*	85	75
Cost of maintenance ($ million)	15	10
Total replacement value	125	100
Maintenance of replacement cost	12	10
Maintenance quality index **	75	60

*Development quality index includes components for trainee satisfaction, instructor satisfaction, maintainability, trainee attainment of objectives, and instructional design efficiency

**Maintenance quality index includes components for % of maintenance items completed, weighted by importance; development quality index items

Figure 24-4   Instructional Materials Development Results

as specified in chapter 14. Tracking maintenance, as we do here, is one important and often overlooked measure.

The area that is most commonly measured by training groups is instructional delivery results. As you have seen, this is only one piece of the overall results measurement. Unfortunately, in this area most often companies measure only what we refer to as the quality index and possibly the total number of training days provided. But as you have seen, it is also important to know how much of the demand is being met and what you are paying to meet this demand per trainee day. Over time, you will have important trend data that will alert you if something is getting out of whack.

Training facilities utilization can be measured in the following categories:

- Trainee days classroom capacity

Result Category	This Year	Last Year
Trainee days delivered	25440	22995
% of needs met where materials available	65	55
% of demand met	90	85
Quality index *	85	80
Cost of delivery ($ milllion)	7.3	6.3
Cost of delivery per trainee day	300	275

*Quality index includes components for trainee satisfaction, timeliness, trainee mastery of objectives, transfer of skills to the job, and client organization satisfaction

Figure 24-5 Instructional Delivery Results

- Trainee days delivered in classrooms
- Percentage classroom utilization
- Classroom cost
- Cost per trainee day
- Classroom quality index includes components for trainee travel distance, comfort, visual effectiveness, sound effectiveness, and housekeeping.

This tells you if your facilities are paying their way, so to speak, and lets you know if you need to do something, like rent out space or some other alternative, to increase facility benefits.

RESULTS DATA SOURCES

The results data that go into making these reports come from many sources. These sources include but are not limited to the following:

- Registration and scheduling data
  - Number of courses scheduled
  - Number of days scheduled
  - Number of students registered per course

- – Number of students attending per course
- – Number of rooms scheduled
- – Days scheduled per room
- Personnel data
  - – Total number of employees
  - – Number of employees per function
  - – Number of employees per job grade or level
- Accounting data
  - – Total budget for training
  - – Field costs for training
  - – Total cost of training
- Trainee feedback questionnaire
  - – Overall effectiveness of course
  - – Applicability to job
  - – Quality of instruction
  - – Subject matter effectiveness
  - – Presentation effectiveness
  - – Quality of training environment
- Instructor feedback questionnaire
  - – Overall effectiveness of course
  - – Quality of course design
  - – Quality of course materials
  - – Applicability of content to job
  - – Quality of training environment
- Supervisor feedback questionnaire
  - – Overall effectiveness of course
  - – Applicability to job
  - – Performance improvement after course
  - – Number of trainees trained
- Mastery test results
  - – Performance-related pre- and post test comparison
  - – Task proficiency results
- Evaluation team data
  - – Overall effectiveness of course
  - – Applicability to job
  - – Quality of course design
  - – Quality of course materials
  - – Quality of training environment
  - – Quality of instruction
  - – Subject-matter expertise

– Presentation skills
– Overall efficiency of processes.

RESULTS SYSTEM DESIGN PROCESS

The process for designing the results measurement system includes the following steps:

Step 1. Identifying Decisions to be Made from Results Data

The first step in designing your results system should be to figure out what you intend to use all this information for, such as:

- Increasing the training budget
- Developing new or updating existing curriculum architectures
- Reassessing number of development or delivery resources
- Building or obtaining additional training facilities

This is basically defining the purpose of your results measurement system.

Step 2. Define All Results to be Measured

Once you know what you want to do with the data, you can decide what your categories of measurement need to be. Previous sections of this chapter give you more details on what possible categories of results might be.

Step 3. Identify Data Required for Results

Once you know what categories you want to measure, you can determine what data is required to figure those results. For example, if you decide to measure percent of need being met, you need to know the total number of employees needing the training and the total number of employees trained for each function or business unit.

Step 4. Define Data Sources and Measurement Means

When you know what data you need, you can figure out where you will get it and how. We previously defined several possible data sources for various types of data in the section on Results Data Sources in this chapter.

Step 5. Specify Reports to be Generated

This step links directly to steps 1 and 2. The reports you generate should provide all the results you need to make decisions. These reports also form the basis for specifying a database.

Step 6. Specify a Database to Store Data for Retrieval

Based on the data you are gathering and the reports you are going to generate, you can specify the database that you will use to store the data. As with other previous systems, a computer-based system is essential for effective and efficient results measurement.

Step 7. Design the Overall Information Flow

Here you are mapping out who is getting what reports when. If the right people do not get the right information on a timely basis, all this results measurement is useless.

Step 8. Design the Administrative System for Collecting and Storing Data and Generating and Distributing Reports

In the end, any system seems to succeed or fail depending on whether good and sufficient administrative resources are put in place to manage the details of the system. If you want your system to work, make sure you have the administrative system and personnel to make it work.

Step 9. Evaluate Cost of Evaluation Compared to Benefits

Finally, you should have a way to determine if the system you have put in place is worth the money and resources it takes to build and maintain it. A good way to make sure that it is worth it is to follow our guidelines discussed in the early part of this chapter:

- Measure only important results.
- Make data collection, storage, and retrieval administratively simple.
- Mechanize as much as possible.
- Keep standard reports simple.

Too much data too frequently in too complex a format has been the death of many a well-intentioned results measurement system.

This system macro design should be completed before developing any of the data collection instruments, database, report etc. The comprehensive system will take time and resources to complete, so a multiyear development and implementation plan for results measurement is usually appropriate.

25

IMPLEMENTATION PLAN

Implementation is largely a project management exercise. We are not going to go into a lot of detail about how you manage your implementation. This chapter provides an overview of how to develop an overall implementation plan and some guidelines for dealing with barriers to implementation.

If your strategic plan calls for significant changes in the way you are currently doing business, such as

- Redesigning and changing processes
- Changing organization structure
- Implementing new delivery strategies
- Establishing a new advisory structure
- Increasing the scope of training operations
- Constructing new facilities or building additions to existing facilities,

then putting a formal implementation plan in place is appropriate. This implementation plan should lay out

- Implementation activities
- Accountability for those activities
- Resource requirements

- Roadblocks and strategies for overcoming them

- Accountability milestones.

With this plan, you are prioritizing the overall implementation that takes place in phase 4 of the strategic planning process (see chapter 2 on the four phase planning process).

IMPLEMENTATION PLAN CONTENTS

There are many possible formats that can be used for an implementation plan. You can document implementation activities in a simple list format, as shown in Figure 25-1. These activities can also be listed and plotted on a projected time line, as in Figure 25-2.

Assigning accountabilities and accountability milestones is also important when developing your overall implementation plan. Standard project management tools such as PERT charts and GANTT charts, are also helpful in laying out your overall plan. One

STRATEGIC PLANNING REPORT _____ 12. Implementation Plan

Initiate Tutorial Programs	• Information session provided to Small Staff and Expanded Staff • Identify program • Identify Subject-Matter Experts and target audience • Map out program plan.
Select Off-the-Shelf Materials	• Pick first ten high-priority courses (T&D) • Have a requirements definition meeting with a project committee on each item • Screen existing programs and select sources • Implement.
Individual Learning (ILC) Implementation	• Classroom layout and design • Consolidate Plato • Equip video learning carrels • Instructional TV • Satellite location at Freeport Road • Establish library of learning materials • Establish Subject-Matter Expert referral network • Establish and communicate administrative systems • Equip learning carrels with PCs/CBE.

Instructional TV Facility	• Earth station
	• Layout and design of small classroom equipped with TV
	• Subject-Matter Expert referral network
	• Pipe to other locations
	  - Theatre
	  - Conference Rooms
	  - Etc.

Figure 25-1   Sample Page of Implementation Plan

Major Milestones	Year 1				Year 2				Year 3				Year 4				Year 5			
	1	2	3	4	1	2	3	4	1	2	3	4	1	2	3	4	1	2	3	4
<u>Human Resources Systems</u>																				
1. Human Resource Plan																				
a. Develop annual plan																				
2. Recruiting																				
a. Develop a recruiting plan																				
- Number of recruits by discipline, experience																				
- Levels of technical and interpersonal talent																				
b. Consider visiting new schools																				
c. Consider recruiting from other disciplines																				
d. Develop recruiting teams																				
e. Obtain Human Resources commitment to manage/coordinate recruiting																				
3. Orientation																				
a. Develop and issue a set of department-wide guidelines for orientation																				
b. Develop and implement plant orientation program																				
c. Develop and implement a mentor program																				
d. Training Department to revise and maintain Orientation Manual																				

Figure 25-2   Implementation Time Line

I. Introduction

- Purpose
- Implementation Goals
- Implementation Recommendations

II. Implementation Guidelines

- Implementation Activities
- Implementation Time line
- Implementation Milestones
- Milestone Dependencies
- Roles and Responsibilities

III. Requirements

- Implementation Resource Requirements
- Implementation Barriers

Figure 25-3   Sample Implementation Plan Contents

of the most successful implementations we have seen used a computerized project management program to produce wall-size PERT charts, which were posted in a project room. Steps were marked off on the chart as milestones were met. If you are looking at a massive and complex implementation, we urge you to make full use of the benefits of computerized project management. Figure 25-3 provides a sample table of contents for an implementation plan that can be presented to executives.

When you have approval for this plan, you can begin your implementation project planning.

IMPLEMENTATION PROJECT PLANS

At this point, you are breaking down the implementation into several manageable projects. Each project will have its own project team, project manager, project budget, and project plan (as described in chapter 3). Figure 25-4 provides a visual example of how this works.

Each project has its own priority, deadline, etc. Note that some projects will be short (one to three months) and some can span a couple of years. In the end, they all roll up to a successful implementation that brings you to world class status, as described in chapter 1.

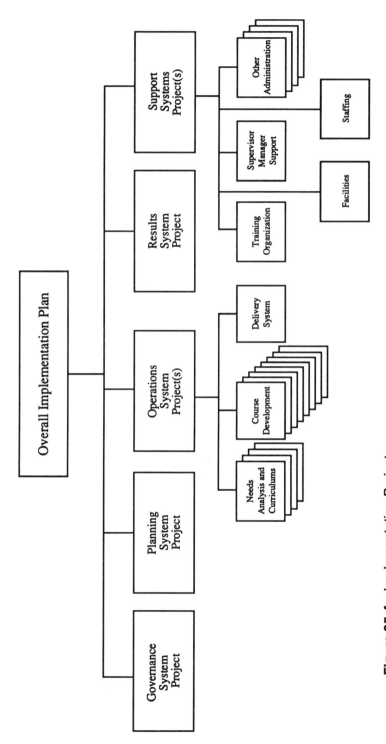

Figure 25-4 Implementation Projects

BARRIERS

Our final word about the strategic planning process relates to barriers. The biggest barrier is that doing the strategic planning project is always in addition to keeping the training function running, so you never have enough resources to do the implementation work. This is why you need to fold all your resource requirements back into the overall summary presented in chapter 18.

Another barrier, of course, is money. Process improvements ultimately pay for themselves, but initially they are not free. You have to make an investment up front.

Overseeing and supporting implementation of all this planning is an extremely important management role that is easy to ignore because of the pressures of daily business. Lack of management attention is another major roadblock. There seems to be a tendency for management to say, "Well, we've got our strategic plan done and approved by the board. Now we can get back to business." Some of the best strategic training plans we have done have ultimately failed when it came to implementation because of lack of top management attention. The key to success in implementation is a solid accountability link between the implementing project teams and management. Regular progress reviews should be held by implementation managers who have direct accountability to the executive training advisory board.

SUMMARY AND CONCLUSIONS

In this book, we have discussd:

- What constitutes a world class training system
- How to develop a plan for such a system
- Why you would want to
- Who you should involve in the process
- How to marry qualitative and quantitative planning and decision making.

We know this is a complex and difficult process, but the benefits are many. A visit with Bob Champion, CEO of our fictitious World Class, Inc. described in Chapter 1 provides some perspective on why it is worth it.

Well, we have to go back ten years. Ten years ago we became aware that we did not have adequate quality in our products and we were rapidly losing market share to the Japenese and European optical products. Market analysis showed us that customers preferred our competitors' products because they produced sharper images, had features the customers wanted and quality and durability were produced at a reasonable and competitive price. A hard-nosed look at this situation convinced us that we could not survive in the long run by simply making incremental changes to our existing way of doing business. The strategic concept we chose to bring us into a winning position is Total Quality Management (TQM). We wanted to move to a whole new way of thinking about our products, the way we make them, the way we identify and measure customer satisfaction. We realized that a major culture change was required from top to bottom.

Management must expect, measure, and reward different things. People must be empowered to make decisions and encouraged to communicate honestly about issues and problems. We realized from the outset that the education and training system was going to be an essential element in making the conversion from our old bureaucratic top-down business style to the new TQM culture. We did not realize just how important it was going to be. Recognizing the importance of training as a tool for executing our corporate culture change, with the executive officers we commissioned a five-year training and education plan that would support our business goals. The recommendation of this plan convinced us of several very important things.

1. Organized training and education programs would be essential to our entire workforce, hourly through executive, in learning the new TQM concepts, tools, and management skills.

2. For us to truly achieve superlative performance in all aspects of our business, we would need to make sure that all of our employees, our suppliers, and our distributors possessed all the skills and knowledge needed to perform their assigned tasks.

3. The concept of a total learning culture in which everyone is learning continuously must become an integral part of the corporate culture.

4. The previous points could not realistically be accomplished without organizing a high-performance training system.

5. Addressing all of our training needs would require a major continuous investment of corporate resources, but the ROI was estimated to be at 10 to 1 or higher.

6. The investment in training and education and the stakes to our success were so high that it would be necessary to put senior management in control of the company's investment decisions in this area.

As a result of the plan and its proposals, we made the following decisions.

- We established world class education systems as the cornerstone of our corporate education system.

- We hired Bill Wagner as the Executive Director of WCES, reporting directly to one of our executive officers.

- We required that each of our business units develops its own training plan and specifies the content of the plan.

- We decided to commit substantial resources to the company-wide training effort and to devise means to avoid the tendency of line management to cut corners on training to improve short term financial results.

- We established the executive education advisory board made up of me and other key officers of the business to oversee and support the implementation of our total learning culture and high-performance training system.

- We established a training results measurement system to give us the control necessary to measure progress against our goal.

The results of all this far exceeded our expectations. We successfully implemented TQM throughout the company and became one of the winners of the Baldrige award. This would have been impossible without the total education system, not just the training related to the quality system itself, but all the training that has been done to teach everyone how to do their jobs more effectively. Customer satisfaction, market share, and profits have all improved dramatically. Employee and distributor morale is up, and cooperation and dedication to results has never been higher. Labor relations has become a partnership rather than an adversarial situation. We are spending more on training and education than I ever dreamed possible or desirable, but our measurements tell us we are getting a high rate of return on this investment. We have implemented a major transformation of our production technology without losing a beat because the training systems were in place to retrain our professional, managerial, and hourly workforce. We have virtually stamped out functional illiteracy among the workers. We certainly have the highest quality workforce that this company has ever had, and I believe we have the highest quality workforce in the industry anywhere in the world. I, and the other officers, firmly believe at this point that it is the quality of the workforce which is giving us the competitive edge. We feel good about it because we know that it is no accident since we have made and will continue to make very substantial investments in workforce competence.

The final thing I want to do is talk about a few features of our training and education system that I believe make it successful.

1. We have clearly defined and communicated the important role training plays in our business success.

2. We measure and reward all our managers for keeping their workforce competent.

3. Every individual and organizational unit has a training plan and is accountable for accomplishing plan goals.

4. We have adopted an ongoing regular planning cycle to identify the training needs of the business and to develop plans to provide the necessary system and resources to meet these training needs.

5. We have a network of advisory boards and councils that formalize the partnership between the training departments and the line and staff organizations that are their customers.

6. Even though as a good-sized and widespread corporation we have several training departments at the corporate, business unit and local levels, these departments are linked together through a common set of training administration systems enabling us to minimize confusion and duplication of effort.

7. We have treated training like other parts of the business and subjected it to our TQM discipline, which has required us to identify all our training processes,

establish quantitative controls over each process, and embark on continuous process improvement.

None of this has been easy. It has been difficult, time consuming, and frustrating. We made mistakes along the way and learned from our mistakes, and it gets easier as we go along. And as you can tell, in our opinion it has been more than worth it.

Putting It All In Perspective

The concepts and practices advocated in this book can be applied over a very wide range of situations, such as:

- An entire world-wide corporation
- A single business unit
- A plant
- A functional department, (e.g., engineering)
- A military organization
- Other public sector and nonprofit organizations
- Public education.

Obviously, the exact same approach does not fit each example of this wide range of applications. Some of the system features and characteristics will be different. The sequence of planning activities may be different, and the participants in the processes may be different. On the other hand, we believe that the general approach and the underlying concepts are universally applicable. You may feel that the approach advocated in this book is much too involved or too complex for your situation. However, the processes and systems we have described can be applied at many different levels of depth and rigor. It may be appropriate for you to completely bypass some of the things we have discussed and to give others the once-over-lightly treatment. Only you can be the judge of the appropriate level of application for your circumstances. As we have pointed out elsewhere, you should be aware that the first time through will be more difficult and time consuming and expensive because you will be establishing the planning processes and databases and spreadsheets as well as gaining experience with a new planning methodology.

Regardless of how comprehensive or intensive your approach is, we strongly recommend that you establish a formalized ongoing planning process that links training to business goals, quantitatively identifies training needs and the resources required to address those needs, establishes the systems and processes to deploy the resources effectively, and links the training department and its customers together formally to jointly make planning decisions and assess results.

We know it all looks like a lot of work. But remember what Goethe said: "Whatever you can do, or dream you can, begin it. Boldness has genius, power and magic in it." Set your vision, and then act. It will prove to be worth it.

Appendix A

EXAMPLE PROJECT PLAN TO DEVELOP A STRATEGIC TRAINING PLAN FOR XTELCO

PURPOSE AND OBJECTIVES

The purpose of this project is to develop a three- to five-year strategic plan that defines and directs a training system to provide employees with the skills, knowledge, and attitudes needed to achieve the business goals of the company. This plan must take into account integration of the XTelco and ACME training systems.

Questions to be answered by the strategic training plan include

1. What are the challenges facing the XTelco/ACME business, and what are the goals for dealing with these challenges?

2. What skills, knowledge, and competencies does the organization need to achieve these goals?

3. How can the business make sure that its employees know what to do and how to do it; what is the role of training?

4. How adequate is the present training system to address these needs successfully?

5. What kind of a training system is needed? What should it look like three to five years from now?

6. What strategic goals should be established for training?

7. What training strategies will most effectively and efficiently achieve these goals?

8. What is the estimated training workload to execute these strategies?

9. How many resources will be required, and what is the expected return on investment?

10. What organizational, management, and administrative systems are needed to deploy the resources effectively and get the job done?

11. How shall the plan be implemented?

PLANNING PROCESS

The strategic training plan will be developed using a four-phase planning process. This process will be linked to curriculum planning projects for

- Sales
- Customer service
- Management
- Quality.

The following figure shows the interrelationship of the strategic planning process and the curriculum planning process. Separate project plans are being created for the curriculum planning effort.

OVERALL PLANNING PROCESS

Strategic Plan

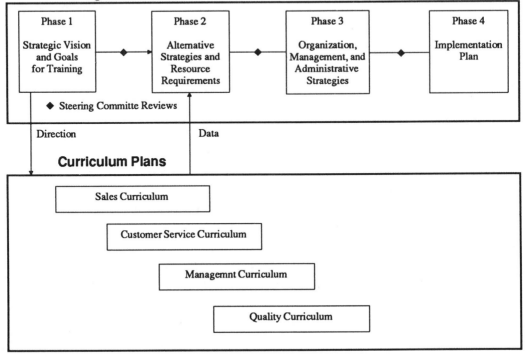

The outputs of each of the four phases are itemized below.

Phase 1: Strategic Vision and Goals for Training

The purpose of phase 1 is to create a vision, mission, and strategic goals for training linked to the business goals of the company. This phase provides the strategic framework for the remaining phases. The outputs of phase 1 include

- Training implications of business plans
- Assessment of the existing training system
- Mission, philosophy, and roles
- Strategic vision and goals for training.

Training Implications of Business Plans The training implications of business goals and challenges is one of the most important aspects of the strategic training plan. This is where training activities are linked to expected business results. This output will include

1. A list of specific challenges facing the business and the strategies and goals that have been established for dealing with these challenges
2. Training implication of each challenge
   - Who is affected?
   - What skills and knowledge will be needed and when?
   - How much will it cost?
   - What is the cost of not doing it?
   - What is the expected return on the training investment?

Assessment of the Existing Training System The assessment of the present training system requires a close look at what exists today in light of the training implications of business plans. This assessment will provide a measure of the gap between what is and what needs to be. This assessment includes the following:

1. An assessment of the capability of the overall training system and its subsystems and processes to do what is needed efficiently and effectively
2. An assessment of the adequacy of basic curricula to train people who are entering new jobs
3. An assessment of the adequacy of training resources to carry the basic training load and address all the specific business challenges that have been identified
4. An assessment of the company's relative position with respect to competitors
5. A benchmark assessment of the company's position relative to best-in-class organizations

6. An estimate of the total cost of training today and the return on investment.

Mission, Philosophy, and Roles   The mission statement for training is a clear statement of the expected contribution of training to the business and the scope of training. The training philosophy statement provides a list of principles and values which the organization will use as a basis for making training decisions. The following items will be included in this output:

1. A mission statement for all training within the organizational scope
2. A philosophy or policy statement about training
3. Mission and roles for the training departments
4. Training roles for line and staff management.

Strategic Vision and Goals for Training   The vision of the future of training should paint a picture of what training will be in the organization three to five years down the road. This vision should include not only what the training department is doing but what line managers are doing and what individual employees are doing with respect to training. It should describe the impact of training on business results and the roles being played by executive management, middle management, and line supervision in the training function. The vision should be clear enough and comprehensive enough so everyone involved can see where they are going and develop a sense of ownership, commitment, and drive to actualize the vision. This output will include

1. A clear vision of the training system needed to support business goals
2. A short list of strategic goals to achieve the vision
3. A one page description of each of these goals.

Phase 2: Alternative Strategies and Resource Requirements

The purpose of phase 2 is to investigate alternative strategies for achieving the vision and strategic goals, to estimate their associated resource requirements, and then to select a strategy mix and adopt a three- to five-year resource plan. The outputs of this phase include

1. Quantitative needs forecast
2. Alternative strategies for meeting the needs
3. Resource requirements for alternative scenarios.

Quantitative Needs Forecast   The needs forecast is completed to develop a quantitative picture of all the work that must be done to achieve the vision, mission, and goals. The work to be forecast can be divided into needs analysis, curriculum architecture design, training materials development, delivery of training, and development and deployment of administrative systems. Included in the quantitative needs forecast are:

1. A three- to five-year personnel forecast

2. Needs assessment for major functions or job groups and for new systems and other initiatives

3. A three- to five-year forecast of needs

4. A three- to five-year forecast of training materials to be developed or procured and maintained

5. A three- to five-year forecast of training delivery requirements.

Alternative Strategies for Meeting the Needs   Based on the numbers and types of requirements identified in the needs forecasts and the logistics involved, alternative strategies must be explored, particularly for development of materials and delivery of training. For example, centralized delivery of training at a single location is much more feasible for a company whose employees are all within a 75-mile radius than it is for a company with locations all over the United States. Interactive computer-based instruction at the worksite is much more feasible when thousands of employees must be trained on common administrative procedures than it is for training corrective action teams in a manufacturing plant. The strategy mix has major implications for the effectiveness, timeliness and cost of training. This output includes

- A list of development strategies

- A list of delivery strategies

- Criteria for using these strategies

- Unit costs for each strategy.

Resource Requirements for Alternative Scenarios   This phase answers the all-important bottom line question: How much can be done at what cost? Usually when the data are in, what is being done today is far less than what is needed to address the challenges of the business. Several scenarios are developed to show what can be accomplished for various levels of resource commitment. This output includes

1. An analysis of the resource requirements implicit in several different three- to five-year scenarios for meeting various fractions of the total estimated need

2. Resource implications of varying the development and delivery strategy mix

3. A workable three- to five-year game plan to present for executive approval.

Phase 3: Organization, Management, and Administrative Strategies

The purpose of phase 3 is to determine what must be done organizationally and administratively to execute the game plan completed in phase 2. Questions to be answered in this phase include

1. How should training be organized?
2. How will the training system be governed by management?
3. How will the training effort be staffed?
4. What facilities are required for the training?
5. How will the business pay for its training?
6. How will the performance of the training system be measured?
7. What systems are needed to support supervisors and managers in performing their training roles?
8. What other administrative systems need to be built or modified (e.g., registration, scheduling, training materials management)?

Organization Structure   There is no single best organization structure for training. A structure is required that will work to achieve the goals that have been established within the culture and framework of the larger organization it serves. The same game plan can usually be executed successfully by a number of alternative organization structures. Included in this output are

1. How many training departments the company will have
2. Their mission, roles, and scope of responsibility
3. How they will coordinate to achieve the overall game plan
4. How they will be structured internally
5. How the organization will evolve to this new structure from a structure that is in place today.

Governing or Advisory Structure   One of the most important administrative issues in training is the governance or advisory linkage between the training departments and the internal and external departments they serve, the customers of training. The governing or advisory structure is the means of forging a true working partnership between the suppliers and customers of training services. The better this partnership mechanism is, the tighter will be the relationship between training activities and the real needs of the business. When this partnership arrangement is working well, training activities are a result of demand from the organizations that are the training customers. When there is no governance or advisory system, the training departments make their own determination of what their customer needs and then try to sell it, or they find themselves reacting to the real or fancied needs of individual managers.

   The most successful training systems have formalized this linkage and tuned it to work like a well-oiled machine. Common components include

- Executive advisory board
- Functional curriculum councils (sales, customer service, management, etc.)
- Administrative council (directors of training from the training departments).

This output will include

1. An overall governance structure
2. Mission, roles, and membership rules for each advisory group
3. A plan for linkage to the training departments
4. A plan for creating or evolving the structure.

Staffing Strategy In the modern training organization, the staff consists of more than just instructors. There are instructors, designers, developers, writers, analyst, specialists in computer-based instruction, and more. This output will include

1. A definition of the needed mix of talents to staff the jobs in the organization structure
2. Sources for these talents (line organizations, consultants, college hires, etc.)
3. Policies for recruiting, selection, retention, and career management.

Facilities Strategy The training facility strategy can be a big deal or a little deal depending on the training strategies that have been selected as part of the game plan. If the company elects to use rented hotel space for most of its training, it is a little deal. If the company elects to build a corporate education center and regional training schools, it can be a big deal. This output will include

1. What kinds of training facilities are needed
2. Where they should be located
3. The capacity requirements over the five- to ten-year forecast period
4. How much it will cost
5. The risk of obsolescence with changing training technologies.

Financing Strategy and Financial Accountability This output determines how the organization is going to pay for the cost of training and how the training department will account for its use of financial resources. There are a number of ways to do this, including

- Overhead staff budgets
- Charge-back systems
- Payroll tax
- The training subsidiary.

All have their advantages and disadvantages. The company will have to pick a strategy that is a good fit for its organizational culture and has the best chance of succeeding.

Financial controls and accountability are equally important. Without good controls, training budgets are commonly overrun and there is inadequate historical data on which to project realistic budgets. The need for financial accountability is axiomatic, but to whom will the training department account and for what?

This output will include

1. Financing strategy
   – Development budget
   – Operations budgets
   – Capital budget
2. A system for data collection and financial control
3. A policy on financial accountability to whom and for what
4. A plan to develop and implement the system.

Results Measurement Plan   The results measurement plan defines how the company will measure and account for training results. These results can include categories such as

- Percent of needs met
- Cost of training
- Customer organization and trainee satisfaction
- Mastery of learning within training
- Transfer of skills and knowledge to job performance
- Payoff in terms of business performance
- Return on investment.

The managers of training, the governance structure, and the customer organizations should use these measures as tools to identify and correct weaknesses and to support and monitor continuous improvement.

This output will include

1. A hierarchy of measures to be used
2. A strategy for collecting and storing the data
3. A plan for a system of regular reports to stakeholders
4. A plan for developing and implementing the system.

Supervisor/Manager Support System   Training departments can be perfectly organized, staffed, financed, housed, and managed and play their roles flawlessly, and still a company will have a marginally performing overall training system if managers and supervisors in the customer departments are not making appropriate decisions and taking effective action. It is important to start with the premise that most managers and supervisors do not know how to make effective use of a world-class training system, and even if they do, they cannot if they do not have the information they need.

Managers and supervisors should be asking and answering these questions:

- What training is needed by each person in my organization?
- When is it needed?
- What is the best source?
- How can I manage my workload with people out for training?
- How do I pay for it?
- What do I need to do to prepare people for training and to make sure it pays off when they get back?
- How can I track my performance and maintain the competence of my workforce?

The training system should have a strategy for providing managers and supervisors with the skills, knowledge, information, tools, and incentives for asking and answering these questions completely.

This output includes specifications for the following:

1. Information systems and communication channels
2. Job aids and procedures
3. Training for supervisors and managers.

Other Administrative Systems   There are a number of other administrative systems that must be planned. This strategic training plan should at least identify the most important systems and estimate the resource requirements to develop and implement these systems. Some of these systems include

- Registration and scheduling
- Training information and record keeping
- Communications (newsletters, announcements)
- Materials management
- Personnel administration
- Procurement.

Phase 4: Implementation Plan

If the strategic training plan is at all complex, it will not be actualized just by making and documenting all the planning decisions and gaining executive support. It will be necessary to lay out a list of implementation activities on a time line, assign accountabilities, and provide resources. For some activities, such as the detailed planning and implementation of a new corporate education center, you may need one or more full-time people and a planning committee.

The implementation plan will include

1. Implementation activities lists
2. Milestones to monitor progress
3. Assignments for accountability
4. Resource allocations for implementation tasks.

OUTPUTS OF CURRICULUM PLANNING PROJECTS

Curriculum planning projects are scheduled between phase 1 and phase 2 to identify more clearly the training needs of the specific target audiences in

- Sales
- Customer service
- Management
- Quality.

The principal outputs of a curriculum planning project include

- A performance model
- A curriculum architecture
- Module specification sheets for each module of training.

Performance Model

The performance models include the following information:

- Mission and responsibilities for the function (e.g., sales)
- Outputs from each of the responsibilities
- Tasks required to produce the outputs

- Skills and knowledge required to perform the tasks

- Importance and priority for developing training in each task and each supporting skill and knowledge.

Curriculum Architecture

The curriculum architecture is a map which defines the modules of training required to meet the skill and knowledge requirements of the target audience and the interrelationships among these modules. Some modules may be orientation modules to the company or the job, some may relate to specific tasks or clusters of tasks, and some may teach individual skill or knowledge items.

Module Specification Sheets

The module specification sheet identifies the following for each individual module in the curriculum:

- Expected learning objectives

- Probable length of training

- Probable best delivery strategy

- Target audience

- Required depth of coverage

- Preliminary content.

The information contained in the definition of the training modules and the priorities for development of those modules is essential to completing phase 2 of the strategic training plan: "Alternative Strategies and Resource Requirements." Without this information, it is difficult to estimate the total training requirements, what the strategy should be for addressing those training requirements, and how many resources will be required to meet the requirements.

SCOPE

The scope of this project plan is to provide the overall planning framework and to provide a detailed project plan for phase 1 only. A separate project plan is provided for the first of the curriculum planning projects, a sales curriculum. Detailed project plans for phases 2, 3, and 4 will be created as outputs of the previous phase.

PROCESS FOR COMPLETING PHASE 1

Participants in the Planning Process

The participants in the planning process will include

- The steering committee
- The project leader
- The project team
- A consultant.

Steering Committee   A steering committee made up of appropriate executives from XTelco and ACME will

- Review and approve the project plan
- Review and approve phase 1 outputs, including a project plan for phase 2
- Appoint the planning team.

Project Leader   John Doe will be the project leader. His roles will be

- Negotiate the project schedule
- Make arrangements for interviews and meetings
- Serve as principal liaison with the consultant.

Project Team   The project team will consist of the project leader and other representatives of the XTelco and ACME businesses. Their roles include

- Interview executives and training department
- Participate in a four-day meeting to assimilate data and develop phase 1 outputs
- Review documents prepared by the consultant
- Present outputs to the steering committee.

Consultant   The consultant will

- Develop the draft of the project plan
- Present the planning process and project plan to the steering committee
- Orient the Project Team to the planning process and Project Plan and to their roles

- Facilitate the planning meetings
- Document phase 1 outputs
- Prepare presentation materials
- Attend the steering committee review
- Revise outputs based on steering committee review.

Planning Activities

There are nine major activities in the phase 1 planning process.

Activity 1: Steering Committee Review of Project Plan The steering committee will meet to review the project plan and appoint the project team. The consultant will prepare and make the presentation to the steering committee.

Activity 2: Orientation of Project Team The Consultant will conduct a one-day meeting with the project team to orient them to the planning project, the planning process, and their roles in the planning process.

Activity 3: Data Collection in XTelco and ACME The project team will conduct interviews with XTelco and ACME executives and the XTelco and ACME training department to elicit the training implications of business plans, identified training needs and priorities, and information regarding the capabilities of the existing training system. These interviews will be conducted by members of the Project Team. It is expected that each project team member will spend approximately three days conducting these interviews.

Activity 4: Planning Meeting The consultant will facilitate a four-day planning meeting with the project team to assimilate the data that has been collected in XTelco and ACME and also to develop all of the phase 1 deliverables.

Activity 5: Documentation The consultant will document the phase 1 results and prepare presentation materials for steering committee review.

Activity 6: Review with Project Team The consultant will conduct a one-day review of the documented outputs and presentation materials with the project team.

Activity 7: Revision The consultant will revise the materials based on project team review.

Activity 8: Steering Committee Review The project team, supported by the consultant, will present the results of phase 1 to the steering committee for their approval or recommended changes.

Activity 9: Revisions The consultant will make any appropriate revisions to the phase 1 materials based on comments of the steering committee.

RESOURCE REQUIREMENTS AND SCHEDULE

| | Estimated Resources (Days) | | | | | Schedule | |
| | Consultant | | XTelco/ACME | | | | |
Tasks	CS	PS	PT	PL	SC	Start	End
Phase 1							
1. Meet with Steering Committee to review Project Plan	2.0	2.0	–	1.0	1.0		
2. Orientation of Project Team	2.0	2.0	1.0	1.0	–		
3. Interview executives and training department	–	–	3.0	3.0	–		
4. Planning meeting to assimilate the data and develop Phase 1 deliverables	5.0	1.0	4.0	4.0	–		
5. Document Phase 1 results and prepare presentation materials	3.0	5.0	–	–	–		
6. Review draft with Project Team	1.0	–	1.0	1.0	–		
7. Revise	1.0	2.0	–	–	–		
8. Present to Steering Committee	1.0	–	1.0	1.0	1.0		
9. Revise	1.0	2.0	–	–	–		
TOTAL	16.0	14.0	10.0	11.0	2.0		

KEY Consultant	XTelco/ACME
CS = Consulting Staff PS = Production Staff	PT = Project Team PL = Project Leader SC = Steering Committee

Figure A-1

Appendix B

XTELCO: STRATEGIC TRAINING PLAN

STRENGTHS, WEAKNESSES, AND GOALS

This section presents an analysis of strengths and weaknesses of corporate education compared to the training implications arising from the corporate challenges and a set of goals for each implication.

Training Implication: 1. Training must become more proactive, professional, responsive.

Strengths	Weaknesses	Goals

• A portion of the training staff is rotational from the user organizations.
• Developing a strategic training plan
• We are well positioned with local community colleges.
• Active executive level advisory council
	• We have not formalized the mechanisms for proactively looking ahead at training needs.
	• Responsiveness has suffered because we have been reluctant to use available outside resources.
	• There is inadequate provision in procurement contracts to require vendors to provide *quality* training with their products.
		• Formalize a planning system to forecast training needs and plan for timely responses. This includes forging stronger linkages to organizations that are planning for change.
		• Develop a system to enhance the professionalism of corporate education
		  –Ratios of rotational to career training people
		  –Professional standards

Strengths

Weaknesses

- Our base of course developer skills is inadequate to responsively develop efficient and effective training.
- Corporate education has no overall measure of employee body reaction to the adequacy of training.

Goals

 –Career development
 –Recruiting.
- Enhance responsiveness by leveraging corporate education staff
 –Cooperative development
 –Outside development resources
 –Purchased training materials
 –Contract instructors
 –Universities, community colleges, vocational schools.
- Implement a periodic survey to measure user satisfaction.

Training Implication: 2. Workforce shrinking but requires higher skills, more training, therefore training must grow.

Strengths

- Aggressively moving to involve educational institutions to fill selected training voids
- Have begun to use contract resources to augment corporate education cadre
- Regional cooperative training has been established as a means of leveraging resources.
- We have a strong training organization to build on.

Weaknesses

- Shortage of training department resources to meet the identified need
- Have not convinced management to recognize required training resources to meet corporate goals
- Have not quantified the need
- Have not taken advantage of contract course development

Goals

- We will develop a quantitative forecast of the resources required to meet all needs within the mission of corporate education (phase 2 of this planning project)

Training Implication: 3. Potential Regionalization of Training.

Strengths

- Already working with re-gional committees to iden-tify common training needs
- We have an index on a re-gional basis that identifies and classifies all training projects.
- The strength of the XTelco training organization will exert a positive influence on the direction of regional training.

Weaknesses

- Not tied in adequately with regional planning commit-tees outside of training
- We do not know what the region will do with train-ing (i.e., there is no pub-lished region training plan).
- We are losing the leverag-ing power of national course development con-sortiums as the regions di-verge in systems and methods.

Goals

- Corporate education will continue to be the principal provider of training devel-opment and delivery for the next three years.
- Outside vendors will begin to play a more significant role in the 1990s.

Training Implication: 4a. Management Training.

Strengths

- Good (expandable) physi-cal plant at Los Angeles for management training
- We have a good base of technical information on which to build manage-ment courses.
- We have good customer contact skills training in place.
- New manager curriculum (regional) coming on line

Weaknesses

- We do not have job admin-istration courses available in most areas.
- We do not have manage-ment-level technical courses in place.
- We do not have training available in generic man-agement skills for second- and third-level managers.
- Our new culture and value system has not yet been in-stitutionalized.
- We have not packaged or marketed our customer contact skills training for managers.

Goals

- Complete the plan for a comprehensive, perfor-mance-based management curriculum, first through third levels, which sup-ports XTelco's culture and values.

Training Implication: 4b. Marketing and Sales Training

Strengths

- We have some products knowledge and selling skills courses.
- We have developed a capability to provide distributed, computer-based product knowledge.

Weaknesses

- The responsibility for imparting this knowledge is split between corporate education and marketing. Therefore, we have no coherent program.
- We do not have a complete family of marketing and selling skills courses.
- This knowledge is required across many disciplines, but we are not organized to deliver training across functions.
- We are not viewed as having marketing and sales skills.

Goals

- Resolve the issue of split responsibility between corporate education and marketing with consideration for
  –Customer impact
  –Effectiveness of employee training
  –Cost/efficiency of training.
- Develop a comprehensive, professional marketing and sales training program with a major thrust in the expanding digital data market.
- Develop a customer contact, sales oriented program for craft and management people who have significant sales opportunities.

Training Implication: 4c. Craft Training

Strengths

- Strong core of technical training
- Well connected to the sources of change, and craft training is up to date
- We are recognized as competent in developing craft technical training.

Weaknesses

- The progression of courses in the curriculum is out of date given today's hiring and job assignment patterns, which leads to unnecessary training.
- We do not have people skilled or available to do curriculum architecture across an entire family of courses.
- Our programs do not keep front-line forces up to date on customer applications.

Goals

- Continue to provide high-quality job skills and technical training.
- Systematically redesign the craft curriculums to
  –Fit today's job
  –Provide various entry points
  –Provide modular flexibility.
- Continue to sponsor pre-technical education for retraining of non-technical employees.

Training Implication: 5. Coordinated effort to achieve broad knowledge base

Strengths	Weaknesses	Goals
• We are a part of the personnel organization.	• Corporate education, labor relations, and employment have different agendas.	• Develop unified strategies with other elements of personnel services, corporate communications, and labor relations to optimize human performance through –Selection –Hiring –Training and retraining –Cooperation with Educational Institutions –Career systems.

Training Implication: 6. Establish a learning culture in XTelco.

Strengths	Weaknesses	Goals
• Company/union training and retraining Committee is an example of an effective effort to establish a learning culture. • The strength and expertise of corporate education positions us to help and influence managers to take appropriate responsibility for employee development.	• Corporate education has not established itself as being capable of providing assistance in employee development.	• Develop a plan to institutionalize training plans for individual employees and organizational units.

Training Implication: 7. Training must market its services on a value-added basis.

Strengths

- We have a systematic process for making cost-effective training decisions.

Weaknesses

- We have not actively marketed our products and services to our users.
- We have not identified all the areas that could benefit from our available products and services.

Goals

- Continue to provide quality training to the corporation and seek opportunities to further reduce the cost of training.
- Actively market our products and services to our XTelco clients.

Training Implication: 8. Customer Training

Strengths

- We have a nucleus of product and service information that could serve as a foundation.
- We have the necessary skills.

Weaknesses

- There is no current policy on whether to provide this training.
- There are no resources currently available to provide this service.
- Our programs are not packaged for customer use.

Goals

- Work with Marketing to establish a policy regarding customer training as a means to help customers make effective use of our products and services.

Appendix C

XTELCO: STRATEGIC TRAINING PLAN

SYSTEM: GOVERNANCE	
Purpose:	Provide a structural means for executive leadership and for the user organizations to direct training resources and control training results in partnership with training management to meet the training needs of the business
Processes:	• Executive board of training or education • Functional curriculum councils; one for each major business function (e.g., marketing) • Training administration council (heads of training units) • Project committees (expert/user support for all projects) • Organizational unit training committees (business units, divisions, plants, etc.)
Outputs:	• Training policy and philosophy • Approved training plans and budgets at all levels • Assessment of training effectiveness by management and users • Resources made available • Political support at all organizational levels
Participants:	• Executives, managers, and employees at all levels in all departments
Performance Measures:	• Executives and representatives of users making key decisions about what training is to be provided and allocating resources for the task • Level of support for training throughout the organization • Skills and knowledge treated as the key assets of the business and training investment systematically managed • Training content matches real needs of the business

SYSTEM: GOVERNANCE	Process: Executive Board of Training or Education
Purpose:	Direct, support, and control the use of the organization's educational resources so the skills and knowledge are developed to achieve its business goals
Key Responsibilities:	• Create mission, philosophy, and policies for training • Provide business input to strategic training plan • Review and approve strategic training plan • Establish relative priorities for the use of training resources • Review and approve annual training plans and budget • Select or appoint top training officer • Review the performance of training against plans • Appoint subordinate advisory structure
Outputs:	• Mission, philosophy, and policies for training • Strategic training plan • Annual training plan and budget • Top training officer appointment and performance appraisal • Assessment of the impact of training on business results • Political support for training
Participants:	• Chaired by a general officer (e.g., President) • Key function heads (e.g., VP Marketing) • Key business heads (e.g., Business Unit General Manager)
Performance Measures:	• Plans created and resources provided for training to support key business goals • Quality of support for training • Quality of appointments • Overall impact of training on the business

SYSTEM: GOVERNANCE	Process: Functional Curriculum Councils
Purpose:	Within its area of jurisdiction (e.g., sales training), oversee needs analysis, approve an overall curriculum architecture, establish priorities, provide support, and oversee effectiveness of training
Key Responsibilities:	• Oversee analysis of training required to support all key job functions and tasks within the function • Oversee analysis of training needs associated with new technology, new methods, or any other planned changes • Review and approve an overall curriculum architecture for the function • Set priorities for developing or acquiring new training programs, materials, systems • Set priorities for maintenance of existing training programs, and materials • Review and approve recommendations to abandon obsolete or ineffective programs • Review reports of efficiency and effectiveness of training • Set priorities for formal follow-up evaluation of programs • Appoint project committees to support new course development • Assist in recruiting content experts for course development or instructions • Review annual functional training plan and budget • Recommend annual budget to executive advisory board
Outputs:	• Needs analyses for job functions and tasks • Needs analyses for planned new systems or other changes • Curriculum architecture • Priorities for developing or acquiring new training • Priorities for maintenance of existing training • Approval to abandon existing training programs • Priorities for formal follow-up evaluation studies • Approval of functional training plans • Recommendations for funding • Political and other support • Appointments to project committees

SYSTEM: GOVERNANCE	Process: Functional Curriculum Councils (continued)
Participants:	• Chaired by corporate function head or delegate • Function heads in business units or key functional middle managers
Performance Measures:	• Completeness and effectiveness of the curriculum for key jobs in the function, including functional management • Effectiveness and timeliness of training to support change • Maintenance condition of the existing curriculum • Comparison of the inventory of functional skills and knowledge to requirements for excellence in functional business results

SYSTEM: GOVERNANCE	Process: Training Administration Council
Purpose:	Plan and oversee the development and operation of administrative systems needed for effective and efficient performance of the training function, including but not limited to • Organization structure • Facilities • Registration and scheduling • Quality standards • Process standards • Information systems • Measurement and evaluation systems • Delivery systems • Needs analysis systems • Courseware development systems
Key Responsibilities:	• Review and approve overall training administrative systems architecture • Develop an administrative systems plan that supports the strategic training plan • Establish priorities for development of new administrative systems or major changes to existing systems • Appoint project committees to oversee administrative systems development • Measure and assess the effectiveness and efficiency of the administrative systems
Outputs:	• Administrative systems architecture • Administrative systems plans • Funding recommendations to executive board of education (e.g., for training facilities) • Project committee appointments • Assessments of administrative efficiency and effectiveness
Participants:	• Chaired by chief training officer • Heads of major training organizational units
Performance Measures:	• Efficiency and effectiveness of administrative systems

SYSTEM: GOVERNANCE	Process: Project Committees
Purpose:	Provide support to training development teams on matters of content and administration during development or major revisions of training materials

Key Responsibilities:	• Review purpose and scope of project
	• Review project plan
	• Provide access to records, reference documents, content experts, master performers, potential students, and management, for purposes of
	  - Task analysis
	  - Content analysis
	  - Developmental testing of materials
	  - Obtaining examples and case studies
	• Review results of analysis phase
	• Approve end-of-training objectives
	• Approve specifications for entry skills and knowledge
	• Review training content for technical accuracy and conformance to policy and standards
	• Approve list of instructor qualifications
	• Select trainees for field trial
	• Review trial results and approve content changes
	• Support implementation

Outputs:	• Approved project plan • Content support • Approved content • Field trial candidates • Implementation support
Participants:	• Chaired by a staff expert if available • Experts and master performers from key organizational units
Performance Measures:	• Appropriateness of training content • Technical accuracy of content • Conformance of content to policy and standards • Quality of field trial candidates • Timeliness of support • Receptivity of the field to implementation

SYSTEM: GOVERNANCE	Process: Organizational Unit Training Committees
Purpose:	Direct and oversee training for an organizational unit (e.g., business unit, plant, sales region) to assure that training is provided to meet the business goals of this unit
Key Responsibilities:	• Develop a strategic training plan for the organizational unit • Develop annual training plans • Recommend training budget for this organizational unit to the executive board of education • Establish priorities for training within this unit • Make recommendations to functional curriculum councils regarding functional training needs and priorities • Oversee development of programs and materials that are unique to the organizational unit • Evaluate the effectiveness of training within the unit • Assign resources to carry out training activities • Make recommendations to the training administration council
Outputs:	• Organization unit strategic training plan • Organization unit annual training plan • Budget recommendation • Priorities • Recommendations to functional curriculum councils and training administration council • Resources assigned • Assessments of effectiveness and efficiency of training
Participants:	• Chaired by head of organization unit • Other key managers • Highest-level training person in the unit (secretary)
Performance Measures:	• Strategic and annual plans approved • Resources allocated match goals and expectations • Strong leadership, participation, and commitment of line management • Training investments managed to support key business goals and achieve high return on investment

SYSTEM: PLANNING	
Purpose:	Develop a hierarchy of training plans to meet the needs of the business (see Figure C-1)
Outputs:	• Strategic training plans; entire organization, major organizational units, major functions • Annual training plans and budgets; entire organization, major organizational units, major functions • Training plans for all subordinate organizational units • Individual training plans • Project plans for all significant projects • Delivery plans and schedule
Particpants:	• Executive board of education • Functional curriculum councils • Organization unit training committees • Training administration council • Project committees • All managers and supervisors • All employees
Performance Measures:	• Foreseeable training needs of the business identified and planned for • Every organizational unit has a training plan • Every individual has a training plan • Planned resources sufficient to achieve planned objectives

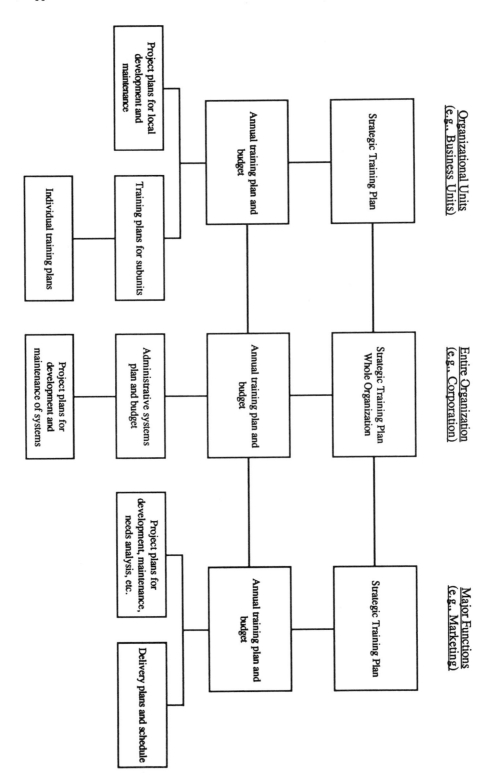

SYSTEM: PLANNING	Process: Strategic Training Plans
Purpose:	Provide a strategic plan that limits training to business goals and challenges, including but not limited to • Training mission and philosophy/values • Training implications of business goals and challenges • Business consequences • Training vision and strategic goals • Development and delivery strategies • Long-range resource plans • Plans for training systems and processes
Key Responsibilities:	• Determine plan contents • Design planning process • Develop and update the plan • Present plan and options • Approve plan
Outputs:	• Annual updates to strategic training plan • Strategic planning process • Implementation plans
Participants:	• Training management work with planning staff to develop the plans, obtaining input from top management and other sources • Executive governance board reviews and approves the plan • All participants in the training process use elements of the plan to shape decisions
Performance Measures:	• Completeness • Usability for management decision making • Timeliness • Cost • Accuracy and validity of data and assumptions

SYSTEM: PLANNING	Process: Annual Training Plan and Budget
Purpose:	Plan annual training objectives and budgets, including but not limited to • Needs analysis and curriculum architecture • Courseware development • Delivery • Maintenance • Results measurement • Administration
Key Responsibilities:	• Establish contents and structure for annual plan and budget • Prepare annual plan and budget in context of strategic plan • Present for approval with options • Approval of plan and budget
Outputs:	• Approved plan and budget • Implementation plan • Planning process
Participants:	• Training management team establishes overall objectives • Each training manager prepares own plan and proposed budget • Training management team reconciles individual plan and develops composite plan • Presentation to governance groups • Approval by governance groups
Performance Measures:	• Conformance to strategic plan • Completeness • Resources sufficient to accomplish objectives • Timeliness • Cost to develop • Establish for management decision making

SYSTEM: PLANNING	Process: Organizational Unit Training Plans

Purpose:	Enable each manager to develop an annual plan for training to be provided to members of his or her organizational unit, including but not limited to
	• Causes of training requirements
	  - New hires
	  - Personnel moves
	  - New technology
	  - New methods
	  - Performance improvement goals
	• Numbers of people to be trained
	• Sources of the training
	• Timing requirements
	• Resource requirements
	  - Budget
	  - Facilities
	  - Staff
	  - Administrative support

Key Responsibilities:	• Identify and prioritize training needs, including timing • Identify and select training strategies and sources • Estimate resource requirements • Develop plan and budget • Present plan • Approve plan
Outputs:	• Training needs • Training objectives • Budget • Implementation • Plan
Participants:	• Managers identify, evaluate, and prioritize training needs • Administrative support identifies and selects training strategies and sources, estimates resource requirements • Managers develop plan and budget and present for approval • Management team reconciles plans and budget across larger organization • Governance structure approves the plan

SYSTEM: PLANNING	Process: Organizational Unit Training Plans (continued)
Performance Measures:	• Completeness and accuracy of needs assessment • Priorities link to business impact • Budget sufficient to accomplish objectives • Efficient and effective strategies and sources chosen

SYSTEM: PLANNING	Process: Individual Training Plans

Purpose:	Develop an annual training plan for each individual member of the organization, including but not limited to
	• Competencies needed for job performance
	• Competencies needed for career development
	• Priorities for learning
	• Training requirements
	• Learning objectives
	• Plan for achieving the objectives, including
	  - Formal training
	  - Job assignments
	  - Coaching
	  - Personal development

Key Responsibilities:	• Identify competencies needed for job performance and for career development • Assess existing competencies to determine developmental requirements and priorities • Develop the learning plan • Evaluate performance against the plan
Outputs:	• Individual learning plans • List of competencies for jobs
Participants:	• Analysts work with managers and job incumbents to identify competency requirements for jobs and job families • Individuals develop their own plans with support from supervisors and others
Performance Measures:	• Percentage of employees with individual plans • Quality and completeness of the plans • Percentage of objectives met

SYSTEM: PLANNING	Process: Project Plans
Purpose:	Provide plans which delimit purpose scope, outputs, procedures, schedule, budget, resource requirements, roles of participant for • Courseware development • Needs analysis/curriculum architecture • Administrative systems development • Planning projects
Key Responsibilities:	• Establish project plan requirements • Develop project plan • Present plan for approval • Approve project plan • Track performance against plans
Outputs:	• Project plan requirements, standards • Project plans
Participants:	• Management develops standards for project plans and project management • Project managers develop and present project plans and use them to control projects • Management and project committees review, critique, and approve the plans
Performance Measures:	• Completeness • Quality of plan and project approach • Performance against plan

SYSTEM: PLANNING	Process: Delivery Plans and Schedules
Purpose:	Provide a plan and schedule for delivery of training, including but not limited to • Class/course schedule, by location • Facility schedule • Instructor schedule
Key Responsibilities:	• Review demand forecasts • Develop 6–12 month schedule • Update monthly as demand figures change
Outputs:	• Class schedule • Facility schedule • Instructor schedule
Participants:	• Administrative staff works with training managers to build initial schedule and monthly updates • Administrative staff issues schedule to everyone with a need to know
Performance Measures:	• Schedules meet the demand in a timely way • Schedules make efficient use of resources • Instructor schedules provide adequate balance between delivery requirements, other instructor duties, and personal life

SYSTEM: OPERATIONS	
Purpose:	Perform the activities directly associated with achieving training results (i.e., skills and knowledge developed and successfully applied on the job)
Processes:	• Needs analysis • Curriculum architecture design • Instructional design/development • Delivery • On-the-job application • Maintenance
Outputs:	• Training needs identified and assessed • Curriculum architectures • Training materials and systems • Learning events • Skills and knowledge acquired • Performance capability
Participants:	• Everyone
Performance Measures:	• Job performance deficiencies due to lack of skills or knowledge eliminated • Cost of deficiencies in terms of business results • Cost of training operations • User satisfaction

SYSTEM: OPERATIONS	Process: Needs Analysis
Purpose:	Identify and analyze all important training needs
Key Responsibilities:	• Analyze training needs associated with major job families • Analyze training needs associated with change (new systems, etc.) • Analyze training needs associated with performance problems (e.g., poor quality)

Outputs:	• Performance models for major job families
	  - Mission
	  - Responsibilities
	  - Major outputs
	  - Tasks
	  - Performance measures
	  - Typical performance deficiencies
	  - Typical causes of performance deficiencies
	  - Skills and knowledge requirements linked to responsibilities or tasks
	  - Importance and priority of training for tasks, skills, knowledge
	• Training requirements to support a change (new system)
	  - Jobs affected
	  - Tasks affected
	  - New or changed skills and knowledge requirements
	  - Numbers of people affected and timing of impact
	  - Importance and priority for training
	• Performance analyses
	  - Performance problem definition
	  - Analysis of causes
	  - Recommendations for training and other solutions
	• Cost/benefit analyses

Participants:	• Analysis performed by trained analysts in the training department or outside resources • Panels of experts and master performers used by analysts to generate the information • Review and assessment of impact performed by curriculum councils

SYSTEM: OPERATIONS	Process: Needs Analysis (continued)
Performance Measures:	• Completeness • Validity • Timeliness • Efficiency

SYSTEM: OPERATIONS	Process: Curriculum Architecture
Purpose:	Organize all training requirements in a function or job family into a structured, modular set of training experiences
Key Responsibilities:	• Overall structural design of the curriculum • Identification of specific training modules and courses • Development of training module and course specifications • Identification of typical learning paths

Outputs:	• Curriculum architecture; structural view of the curriculum linked to job performance models
	• Module and course specifications
	   - Name of module
	   - Purpose
	   - General objectives and content
	   - Length of training
	   - Type of training (e.g., classroom)
	   - Prerequisites
	   - Content volatility
	   - Target audiences
	• Typical learning paths or sequences

Participants:	• Designed by trained instructional designers with input from content experts • Reviewed and approved by curriculum councils
Performance Measures:	• Flexibility of learning paths to accommodate individual and subgroup needs • Minimum content overlap among modules • Appropriateness of course modules for specific primary target audiences • Easy to connect training to expected job performance via job performance models • Conforms to important administrative constraints (e.g., length of time off for training), minimized need for trainee travel • Effective and efficient use of available delivery strategies (e.g., self-paced, OJT, computer based)

SYSTEM: OPERATIONS	Process: Instructional Design and Development
Purpose:	Create the courseware (courses/modules)

Key Responsibilities:	• Detailed analysis of training required within the scope of module specification from curriculum architecture
	• Instructional design
	  - Sequence of learning activities
	  - Materials specifications
	  - Equipment specifications
	  - Instructional staff specifications
	  - Prerequisite specifications
	  - Testing and evaluation specifications
	• Development
	  - Instructional materials
	  - Exercises, case problems
	  - Media
	  - Software (if computer-based training)
	  - Laboratory setup/simulators
	• Field test and revise
	• Training of delivery team

Outputs:	• Project plan • Analysis report • Design document • Materials, media, software, simulators • Field test report • Trained delivery team

Participants:	• Development team
	  - Project leader
	  - Trained analysts
	  - Trained instructional designers
	  - Content experts
	  - Writers
	  - Editors
	  - Media specialists
	  - CBT specialists
	  - Production support (graphics, word processing, etc.)
	• Development project committee (see governance system in this appendix)
	  - Content experts
	  - Appointed by curriculum council

SYSTEM: OPERATIONS Process: Instructional Design and Development (continued)	

Performance
Measures:
	• Relevance of content to job performance
	• Training evaluation data
	  - Level 1: Reaction of trainees and instructors
	  - Level 2: Trainees' mastery of objectives
	  - Level 3: Transfer of skills and knowledge to performance on
	        the job
	  - Level 4: Effectiveness and efficiency of instructional design
	        (as measured by ROI)
	• Cost of development
	• Timeliness of completion
	• Content completeness, accuracy, and conformance to policy and
	  standards

SYSTEM: OPERATIONS	Process: Delivery
Purpose:	Provide the designed, structured learning experiences through a variety of learning channels, including but not limited to • Classrooms • Laboratory/simulation • Structured OJT • Computer-based delivery • Video teleconferencing • Correspondence systems • Video/audio library systems

Key Responsibilities:	• Supply trainees and their supervisors with pretraining information
	• Set up and test classroom, laboratory, simulators, etc.
	• Pretest trainees, if appropriate
	• Administer actual training experience
	• Test trainees' mastery of objectives
	• Collect trainee opinion feedback
	• Identify needed maintenance to the courseware
	  - Content problems
	  - Instructional design problems
	  - Courseware quality and usability
	• Training of delivery team

Outputs:	• Pretraining information • Trained trainees • Pre- and posttest data • Opinion survey data • Maintenance requirements list

Participants:	• Delivery team provides the learning experience
	  - Instructors/facilitators
	  - Production support
	  - Training manager
	• Trainees learn
	• Trainee supervisor establishes expectation in pretraining briefing and debriefs trainee upon completion

Performance Measures:	• Trainees' mastery of learning objectives • Trainee opinions toward training • Transfer of learning to job performance • Completeness of maintenance requirements

SYSTEM: OPERATIONS	Process: On-the-Job Application
Purpose:	Assure transfer of new skills and knowledge to actual job performance
Key Responsibilities:	• Assign tasks that require the use of newly acquired skills and knowledge • Monitor application and provide coaching where necessary • Provide additional or remedial training, if needed • Provide feedback to training evaluation system
Outputs:	• Transfer of new skills and knowledge to job performance • Feedback to training evaluation system
Participants:	• Trainees' supervisors assign tasks, provide for monitoring and coaching, and provide feedback • Master performers may perform monitoring and coaching and provide feedback • Trainees apply skills, provide feedback
Performance Measures:	• Time to achieve mastery performance using new skills and knowledge • Quality of job assignment and coaching for learning purposes • Timeliness and completeness of feedback to training evaluation system

SYSTEM: OPERATIONS	Process: Maintenance
Purpose:	Keep courseware in a high state of maintenance • Content up to date and valid to job requirements • Instructional design problems corrected • Courseware problems corrected

Key Responsibilities:	• Maintenance planning based on inputs from delivery, evaluation system, curriculum council
	• Routine maintenance (small changes)
	• Major maintenance
	  - Analysis
	  - Design
	  - Development
	  - Field test and revision
	  - Delivery team training

Outputs:	• Maintenance plan
	  - Requirements lists
	  - Assessment and priorities
	  - Schedule
	  - Resource requirements
	• Updated courseware
	• Maintenance reports

Participants:	• Development team
	  - Project leader
	  - Trained analysts
	  - Trained instructional designers
	  - Content experts
	  - Writers
	  - Editors
	  - Media specialists
	  - CBT specialists
	  - Production support (graphics, word processing, etc.)
	• Development project committee (see governance system in this appendix)
	  - Content experts
	  - Appointed by curriculum council

Performance Measures:	• Courseware changes made only through disciplined system of control • Timeliness • Changes effective • Cost of maintenance

SYSTEM: RESULTS	
Purpose:	Measure and evaluate the effectiveness and efficiency of the entire training system and its processes in supporting the business goals of the organization, including but not limited to • Percentage of training needs met • Cost of training • Cost of not training (CONC—Cost of Nonconformance) • Impact on business results • Transfer of skills and knowledge to job application • Mastery within training • Opinions of trainees and others
Processes:	• Overall performance • Trainee opinions • Mastery testing • Transfer of learning to job performance • Impact on business results • Financial results
Outputs:	• System architecture • Measurement plan • Measurement and evaluation reports
Participants:	• Evaluation specialists design the system and assist in interpreting results • Training managers and professionals use the data to assist in decision making • Governing groups use the data to assist in decision making • Managers at all levels of the business use the data • Administrative support group collects and stores data, generates reports
Performance Measures:	• Validity and reliability of the data • Value of the data to decision makers • Cost of the system • Timeliness of reports • Usability of reports • Accessibility of data for special reports

SYSTEM: RESULTS	Process: Overall Performance
Purpose:	Measure the overall effectiveness and efficiency of training, including but not limed to • Percentage of training needs met • Percentage of needed curriculum in place • Cost of training • Cost of nonconformance to training standards • Return on investment for training • Timeliness of training for new employees, new systems, other time-dependent initiatives • Overall attitudes of employees, management, and others toward the training system • Managerial and individual behavior consistent with values, philosophy, goals, and objectives
Key Responsibilities:	• Determine overall results measured • Develop methods for collecting, storing, and reporting results data • Analyze results data
Outputs:	• Results reports • Results definitions • Data collection instruments and systems • Analysis reports and recommendations
Participants:	• Measurement specialists work with management to determine the measures and design the system and interpret results • Administrative staff collects and stores the data and issues reports • Management uses results data to support decision making
Performance Measures:	• Results are believable and useful to top management in making decisions to manage the organizations investment in training • Reports are easy to interpret, timely and accurate • The cost of the system

SYSTEM: RESULTS	Process: Trainee Opinions

Purpose:	Measure trainee opinions toward training experiences, including but not limited to • Relevance of content to trainees' jobs • Instructor effectiveness • Effectiveness of instructional design • Effectiveness of instructional materials and equipment • Quality of training facilities • Quality of pretraining information and registration process • Confidence in own ability to apply training back on the job
Key Responsibilities:	• Design and maintain the opinion survey instruments • Collect and store data • Prepare and analyze reports
Outputs:	• Opinion surveys • Opinion data • Summary reports • Administrative system
Participants:	• Measurement experts' work with training staff to design the instruments and the administrative system, assist in interpreting data • Instructors or others administer surveys at the end of each learning event, and use the data to improve instruction or recommend course maintenance • Administrative staff enters data into the system and generates reports • Training managers use the data as part of performance appraisal system
Performance Measures:	• All important opinion issues measured • Reliability and validity of the data • Timeliness and usability of reports • Appropriateness of decisions using the data

SYSTEM: RESULTS	Process: Mastery Testing
Purpose:	Measure trainees' mastery of end-of-training learning objectives through paper and pencil, computer, simulated performance, or actual job performance
Key Responsibilities:	• Design overall testing policy, strategy, and system • Develop tests and simulation exercises for individual learning modules and performance checklists • Administer tests or observe performance • Record and store test data • Report mastery results to trainees and their supervisors • Analyze test data
Outputs:	• Testing policy, strategy, and system • Tests, simulation exercises, performance checklists • Test results • Reports to trainees and supervisors • Analysis reports and recommendations
Participants:	• Measurement specialists work with management, developers, and instructors to design the system, develop tests, and interpret results • Instructional designers/developers develop tests and use test data in course maintenance • Instructors administer test • Administrative staff inputs and stores data and generates reports • Training managers use reports as input to performance appraisals
Performance Measures:	• All learning objectives measured • Validity and reliability of measures • Data storage and retrieval complete, accurate, timely • Reports to trainees and supervisors comply with legal requirements • Analysis reports timely and useful to instructors, developers, and managers

SYSTEM: RESULTS	Process: Transfer of Learning to Job Performance

Purpose:	Measure the transfer of skills and knowledge acquired in training to actual performance on the job, including but not limited to
	• New skills used on the job
	  - Proficiency
	  - Problem areas
	• New skills/knowledge not used on the job
	  - Reasons for nonuse
	  - Prospects for future use

Key Responsibilities:	• Determine the specific measures to be used • Design the strategies for collecting the data (e.g., questionnaire, job observation, qualification tests) • Develop data collection instruments • Collect and store data and issue reports • Interpret results and make recommendations
Outputs:	• Results reports • Results definitions • Data collection system and instruments • Analysis reports and recommendations
Participants:	• Measurement specialists work with training managers to define results categories and systems • Measurement specialists work with developers and instructors to design data collection instruments and interpret results • Developers and instructors use results data for continuous improvement of instructional programs • Supervisors and managers of the trainees use the data to improve posttraining support for trainees • Training managers use the data in performance appraisal and to help improve the design and delivery systems
Performance Measures:	• Reliability and validity of the data • Percentage of courses/learning events covered by the system • Timeliness and usability of reports • Cost

SYSTEM: RESULTS	Process: Impact on Business Results
Purpose:	Measure the impact of training on business performance, including but not limited to • Quality results • Productivity • Profitability • Customer satisfaction
Key Responsibilities:	• Determine specific measures to be used • Design data collection strategies • Develop data collection instruments • Collect and store the data and issue reports • Interpret results and make recommendations
Outputs:	• Results data • Results definitions • Data collection system • Analysis reports and recommendations
Participants:	• Measurement specialists work with management, developers, and instructors to define the measures and design/develop the system • Instructors, developers, training management, and governance systems use the data to support investment decisions
Performance Measures:	• Validity and reliability of the data • Cost • Timeliness and usability of reports • Percentage of courses/learning systems covered by the measurement

SYSTEM: RESULTS	Process: Financial Results
Purpose:	Measure the financial results of the training system, including but not limited to • Income and expenses for all budget categories • Assets and liabilities • Conformance to project budgets
Key Responsibilities:	• Develop a chart of accounts • Determine results measures • Design data collection and accounting system • Collect and store data, issue reports • Analyze reports and make recommendations
Outputs:	• Financial reports • Chart of accounts • Data collection and accounting system • Analysis reports and recommendations
Participants:	• Accountants work with training management to develop the chart of accounts, determine the financial performance measures, and design the data collection and accounting system • Training managers and others in the training system use the data to control expenditures in their areas of responsibility • The governance system holds training management accountable for results
Performance Measures:	• Accuracy • Timeliness and usability of reports • Cost

SYSTEM: SUPPORT	
Purpose:	Provide administrative systems, facilities, materials and other resources need for the overall training system to function smoothly
Processes:	• Information system • Registration and scheduling • Communications • Production support • Facilities and equipment • Technologies • Specialists • Administrative manuals • Organization structure • Financial systems • External resources • Staffing • Supervisor/manager
Outputs:	• Information • Facilities and equipment • Materials • Staff organized and in place • Financial resources • Other resources
Participants:	• Administrative support staff • All providers and users in the training process

Performance Measures:	• Resources
	  - Adequacy
	  - Quality
	  - Cost
	  - Timeliness
	• Information
	  - Adequacy
	  - Quality
	  - Cost
	  - Timeliness

SYSTEM: SUPPORT	Process: Training Information Systems
Purpose:	Provide for storage and retrieval of important training data, including but not limited to • Delivery volume • Development of materials • Maintenance records • Curriculum histories • Individual training records • Budgets • Expenditures

Key Responsibilities:	• Design overall information system architecture
	  - Information to be kept
	  - System structure
	  - Specification for data and processes
	• Develop information systems plan
	  - Systems development
	  - Implementation schedule
	  - Resource requirements for development, implementation, and maintenance
	• Administer information system
	  - Collect and store data
	  - Generate reports

Outputs:	• System architecture • Information system plan • Reports
Participants:	• Information system specialists work with training administrative council to specify and design the system • Training managers and professionals use the data to assist in decision making • Governing groups use the data to assist in decision making • Managers at all levels of the business use the data • Administrative support group collects and stores data, generates reports
Performance Measures:	• Accuracy and completeness of data • Usefulness of data • Cost of the system • Timeliness of reports • Usability of reports • Accessibility of data for special reports

SYSTEM: SUPPORT	Process: Registration and Scheduling
Purpose:	Schedule learning events and the resources needed to support them, to register participants and record completions
Key Responsibilities:	• Forecast demand for learning events • Schedule events based on demand and business priorities • Schedule resources for events (instructors, classrooms, etc.) • Register participants • Maintain waiting list • Record completions • Send completion notices
Outputs:	• Schedule of events • Resources schedules • Waiting lists • Registration notices • Completion notices
Participants:	• Administrative staff operates the system • Employees and their supervisors use the system to register for events • Training managers use the system to schedule events and resources
Performance Measures:	• Ease of use for registration by employees and their supervisors • Schedule efficiency • Efficient loading of resources • Timeliness of events • Accuracy of registration and completion data • Cost to operate and maintain the system

SYSTEM: SUPPORT	Process: Training Communications
Purpose:	Provide timely information to all affected employees and managers, including but not limited to • Descriptions of available training • Schedules • Notice of new training releases • Key training results • Recognition for important accomplishments

Key Responsibilities:	• Design overall communications system
	  - Identify key audiences and their information needs
	  - Plan and specify communications vehicles
	• Develop communications plan
	  - Systems development
	  - Implementation schedule
	  - Resource requirements for development, operation, and maintenance
	• Collect information, prepare releases, and publish them
	• Maintain distribution lists

Outputs:	• Training catalogs and descriptions • Brochures for training events or curricula • Newsletters • News releases to company news media • News releases to outside media • Articles for company and outside media
Participants:	• Communications (PR) specialists design the system, collect information, prepare releases • The entire training community provides input • Everyone uses the information • Administrative staff keeps mailing list and manages production and distribution
Performance Measures:	• Value of information to user • Timeliness of information to user • Accuracy of information to user • Cost to provide the information

SYSTEM: SUPPORT	Process: Production Support
Purpose:	Provide production support for the training function, including but not limited to • Graphic arts • Word processing • Editing and formatting • Materials production • Materials storage and shipment • Procurement • Archiving master copies of material • Classroom setup • Laboratory and equipment construction, setup, and maintenance
Key Responsibilities:	• Identify support customers and their needs • Develop services and plans to meet customer needs • Provide service • Measure effectiveness and customer satisfaction • Develop a high-quality support staff
Outputs:	• Reproduction masters • Printed materials • Media copy (video, audio, slide, etc.) • Lab and equipment setups • Classroom setups
Participants:	• Production staff produces the outputs in support of the entire training system • Users of the system provide requests and feedback

Performance Measures:	• Timeliness
	• Quality
	  - Accuracy
	  - Appearance
	  - Format
	• Cost
	• User satisfaction

SYSTEM: SUPPORT	Process: Facilities
Purpose:	Provide the necessary facilities for the delivery of training events and housing of training staff, including but not limited to • Classrooms • Laboratories/simulators • Learning resource centers • Video teleconferencing systems • Computer-based training systems and networks • Office space • Production space • Storage space • Conference rooms • Trainee and training staff recreational facilities • Trainee living quarters

Key Responsibilities:	• Forecast facility requirements (long and short term)
	• Develop facility plan
	  - Number
	  - Location
	  - Specifications
	  - Timing
	• Oversee construction
	• Manage facility utilization
	• Operate and maintain facilities

Outputs:	• Facility plans • Facilities in place • Facilities operated and maintained
Participants:	• Facility management works with training staff to forecast requirements and develop plans • Executive board of education approves overall facility plan and budget • Facility staff operates and maintains facilities • All users provide requests and feedback

Performance Measures:	• Facilities available to meet requirements
	• Facility utilization efficiency
	• Efficiency of location
	  - Trainee travel and living costs
	  - Convenience for expert resources
	• Quality of facilities to meet the varied needs
	• User satisfaction
	• Cost

SYSTEM: SUPPORT	Process: Technologies
Purpose:	Develop and/or exploit emerging technologies to improve the effectiveness and efficiency of training, including but not limited to • Computer and information technologies • Expert systems and other forms of artificial intelligence (AI) • Videodisc • CBT authoring and delivery • Graphics and text publication • Teleconferencing • Simulation
Key Responsibilities:	• Systematic surveillance of a list of key technologies • Assessment of applications potential • Experimental application • Develop exploitation recommendations and plans • Support initial implementation
Outputs:	• Technology assessment reports • Experimental application reports • Exploitation plans • Implementation effectiveness reports
Participants:	• Technology specialists perform surveillance, assessment, and work with training staffs on experimental application, exploitation plans, and support implementation • Training staffs participate in experimental application, exploitation plans, and implementation • Governing structure makes strategic implementation decisions
Performance Measures:	• Improved effectiveness or efficiency of training • Cost of the technology system • Trainee and client organization satisfaction • Cost reductions achieved by applying the technology • Training staff satisfaction with the system

SYSTEM: SUPPORT	Process: Specialist Support
Purpose:	Provide specialist support to the training staff in areas, including but not limited to • Instructional design • Testing and measurement • Performance analysis • Statistics • Learning theory
Key Responsibilities:	• Forecast support requirements and provide access to specialists (internal or external) • Provide consulting support on demand • Maintain overall quality surveillance • Train training staff
Outputs:	• Technical advice • New skills for training staff • Quality assessments
Participants:	• Internal and external technical specialists provide consulting support • Training staff makes requests and provides feedback
Performance Measures:	• Advice received, understood, and accepted • Improved effectiveness or efficiency of training • Improved skills of training staff • Responsiveness to requests • Cost of the support • User satisfaction

SYSTEM: SUPPORT	Process: Administrative Manuals
Purpose:	Document key administrative issues, including but not limited to • Training mission • Training philosophy statement • Training organization structure • Training governance structure • Training processes and process standards • Training administration systems; roles, responsibilities, and information flow • Position descriptions and performance models
Key Responsibilities:	• Develop and maintain administrative manuals • Produce and distribute (either paper or electronic)
Outputs:	• One or more manuals • Updates
Participants:	• Management of training • Training staff • Writers
Performance Measures:	• Completeness • Usability • Timeliness of updates • Cost • User satisfaction

SYSTEM: SUPPORT	Process: Training Organization Structure
Purpose:	Provide an organization framework for the training staffs that accomplishes • Linkage to client organizations • Efficient and effective operation of all training systems and processes • Effective communication internal to training • Efficient information flow and workflow • Decision making at lowest possible levels • Support for specialized expertise
Key Responsibilities:	• Design an evolutionary structure that changes to meet the needs of the business
Outputs:	• Evolutionary organization chart • Team structures • Rationale
Participants:	• The training administration council plays a key role in estalishing organization structure • Training managers, possibly with expert support, perform actual organization design • The executive board of education approves the major design features
Performance Measures:	• Clear channels of communication with client organizations • Clear and unambiguous assignment of roles • Efficient and effective performance of training roles • Responsiveness

SYSTEM: SUPPORT	Process: Financial Systems
Purpose:	Provide the financial resources needed to accomplish training goals
Key Responsibilities:	• Design the financing system and periodically assess its effectiveness • Establish budgets • Billing and paying • Accounting for expenditures • Evaluating financial results
Outputs:	• Financial system design document (becomes policy) • Financial system administrative procedures • Budgets • Financial reports • Invoices, payments, purchase orders • Cost tracking on projects and training events
Participants:	• The training administration council designs the financing system with help from financial experts • The executive board of education approves the features of the financing system, approves annual budgets, and evaluates overall financial results • The training administrative staff compiles budgets, does billing and paying, accounts for expenditures, and issues financial reports • Training managers propose budgets, use financial reports to control results, and account for results to the executive board of education
Performance Measures:	• Accuracy • Responsiveness • Sufficient resources available to achieve goals • Fair allocation of costs to client organizations • Cost of operation • Easy to understand and use

SYSTEM: SUPPORT	Process: External Resources

Purpose:	Leverage the effectiveness of a minimum-size training staff by using resources outside the training organization, including but not limited to • Proprietary prepackaged training programs and materials • Learning events sponsored by universities, community colleges, vocational schools, professional societies, trade associations, and others • Contractors for instructional design and development, needs analysis, curriculum architecture, instruction, etc. • Managers, supervisors, and master performers from the client organizations to participate in needs analysis, curriculum architecture, instructional design and development, delivery, on-the-job application, maintenance, and governance system
Key Responsibilities:	• Establish a policy regarding the use of the various types of external resources • Establish selection criteria and selection systems • Select resources • Manage resources • Evaluate performance
Outputs:	• Policy and procedures for use of external resources • Selection criteria and systems • Contracts and agreements • Purchased materials and services • Performance evaluation data
Participants:	• Training administrative council develops policy and procedure • Executive board of education approves overall policy • Training managers and professionals use the policy and procedures for individual decision making
Performance Measures:	• Quality of products and services procured • Cost effectiveness • Client satisfaction

SYSTEM: SUPPORT	Process: Staffing
Purpose:	Provide for selection, training, and career management of the training staffs
Key Responsibilities:	• Design jobs • Analyze jobs for competency requirements • Design and develop or acquire staff training curriculum • Design and develop staff selection guides • Recruit and select staff • Provide staff training and development • Develop career policies and planning system • Develop and manage individual career plans
Outputs:	• Job designs and performance specifications for all positions • Competency requirements and other selection criteria for all positions • Selection guides • Training curriculum • Career development practices and policies • Competent staff in place • Individual career plans • Staff career development needs met
Participants:	• Specialists work with training mangers to design the jobs, analyze competency requirements, and develop the selection guides, training curriculum, and career system components • Training managers recruit and select staff • Specialists provide staff training • Individual staff members develop their own learning plan and career plan in collaboration with their managers
Performance Measures:	• Competent staff in place when needed • Individual career development needs met • Turnover rate due to performance problems or poor match between people and jobs • Training staff reputation

SYSTEM: SUPPORT	Process: Supervisor/Manager
Purpose:	Provide supervisors and managers with the support they need to carry out their important training roles, including • Values and expectations regarding appropriate management roles and behavior • Training • Information • Tools and other resources • Feedback and consequences
Key Responsibilities:	• Design/develop the support system elements • Training supervisors and managers • Provide information, tools, and other resources • Measure effectiveness of manager/supervisor behavior • Provide feedback, recognition, and other consequences
Outputs:	• Statement of values and expectations regarding supervisor/manager roles and behavior • Information to managers and supervisors • Job aids to help in assessing performance requirements and training needs and developing individual and organizational training plans • Training for supervisors/managers • Specialist support for supervisors/managers • Performance feedback and consequences to supervisors/managers • Supervisor/manager behavior
Participants:	• Specialists work with training managers and representative supervisors/managers to design/develop the systems • Training department trains supervisors/managers • Training department provides information, job aids, and specialist support • Training department measures performance and provides feedback • Manager provides performance consequences to subordinate managers and supervisors • Managers play their expected roles in the training system
Performance Measures:	• Effectiveness of supervisor/manager behavior • Employee satisfaction with training roles played by management • Supervisor/manager satisfaction with support received

BIBLIOGRAPHY

Austin, Nancy & Peters, Tom *A Passion for Excellence* New York, Random House, 1985

Bennis, Warren & Burt Nanus *Leaders: The Strategies for Taking Charge* New York, Harper & Row, 1985

Bowsher, Jack *Educating America* New York, John Wiley and Sons, 1989

Camp, Robert C. *Benchmarking* Milwaukee, WI, Quality Press, 1989

Carnevale, Gainer, & Schulz *Training the Technical Workforce* San Francisco, Jossey Bass, 1990

Cleland, David & King, William R. *Project Management Handbook* New York, Van Nostrand Reinhold, 1983

Competencies International Board of Standards for Training and Performance, 1986

Craig, Robert L. *Training and Development Handbook, A Guide to Human Resources Development* Washington, DC, ASTD, 1979

Deal, Terrence E. & Kennedy, Allan A. *Corporate Cultures* Reading, MA, Addison Wesley, 1988

DePree, Max *Leadership Is An Art* New York, Doubleday, 1989

Drucker, Peter F. *The Changing World of the Executive* New York, Times Books, 1982

Drucker, Peter F. *The Frontiers of Management* New York, Harper & Row, 1986

Drucker, Peter F. *Managing for Results* New York, Harper & Row, 1964

Galbraith, Jay *Organization Design* Reading, MA, Addison Wesley, 1977

Gilbert, Thomas F. *Human Competence* New York, McGraw-Hill, 1978

Hax, Arnoldo C. *Planning Strategies That Work* New York, Oxford University Press, 1987

Houle, Cyril O. *Continuing Learning in the Professions* San Francisco, Jossey Bass, 1980

Kanter, Rosabeth Moss *The Change Masters* New York, Simon & Schuster, 1983

Kaufman, Roger *Planning Educational Systems* Lancaster, PA, Technomic Publishing Company, 1988

Kearsley, Greg *Costs, Benefits, and Productivity in Training Systems* Reading, MA, Addison Wesley, 1982

Kotter, John P. A *Force for Change* New York, The Free Press, 1990

Kotter, John P. *Power and Influence* New York, The Free Press, 1985

Laird, Dugan *Approaches to Training and Development* Reading, MA, Addison Wesley, 1978

LeBoeuf, Michael *How to Win Customers and Keep Them for Life* New York, G. P. Putnam's Sons, 1987

LeRoux, Paul *Selling to a Group: Presentation Strategies* New York, Barnes and Noble, 1984

Lynch, Dudley & Kordis, Paul L. *Strategy of the Dolphin* New York, Fawcett Columbine, 1988

Mager, Robert F. *Preparing Instructional Objectives* Belmont, CA, Lake Publishing Company, 1984

Martin, Charles C. *Project Management: How to Make it Work* New York, AMACOM, 1976

Miller, Kathleen *Retraining the American Workforce* Reading, MA, Addison Wesley, 1989

Mohrman, Mohrman, Ledford, Cummings, Lawler, & Associates *Large Scale Organizational Change* San Francisco, Jossey Bass, 1989

Nadler, Leonard & Wiggs, Garland D. *Managing Human Resource Development* San Francisco, Jossey Bass, 1986

Neustadt, Richard E. & May, Ernest R. *Thinking in Time* New York, The Free Press, 1986

Niebuhr, Herman *Revitalizing American Learning* Belmont, CA, Wadsworth Publishing Company, 1984

Odiorne, George S. & Rummler, Geary A. *Training and Development: A Guide for Professionals* Chicago, IL, Commerce Clearing House Inc., 1988

Ohmae, Kenichi *The Mind of the Strategist: The Art of Japanese Business* New York, McGraw-Hill, 1982

Pace, R. Wayne *Organizational Communications* Englewood Cliffs, NJ, Prentice Hall, 1983

Peters, Thomas J. & Waterman, Robert H. *In Search of Excellence* New York, Warner Books, 1982

Porter, Michael E. *Competitive Strategy Techniques for Analyzing Industries and Competitors* New York, Macmillan Publishing Company, 1980

Senge, Peter M. *The Fifth Discipline* New York, Doubleday Currency, 1990

Smith, Theodore A. *Dynamic Business Strategy: The Art of Planning for Success* New York, McGraw-Hill, 1977

Solman, Paul and Friedman, Thomas *Life and Death on the Corporate Battlefield* New York, Simon & Schuster, 1982

Tichy, Noel M. & Devanna, Mary Anne *The Transformational Leader* New York, John Wiley and Sons, 1986

Toffler, Alvin *Powershift* New York, Bantam, 1990

Toffler, Alvin *The Third Wave* New York, Bantam, 1980

Townsend, Patrick L. *Commit to Quality* New York, John Wiley & Sons, 1986

Tregoe, Benjamin B. & Zimmerman, John W. *Top Management Strategy: What It Is and How to Make it Work* New York, Kepner-Tregoe, 1980

Weiss, Donald H. *How to Delegate Effectively* New York, AMACOM, 1988

INDEX

A

Accounting for training cost, 119–35
Actions plans, 117
Administrative coordination, 20, 326
Administrative network, 14
Administrative systems, 39–40
Advisory or governing structure, 11,
    40–41, 309, 322–36
Alcoa Laboratories philosophy of training,
    142
Alternative strategies, 36–37
Analysis:
    cost/benefit, 81–83
    process, 70–76
    training implications of business
        challenges, 77–83
    written business plans, 71–72
Annual updates to strategic training plan,
    44
Architecture, curriculum, 202–18
Assessment:
    existing training system, 32
    training needs, 183–201

Assumptions:
    delivery scenario, 270
    unit cost, 270

B

Barriers, 376–78
Bell System Center for Technical
    Education, 154, 323–27
Benchmarking, 109–18
Bibliography, 384–85
Board of advisors, 323–24
BSCTE, 154, 323–27
Budget:
    capital, 354
    development, 347–49
    field for training
        operations, 349–54
Budgeting process, 347–55
Building consensus, 64–65
Building your advisory structure, 327–36
Business plans, training implications of,
    32